DEPARTED WARRIORS

The story of a family in war

Kind regards

Jerry Whitland

DEPARTED WARRIORS

The story of a family in war

Jerry Murland

Matador
9 De Montfort Mews
Leicester LE1 7FW, UK
Tel: (+44) 116 255 9311 / 9312
Email: books@troubador.co.uk
Web: www.troubador.co.uk/matador

ISBN 978 1906510 701

A Cataloguing-in-Publication (CIP) catalogue record for this book
is available from the British Library.

Typeset in 11p.5pt Bok Antiqua by Troubador Publishing Ltd, Leicester, UK
Printed in the UK by The Cromwell Press Ltd, Wiltshire, UK

Matador is an imprint of Troubador Publishing Ltd

Dedicated to my granddaughter Alisha
so that she and her children will continue to remember

Contents

Acknowledgements

Departed Warriors has taken over four years to research and write and during that time, my wife Joan has borne the brunt of a house full of books, papers and photographs that filled my conversation and kept me all hours in front of a computer screen. She was always a welcome companion to the many battlefields and cemeteries we visited, generously heeding to my requests to plod across fields and through woods in pursuit of long since abandoned and obscure trench lines. To her I give my heart felt thanks for her encouragement and support.

I am very grateful to George Harris for writing the preface. George and my father first met on the Edinburgh University course in 1941 and after flying training in the States, went on to eventually fly the Lancaster bomber with 101 Squadron until the end of the war.

I am also indebted to Chris Holland who bravely agreed to read my manuscript, making a number of very helpful and constructive suggestions that have undoubtedly improved the presentation of the text. If I ever write another book, I promise not to ask him to read the draft text just before Christmas again.

In addition to those individuals I have acknowledged in the text, I must also thank the following who have been of great help to me in various ways: Gerry Chester (North Irish Horse history), Bob Cossey (74 Squadron operational records), Geoff Faulkner (99 Squadron operational records), Paul Gillies (15th Battalion AIF history), Jeff Goodwin (144 Squadron operational records), Dr. Geoffrey Hoon (interpretation of army medical board notes), Dr. Anthony Morton (Sandhurst Archives), Richard Murland (Maps), Andy North (Northamptonshire Records Office), Vic Nurcombe

Departed Warriors

(15th Battalion AIF war diary), Paul Reed (13th Battalion Royal Sussex Regiment history), Hugh Vaugh (service records), and the members of the Great War and RAF Commands Forums who responded so generously to the many questions and requests for information I posted.

Jerry Murland
June 2008

Preface

Few families can offer the same span of service and sacrifice as the extended Murland family. Fewer still can boast of a family member with the curiosity and determination to ferret out in such detail the history of their family and the nature of their forbears – even the black sheep, that most families would prefer to forget about!

Not all the men described achieved high rank and awards for heroism or distinction and, apart from one, all were ready to give their lives. Those who did gain distinction contributed three DSOs, three MCs and eight mentions in despatches, a proud legacy for any family. The fighting spirit of the Irish shines throughout. Their story brings to life – and death – the appalling statistics of war. We should indeed remember them.

Jerry's father, Howard, and I first met in April 1941 at Edinburgh University. We and twenty other 18 year old school leavers had been selected to join the first RAF University Course, combining academic studies with University Air Squadron training. It was intended as a quick way of replacing former UAS members who had been killed in the Battle of Britain. We were expected to become pilots and officers, potentially future leaders, the RAF having realised that their officer corps had already been much reduced. For six months we all enjoyed an undergraduate life-style in study and sport, coupled with the benefit of an introduction to service requirements. Looking back, I am sure that we would all describe it as an idyllic part of our war service.

When we moved on to full-time flying training we were lucky to be given a choice of location. Howard chose South Africa and I chose the United States, arriving shortly after Pearl Harbour. This meant that my course was the first to be allowed to wear RAF uniform, a fact which excited much curiosity and hospitality. The flying in Alabama and Georgia was stunning. I returned to the European theatre, whereas Howard went to the Middle East.

Twenty five years later we tried to find out what had happened to the rest of the Edinburgh course but only succeeded in finding dead men. Could telling the story of the RAF University Short Course history be a worthy future challenge to Jerry Murland's talent for research?

George H.G. Harris, DFC

1

Introduction

I began writing this book with my granddaughter in mind. I wanted her to be able to read about her family and, in particular, the part they played in the wars of the Twentieth Century. It is not intended to be a jingoistic celebration of heroic deeds, but a tribute to young men who served their country in time of war. In so doing, I have concentrated on the experiences of fourteen individuals and although four of them were professional fighting men, the remainder were citizen volunteers.

Citizen armies were essentially a Twentieth Century phenomenon that were first raised for service during the second Boer War. For the first time, the country called upon civilians with no previous military experience, to support the regular forces. One of those early volunteers was my great-uncle, Thomas Stanley Murland, who served two years in South Africa before returning to civilian life. This was repeated, on a much larger scale, during the Great War, with the formation of Kitchener's New Armies; a model that would re-emerge during the Second World War, with volunteers, like my father, putting on uniform and going off to war.

I have called them 'warriors', for that is what they were: fighting men in the uniform of their country answering the call to arms. Yes, it was a violent trade, but it was generally a disciplined violence that was tempered by the very uniform they wore. The majority of them did their duty conscientiously and courageously, some were decorated for gallantry, but others inevitably chose a path that would, as far as possible, circumvent the dangers of front-line service and increase their chances remaining relatively unscathed.

The search for family warriors who qualified for inclusion took me beyond the immediate blood relations of my mother and father. Joan had a number of her relatives, including both her grandfathers, who had enlisted and fought in the Great War. She also had three uncles who served in the Second World War, one of whom was a bomber pilot in the RAFVR[1]. I was reminded that they were also family members, albeit through marriage, and thus should be included in any narrative.

Ultimately, the individuals I chose to write about in depth were a self selecting group. If I was to tell their story, I needed to have a story to tell. For many of those who fought in the ranks during the Great War there is little or no personal information beyond family recollection. Officers tended to generate far more evidence of their service history, but even then, without other sources of information, it is not always easy to find the detail. For some of those who served in World War Two there is more material available, but at the same time, some of it, such as service records, are not always available to the general public on demand. Regretfully, I could find little more than the basic details of name, rank, number and unit for the majority of Joan's family. Ironically, there was more information available about those that had been killed in action, than those who had survived.

—◆◆◆—

The Murland family had their roots in County Down, Northern Ireland. They owed their wealth to the Irish linen industry and the discovery of the wet spinning process in 1825. Irish linen manufacturers were quick to adopt James Kay's invention which allowed flax fibres to be drawn into a very fine yarn. Possibly the first of these manufacturers were William and James Murland who built their mill in 1828 at Annsborough in County Down. By 1840 there were over 300 workers in the Murland mills with some 700 hand loom weavers working in the associated cottage industry. The greatest expansion of the family business came 20 years later when

1. Royal Air Force Volunteer Reserve

the American Civil War cut off supplies of material for the cotton industry, thus enabling James' eldest son, Charles Murland, to preside over a huge expansion of the firm and the resulting increase in prosperity. By 1887 the Annsborough business had 229 acres of bleach-greens, two spinning mills, a power loom factory and housing for 138 mill workers, providing work for over 1000 people.

Charles Murland transformed the business from a local concern to one which was known worldwide with offices in Belfast, London, Berlin, Paris, New York and Glasgow. The family were also involved in the development of the nearby Dundrum harbour, where they had a steam packet built to run a weekly passenger and cargo service to Whitehaven. Later they were partners in the financing of the railway link between Castlewellan and the coastal town of Newcastle.

The extent of the family wealth during this period is no better illustrated than by the Murland family tomb at Clough. This impressive vault, the size of a small bungalow, houses twenty members of the family. The last to be interred there was James Murland, the Crown Solicitor, in December 1890, although the ashes of my great-uncle Charles Henry Murland were placed there in 1969

After his death in 1887 Charles was succeeded by his second son Clotworthy Warren Murland, who married Sarah Ferguson in 1873. Sarah was the daughter of another mill owner, Thomas Ferguson of Banbridge. Clotworthy and Sarah were my great grandparents and, in the eight years between 1876 and 1884, Sarah gave birth to two daughters and five sons.

During this time, the family were living at Ardnabannon, a house built by Charles Murland that the 1901 Irish Census describes as a substantial private dwelling. The house stood in a large estate with a view that took in the panorama of the Mourne Mountains and looked across to the mills and bleach greens[2] nestled in and around the valley. It was quite simply a splendid location. The 1901 Irish Census lists the family who were living at Ardnabannon at the time:

---

2. Unbleached linen cloth was brown and before it was ready for sale it had to be bleached. During the early decades of the eighteenth century, the bleaching process was rather slow and primitive. It took up to five months to produce white cloth. Bleaching was carried out on 'bleachgreens' which had to be located close to a steady supply of fresh water. The webs of liner were laid out on the grass to dry in the sun during good weather.

Clotworthy Warren (my great grandfather) aged 54
James Warren , aged 25
Clotworthy Warren, aged 21
Evelyn, aged 20
Charles Henry, aged 19
Florence, aged 16.

Sarah died in 1896, leaving her husband with the family. The census confirms the occupations of James, Warren and Charles as flax spinners and linen bleachers. Elder brother James was universally known as 'Jim' and Charles Henry was always referred to as 'Charlie'. Clotworthy Warren, despite having the same forenames as his father, and presumably to avoid confusion, was known by his middle name, Warren. Two of the family were missing from the census return, Thomas Stanley Murland, aged 24, who was in South Africa and my grandfather, Howard Ferguson Murland, aged 18. Howard was in Portsmouth in 1901 studying for the Civil Service Examination, prior to entering the Royal Military College, Sandhurst[3].

Their lifestyle in County Down was privileged to say the least. Their social life revolved around house parties where the landed linen families met and entertained themselves. The Royal County Down Golf Club and the Sieve Donnard Hotel at Newcastle were frequent venues for social events, as was Lord Annesley's home and estate at Castlewellan Castle. The family were passionate about horses; the stables at Ardnabannon and later Greenvale House, where Warren took up residence in 1911, were full of some of the finest horses in the county.

Gerald Brice Ferguson Smyth and George Osbert Stirling Smyth were cousins to the Murland family and both regular army officers. Their mother, or Aunt Helen as she was known to my grandfather, was brought up at Edenderry, the Ferguson family home at Banbridge. Edenderry had also been home to the eldest of the Ferguson sisters, my great grandmother, Sarah. The house, a symbol of the family prosperity, was built by her father, Thomas Ferguson, in

---

3. Sandhurst was known as the RMC (Royal Military College, Sandhurst) from its inception in 1802 until 1947, when it amalgamated with the RMA (Royal Military Academy, Woolwich, established in 1741) to become the RMAS (Royal Military Academy Sandhurst).

1865 shortly after he established the family firm of Thomas Ferguson & Co. Ltd on the banks of the River Bann. In 1881, aged 26, Helen married George Smyth, a member of the extensive Smyth family whose wealth also came from the linen trade. After her marriage she retained the Ferguson name, becoming known as Helen Ferguson Smyth, and moved to India with George who went on to have a distinguished career in the Indian Civil Service, ultimately rising to the position of British High Commissioner in the Punjab.

James Martin Gerald Murland and his brother William Sydney Murland were known by family and friends as 'Gerry' and 'Bill'. They too, enjoyed a privileged lifestyle on their father's country estate near Badby in Northamptonshire. Both boys were sent to Harrow and according to Bill's service record, he was for a time brought up in France, becoming fluent in French. Their father, William Murland, or 'Willie', as he was more commonly known, was a horse breeder of some repute[4] and the son of James William Murland, a one time Chairman of the Bank of Ireland and the Great Northern Railway. Willie was educated at Trinity College, Dublin where he graduated in 1877 and, despite being called to the Bar in 1880, pursued his one love in life: horses and racing. Amongst the 98 races he won as a rider were the Dunboyne Cup, the Conyngham Cup and the prestigious Downshire Plate at Punchestown in 1884. A year later, in 1885, he won the Irish Grand National, riding *Billet Doux*. Sometime around 1887 Willie moved to England with his wife, Mary, and founded the Findon Racing Stables and Stud in Sussex, situated a few miles south of my maternal grandmother's family home in West Chiltington.

In 1913, having moved from Sussex sometime at the turn of the century, Willie was appointed High Sheriff of Northamptonshire, a post he combined with his continuing membership of the Jockey Club and the National Hunt Committee. Records show the family were keen huntsmen and subscribed annually to the Pytchley and Grafton Hunts. My grandfather was a guest at Badby House[5] on

4. His most celebrated colt was *Hurry On* which was sold in 1914 to Lord Woolavington for 500 gns. In 1916 *Hurry On* won the Substitute St. Leger, the Newmarket St. Leger and the Jockey Club Cup. In retirement *Hurry On* sired numerous winners which included three Derbys, two Oaks and one St.Leger.
5. Badby House is now part of a residential complex for the elderly and situated just outside Daventry.

several occasions, taking full advantage while he was there of the opportunity to ride with the Pytchley.

The Murland family and their Smyth cousins would have seven of their number in uniform by 1915, and in keeping with their education and social standing, were all commissioned officers. Apart from my grandfather, who, in 1915, was in Burma with his regiment, the remainder were either already on the European mainland with the British Expeditionary Force, or waiting for orders that would take them one step closer to getting there.

My mother's family had been resident in West Sussex for two generations. My great grandfather, Charles Henry Goode, was an Architect and landowner and the family lived comfortably at Vaux Grange in the West Sussex districts of Thakeham and West Chiltington. They were listed in the census of 1901:

> Charles Goode (my great grandfather), a farmer and landowner, aged 64
> Ada Jessie Goode (my great grandmother), aged 33
> Margery (my grandmother), aged 3
> Walter aged 10
> Ethel aged 9
> Lynton aged 7
> Archibald aged 5
> Harriet Golds, Cook and domestic
> Florence Rolf, Housemaid

A second search of the census revealed a Violet Goode, aged 14, who was living at the time of the census, at Lyndale College in Heene. I had distant memories of my aunts, Ethel and Violet, from childhood and now it would seem I had discovered several great-uncles whose names I was unaware of. Another family member absent from the 1901 Census listing was the eldest son, Charles Herbert Goode, who was 13 years old at the time and attending boarding school at New College, Heene.

Charles Henry Goode had married his first wife Elizabeth

Introduction

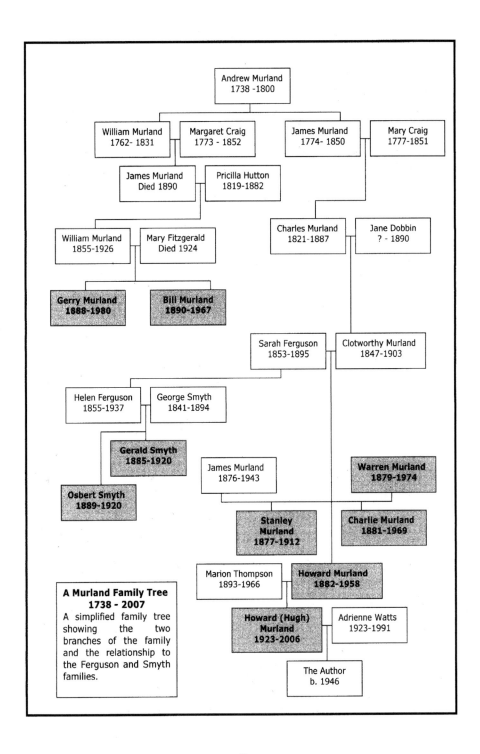

Andrew Murland
1738 -1800

William Murland
1762- 1831

Margaret Craig
1773 - 1852

James Murland
1774- 1850

Mary Craig
1777-1851

James Murland
Died 1890

Pricilla Hutton
1819-1882

William Murland
1855-1926

Mary Fitzgerald
Died 1924

Charles Murland
1821-1887

Jane Dobbin
? - 1890

Gerry Murland
1888-1980

Bill Murland
1890-1967

Sarah Ferguson
1853-1895

Clotworthy Murland
1847-1903

Helen Ferguson
1855-1937

George Smyth
1841-1894

Gerald Smyth
1885-1920

James Murland
1876-1943

Warren Murland
1879-1974

Osbert Smyth
1889-1920

Stanley
Murland
1877-1912

Charlie Murland
1881-1969

Marion Thompson
1893-1966

Howard Murland
1882-1958

**A Murland Family Tree
1738 - 2007**
A simplified family tree
showing the two
branches of the family
and the relationship to
the Ferguson and Smyth
families.

Howard (Hugh)
Murland
1923-2006

Adrienne Watts
1923-1991

The Author
b. 1946

7

Stoveld in Worthing on 12th July 1859; the marriage was childless and ended in divorce in 1877. Some time after this, Charles Henry was living in Sussex at Nutbourne Place, just outside West Chiltington, with his young housekeeper Ada Jessie Poole. Ada came from a large family in Chichester where her parents, Edwin and Emma Poole, brought up Ada's seven brothers and sisters at Number 30, Orchard Street.

Her relationship with Charles Henry clearly developed beyond the duties of housekeeper, and by 1893, she had given birth to seven children out of wedlock, one of whom died at birth. Of these children, Violet Anne was born in 1887, Charles Herbert in the following year and Walter two years later in December 1890. A second girl, Ethel, arrived in 1892, a year later Lynton was born and then Archibald in 1895. Charles Henry eventually married Ada in London in December 1896 and the surnames of the children were changed to Goode. Two years later my grandmother Margery was born, followed by Leslie in 1902, and Richard in 1905. Sadly in 1904, Ada gave birth to another girl who died at birth. Of Margery's four brothers who served in the Great War, only two would survive beyond 1918.

Another who would survive the war years was my maternal grandfather, Douglas Allen Watts, who was also a Sussex man. The Watts family Drapery in Arundel was an established high street business, one which enabled Alfred and Emily to employ two servants and live relatively comfortably with Douglas and his four sisters. I am not absolutely sure when Douglas met my grandmother, I have a suspicion it was in 1914, but they certainly didn't marry until after the war.

———

By way of contrast, Joan's family were much less fortunate. Three generations of Royles and Clarkes have made their home at Kingston-upon-Hull in East Yorkshire. The 1901 Census loosely describes many of her family as 'workers', a term that appeared to include the semi-skilled as well as the unskilled. There is evidence that, when opportunity arose, each successive generation sought to improve their circumstances. On her father's side, John Royle, her great grandfather, was a labourer, while her grandfather, Harry, had become a postman after leaving school at 14. Her father, Albert Royle, took advantage of a greater access to education and qualified as a teacher in 1930, teaching all his working life at schools in Hull. It was a similar story on her mother's side. Great grandfather Charles Henry Clarke was a Plasterer, his son, William, became a railway clerk after leaving school but Charles Owen Clarke, who was born in 1920, attended the Malet Lambert Grammar School and began his working life with a shipping company in Hull.

Joan's grandfathers, Harry and William, both enlisted in locally raised Royal Artillery units and by 1916, were on active service. Gunner Harry Royle landed in France at the end of June 1916 with the 146 (Hull) Heavy Battery, and served in all the major battles of the Great War, firing his last round on October 27th 1918. He survived the war and returned home after being demobbed in July 1919. The local Hull newspaper recorded the arrival of the 146 Battery marching through the city after disembarking at King George Dock. Harry died in 1966, aged 82. Ex Gunner William Clarke died on the cross channel ferry, *SS Dewsbury*, in 1935, on his way to visit Ypres and the notorious Salient for the first time since 1918. His war was fought with the Royal Field Artillery and family fable has it that he named his youngest son Charles, in memory of a close friend who had been killed. There is no doubt that the two men, despite surviving physically intact, took several years to recover from their experiences in the trenches of the Western Front. Those who knew William Clarke would argue he never really fully recovered.

There were others in Joan's family that volunteered for Kitchener's New Armies. Few, if any, of their records survived as a testament to their service and, like ten of thousands of their comrades, they remain largely anonymous. The final phase of the Somme Offensive claimed the life of her great-uncle, Charles Percy Weatherill[6] in November 1916, when the 7th Battalion, Royal Fusiliers attacked the German line near Hamel. Badly wounded, he died in a base hospital at Rouen a week later. He was 32 years old. There is little beyond a CWGC headstone and fading family memories to mark his service to his country.

6. 26217 Private Charles Weatherill, aged 32. Buried in the St. Sever Cemetery Extension, Rouen. Ref: O.II.I.10.

Departed Warriors

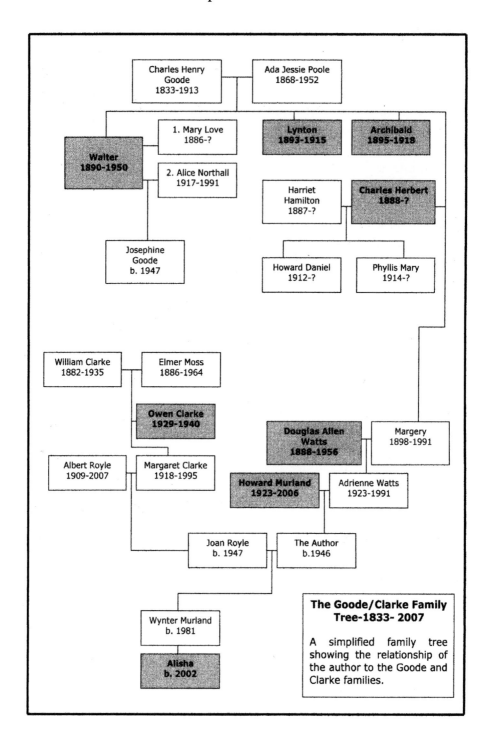

Charles Henry Goode 1833-1913 — Ada Jessie Poole 1868-1952

1. Mary Love 1886-?

Walter 1890-1950

2. Alice Northall 1917-1991

Lynton 1893-1915

Archibald 1895-1918

Harriet Hamilton 1887-?

Charles Herbert 1888-?

Josephine Goode b. 1947

Howard Daniel 1912-?

Phyllis Mary 1914-?

William Clarke 1882-1935 — Elmer Moss 1886-1964

Owen Clarke 1929-1940

Douglas Allen Watts 1888-1956

Margery 1898-1991

Albert Royle 1909-2007 — Margaret Clarke 1918-1995

Howard Murland 1923-2006

Adrienne Watts 1923-1991

Joan Royle b. 1947 — The Author b.1946

Wynter Murland b. 1981

Alisha b. 2002

The Goode/Clarke Family Tree-1833- 2007

A simplified family tree showing the relationship of the author to the Goode and Clarke families.

Introduction

My research began after my maternal grandmother, Margery, died. It was only then I began to ask questions about previous generations and to add to a family tree that my father had begun many years earlier. The catalyst for this interest was the discovery of a picture postcard that was found in a box of assorted memorabilia that had belonged to my grandmother. The face of a young girl stared out from behind two boys who were seated on a garden bench. The girl was instantly recognisable as Margery, aged about twelve or thirteen, but the two boys she was pictured with were a mystery. I knew Margery had grown up with several brothers, but they were rarely spoken of and she only once mentioned to me that her two favourite brothers had died in the Great War of 1914-18. I also remember her telling me that one of the boys had emigrated to Australia. Were these two boys, sitting on either side of her, two of her brothers? The photograph, dated 1911, was a window into the past and served to illustrate sharply how little I knew of my grandmother's family and her early life in Sussex.

It seemed reasonable to presume from census evidence the faces on the picture postcard belonged to two of the four boys listed as Margery's brothers. The photograph itself suggested it was more likely that they belonged to the two youngest boys, Lynton and Archie. Charles would have been 26 years old in 1914 and brother Walter, 23 years old. The boys seated with Margery were much younger, so were these the two brothers who were killed in the Great War?

Although it looked as though the boys were Lynton and Archie, I was still unable to match faces to names. Fortunately, the Australian War Memorial Museum was able to confirm Lynton had enlisted in the Australian Imperial Force in 1915 and provided me with new information about his service with the 15th Battalion. In the photograph, one of the boys is smaller in stature than the other. Lynton's attestation papers described him as five foot eight and a half inches tall and weighing 145lbs. It looked very much as though he was the boy seated on the left, with Archie, the younger and taller boy seated on the right.

Once I had begun to dig into the past, a wealth of information in the form of photographs, medals and diaries began to surface. The most remarkable discovery was the twelve volumes of diaries which my paternal grandfather began writing in 1906. The diaries introduced me to my Irish heritage and a family tree I had no idea existed. It was through the diaries that I discovered the remarkable careers of the Smyth brothers and the impact the Great War had on my grandfather's circle of friends and colleagues. Fortunately my father had the foresight to keep the diaries in the family and made them available to me when I began researching this book. To my astonishment, my grandfather's assortment of letters and newspaper cuttings relating to the family had also survived, adding to the archive of personal detail that otherwise would have been lost.

After my father died, my sister and I had the task of sorting through his personal effects. Not only did we find five large albums of photographs that illustrated over forty five years of Murland family life from 1900 to the late 1940s, but wrapped in newspaper was a tarnished group of Great War medals, one of which was a Military Cross. Incredibly, these family heirlooms had been tucked away for safe keeping and forgotten about. The Military Cross belonged to Gerry Murland who had been an officer in the Northamptonshire Yeomanry, and in later life, godfather to my brother. As children we had no idea that he had been decorated for gallantry or even considered for a moment he had fought in the Great War.

Fortunately my maternal grandfather Douglas also left a photographic legacy of his time in Gallipoli and Egypt, as well as his short career in the Royal Flying Corps. His photographs were taken in the trenches during his time on the Gallipoli peninsula at Cape Helles and later in Egypt where he served with the Egyptian Expeditionary Force. There were several others, presumably taken after he was commissioned into the Royal Air Force in 1918. Unfortunately he did not annotate every picture in the album and I couldn't but help wonder how many of those faces caught in the lens, survived the war to return home after the Armistice.

It was photographs and personal diaries that provided a similar record of my father's service in the RAFVR during the Second World War. The photographs and diaries of his wartime flying proved to be a documentary of the life of a fighter pilot, a life he had rarely spoken about to the family. A photograph of another pilot, which I found during a search for family photographs in my late father-in-law's house, proved to be one of Joan's uncles, Charles Owen Clarke. He had joined the RAFVR in 1939 and flew with Bomber Command in 1940. In a second photograph, he was standing with another sergeant pilot, in what looked like a small back garden. These fresh-faced boys reminded me of the photograph I had found of my grandmother with her brothers. My curiosity was aroused again, I wanted to know more about these two pilots and what exactly had happened to them.

In the same drawer as Owen's photograph, I found a small registered package containing a British War Medal and a Victory Medal, both in mint condition and still in their original boxes. The medals belonged to Joan's grandfather, Harry Royle. The service number on the medals pointed to his three years with the Royal Garrison Artillery[7]. The medals, I suspect, were a reminder of the horrors of the battlefield and of the deaths of friends and, accordingly, had ended up consigned to the bottom of a drawer and forgotten about. This was a scenario that must have been repeated in many households throughout the country, after the small registered packages arrived through the post from regimental records offices. Over 13.5 million British campaign stars and medals were issued in the 1920s. Many were not given another thought by the recipients, ending their days as children's playthings, while countless others were sold for their silver content in the economic depression of the 1930s.

The research trail took me to the National Archives, the RAF Museum, the British Library and the Imperial War Museum. I also spent time in local archives, such as the Northamptonshire and West Sussex Record Offices. Local collections are very often a valuable source of information on county regiments and the individuals who served in them. I was also surprised at how much information could be found by searching the internet. One of the great online assets is the dedicated websites that bring together like minded individuals to share and discuss topics of common interest. One of the leading

7. The heavy artillery was manned by units of the Royal Garrison Artillery.

sites for the Great War is Chris Baker's, *Long Long, Trail.* Chris has put together an outstanding and informed resource which every serious Great War researcher should visit. There are similar sites that cover the Second World War, in particular I found the *RAF Commands Forum*, to be of great assistance while I was checking background information on Owen Clarke and my father.

Researching the past deeds of the family was a captivating activity that I thoroughly enjoyed; but as the amount of information increased and began to fill several large files, there had to come a point when I first put pen to paper in an attempt to make sense of it all. In doing that, I returned to the photograph that first aroused my curiosity and had begun the whole process. Looking at the faces of those three young people, I couldn't help but think how the innocence of that composed family portrait was about to be shattered by the nation's collision with the Great War.

2

A Respectable and Honest Man of Good Character

Archibald Goode

Now that I knew the likely identity of the two boys in my grand-mother's photograph, I focused my attention on Archie, reasoning that his records and any war diaries kept by his unit would be relatively straightforward to locate. To an extent this was true but, as he was a private soldier, and later a junior NCO[1], the likelihood of finding any personal reference to him in any battalion war diaries was slim. It also became apparent that the chances of finding his army service records were not good, as the majority of these records were destroyed in 1940 by fire during the Blitz. Those that were not burned were largely smoke or water damaged and it was not until relatively recently that the remaining records, referred to as the Burnt Series papers, were microfilmed and made available to the general public at the National Archives. The ravages of time and the lost legibility through microfilming have meant that in many cases the surviving paperwork can be difficult to read and many files contain only fragments of papers, with the evidence of fire only too apparent.

As luck would have it, two sets of files survived intact, having been removed from the main archive and stored elsewhere. One of

1. Non Commissioned Officer

these sets was the service records of those who had been discharged as unfit for further service and granted a pension. A number of these individuals died later as a result of their injuries and wounds. The surviving records are known rather appropriately as the Unburnt Series and, as Archie had been wounded and discharged from the army in 1918, there was a chance some of his service records had survived intact.

To my delight, I found them relatively quickly on my next visit to the National Archives at Kew and, although difficult to read on microfilm, they unfolded the tragic story of another young life destroyed by war. His service records described him as being five foot eleven inches tall and weighing 150 pounds, confirming my belief that he was the larger boy seated on my grandmother's left in the photograph. He was nearly 20 years old when he enlisted in January 1915 and his records included his attestation papers and casualty records, along with two pages of medical notes completed, probably during his stay at the King George's Hospital in London, prior to discharge. I found it quite poignant that, apart from these limited records – a memorial stone in a small Sussex churchyard and a photograph – nothing else remained to remind us of Archie's service to his country. Despite this, the information contained in his records was enough to provide me with the basis for an accurate timeline of his army service and for me to trace his movements up until the end of 1918.

My great grandfather, Charles Henry Goode, died in November 1913 and Archie emigrated to Canada five months later in April 1914, sailing from London on an Allen Line steamship, the *SS Scotian*. The passenger manifest records the 18 year-old Archie as travelling in second class and being a farmer by occupation. Britain's declaration of war on Germany on 4th August presumably put this young man in a dilemma: should he remain in Canada and enlist, or return home to join the Royal Sussex Regiment? His decision saw him returning home after only three months in Canada, his plans for farming now overshadowed by the German invasion of Belgium. He would in all probability have arrived home in time for Christmas 1914.

His mother Ada was still living at the family home in West Chiltington with Margery, now 16 years old, her older sister Ethel, and two younger brothers, Richard aged 10 and Edwin aged 12. Ada had given birth to four more children after 1901; sadly two of the children died at birth, but she was still left as matriarch of a large family. The family estate was being managed and run by her son Walter, aged 23, who would soon respond to Kitchener's call to arms and enlist in the Sussex Yeomanry in April 1915.

Archie's elder sister Violet and her husband Arthur Barnes were living in the village; their family had increased to three with the arrival of Joyce in 1912, giving Ada her first grandchild. It is highly likely that they were joined at Christmas by Ada's eldest son Charles Herbert who, having enlisted in the 2nd King Edward's Horse as a trooper in September, was about to be commissioned into the Royal Field Artillery. I am also quite sure that his wife Harriet and their children were also there.

Once war had been declared, it had not taken long for the idea of Pals Battalions and units to be seized upon as a platform for recruiting men of similar backgrounds and professions into the ranks of the Army. Although by far the greater proportion of these came from the urban conurbations of the industrial north of England, the southern counties also did their bit in contributing men from similar walks of life, and certainly in Sussex there was no shortage of men willing to enlist in locally sponsored battalions.

Prominent in raising the Sussex South Downs battalions was Lieutenant-Colonel Claude Lowther, an Edwardian aesthete and the Conservative MP for North Cumberland. Lowther was a well-known local figure who had bought the ancient ruins of Herstmonceux Castle in 1911 and begun to restore it to its former glory, using local craftsmen to carry out the building work. He was also an outspoken figure in Parliament, arguing for a pound a week for every man on service, which was considerably more than the shilling a day the vast majority of enlisted men did actually receive. In September 1914, this Boer War veteran began the task of raising three battalions of the Royal Sussex Regiment at his own expense, embracing the Pals principle of joining, training, fighting (and dying) together. Once the South Downs battalions' recruiting offices opened, it took very little persuasion for the men of the towns and villages of Sussex to join the ranks of Lowther's Lambs.

Standing in line waiting his turn to join up was Archie Goode, who enlisted in the 13th Battalion at Worthing on 18th January 1915. By January the recruiting fervour of the previous year had begun to slow down and, despite being formed in November 1914, the battalion was not up to strength until March 1915. The 11th and 12th Battalions had drawn off much of the willing manpower of the county, requiring the regiment to widen its trawl in order to fill the gaps in its ranks. While the majority of enlisted men in the battalion had Sussex roots, many came from the surrounding counties of Kent, Middlesex, Hampshire and Surrey. Battalion records also show a small proportion of men joining from as far away as Staffordshire and Northamptonshire in the north, and Norwich in the east. To retain their South Downs identity, the regimental numbers of men enlisting during this period were prefixed with SD, although by the end of 1916 there were very few of the original Southdowners left.

Moving to Cooden Hill Camp near Bexhill, SD 3773 Private Archie Goode began his basic training soon after enlistment. The battalion was destined to remain in England for the next fourteen months, moving from Bexhill in July 1915 to Maidstone and finally to Witley Camp, Aldershot, in September. In October 1915 the three South Downs battalions together with the 14th Battalion of the Hampshire Regiment became part of 116 Brigade, 39th Division, under the command of Major-General Nathaniel Barnardiston[2]. No doubt Archie managed to return home on leave during this time but the majority of his time would have been taken up with a training programme that focused on route marches, drill, lectures, physical training, inspections and becoming proficient with the Short Model Lee Enfield Rifle. He possibly even got home again for Christmas 1915 before the battalion received their orders to embark for France in March 1916.

Leaving Aldershot on 5th March, it took three trains to get the Southdowns battalions and the rest of 116 Brigade to Southampton where they embarked on the *SS Viper* and *SS Australind* for the night crossing to Le Harve. Disembarking in the late morning of 6th March, the brigade marched in the snow to the tented accommodation at Number 5 Rest Camp, a little different from the huts they had been used to at Witley but serving a hint of the hardships to come.

---

2. Major-General General Nathaniel Walter Barnardiston (1858-1919).

There was little time to grumble. Early the next morning, they began a nineteen and a half hour rail journey in cattle trucks which took them across northeastern France. One can only assume the officers travelled in slightly more comfortable surroundings, but for Archie and his fellow soldiers it must have been an arduous journey. When they reached their destination at Steenbecque, stores and baggage were unloaded and the men marched the two miles to Morbecque, where once again they were billeted in a rest camp. Three days later the whole brigade was on the road again marching to Rue Du Quesnoy. They had finally arrived at the Western Front.

Once in France, every battalion was obliged to keep a daily war diary, copies of which were sent monthly up to Divisional Headquarters. Many of the surviving diaries can be found at the National Archives, and more recently a number of them have been made available online. The war diary recorded the daily activities of the battalion, where they served and how they were deployed. The 13th Royal Sussex diary was no different to countless other war diaries of the period: very few of the other ranks were mentioned unless decorated for gallantry and there was no mention of Archie, even on the two occasions he was wounded. Nevertheless, it provided a detailed account of the battalion's activities during their service on the Western Front.

On 18th March the battalion was formally attached to the 8th Division for purposes of familiarisation with front-line trench duties. This was quite a normal procedure. A new battalion was not deemed able to take over their own sector of the front until they had completed a probationary period with more experienced troops. Broken up into companies, the battalion spent twenty-four hour sessions in the trenches, sharing them variously with the 2nd Royal Irish Rifles, 2nd Royal Berkshires, 2nd Lincolns and the 2nd Rifle Brigade.

By late 1915 the British Army in France consisted of five armies. Each army was subdivided into a number of corps, a corps being made up from a number of infantry divisions and sometimes a cavalry division as well. The infantry division of 1915 was commanded by a Major-General and had three brigades, each brigade containing four infantry battalions, although this was reduced to three by 1918. At the time the Royal Sussex joined the 8th Division for instruction in the art of trench warfare, the division consisted of four infantry brigades, three battalions of pioneers, eight divisional artillery and engineer units and three field ambulance units.

Any misconceptions that may have been held by the men about trench life would have been lost very quickly as the battalion settled in with their more experienced tutors. For the private soldier in the trenches much of the time was spent as part of a working party in repairing and maintaining trenches which were constantly in need of attention. It was while on various working parties with their hosts that the battalion suffered its first casualties, with four men wounded by shellfire. The lessons had begun and were being learnt the hard way.

One of the other lessons learnt during the battalion's time in the 8th Division's lines would have been the importance of an established daily trench routine. For the 13th Battalion that routine would involve the essential task of defending the front-line and allowing sufficient time, where possible, for the troops to rest and be fed. The established practice in the Army was to stand-to every morning at first light and again at last light as dusk was falling. In effect, this involved having every man in the line in full kit, at the alert and ready to fire his weapon. Not only did this ensure each man was ready for a possible enemy attack, but also enabled battalion officers to see that every soldier was fully kitted-out, was fit, well and fully prepared.

The organisation of an infantry battalion in 1916 was a simple one. Broken down into four rifle companies, each commanded usually by a Major or Captain, a machine gun section and a headquarters, the whole unit of around 800 men was commanded by a Lieutenant-Colonel. In this instance it was Lieutenant-Colonel G.W.C. Draffen. In C Company, under the command of Captain C.M. Humble-Crofts, Archie would have been a member of one of four platoons commanded by a Lieutenant or Second Lieutenant and assisted by a platoon sergeant. Within the platoon organisation there were usually four sections, each of eight to ten men, who would answer to a corporal or lance corporal. When in the line, each section would occupy one bay of the trench, with one man on guard observing the enemy lines through a periscope or observation slit, the remainder either engaged in improving the trench, sleeping in bays dug into the sides of the trench or eating. By night the sentries were doubled and working parties could take advantage of the cover of darkness and repair and strengthen the wire, bring up supplies and, when ordered, send patrols out into No Man's Land.

Occasionally, either side would mount a raid on the opposing trenches. A trench raid would focus attention on a small sector of the enemy lines and attempt to destroy their fortifications, capture prisoners and documents and kill as many of the rival forces as possible. Such a raid would often be carried out by a single platoon, but occasionally whole companies or battalions would be tasked with temporarily invading the enemy trenches. This was part of the British Army's practice of aggressive defence, built on the principle that in defence the dominance of No Man's Land was paramount. To allow troops to sit in defensive positions for too long, it was argued, would inevitably undermine the aggressive spirit. Raids were certainly not popular with the men, for they inevitably resulted in casualties, and for the front-line soldier it was understandably difficult to appreciate how such raids furthered the progress of the war.

By the end of March, the battalion was judged to be capable of occupying its own sector of the line and, after moving south from Robermetz to Givenchy Village, they relieved the Royal Welsh Fusiliers, taking over the trenches just to the north of the La Bassée Canal. They were now in the front-line with the 14th Hampshires on their left and the 12th Royal Sussex behind them in the support trenches of the Village Line. The Village Line was the British second line that ran through Givenchy taking full advantage of the numerous cellars and basements that remained intact. The sector included the notorious Duck's Bill, a salient which had been subjected to repeated enemy mining activity and which, by this time, resembled a lunar landscape. A month before, the Germans had exploded a mine under the salient, destroying much of the trench line and killing large numbers of the defending troops. Only prompt action by the South Wales Borderers had prevented the German forces from occupying the rim of the crater. The German line in this area was formidable, with very deep trenches and dugouts and, in some places, the two front-lines were only separated by a matter of yards. This was certainly not a quiet sector, as B Company was to discover on 16th April. The war diary recorded the day's events:

Fine Day. Enemy shelled Gunner Siding and Village Line in morning. No material damage was done. At about 12.30pm, he made a direct hit on our parapet in B Coy's [Company] trenches killing and wounding 10 men. A great number of rifle grenades were fired on both sides. Enemy machine guns very active at night. Patrols were sent out at night to reconnoitre No Man's Land – a large amount of work was done in various parts of the line. Total casualties 5 killed and 16 wounded.

Fortunately, the British soldier did not spend all his time in the trenches or even in the front-line. The war diary records the battalion's rotation between the firing line, support and reserve lines and billets, referring to trenches by name, such as Hunter Street or Fourth Avenue. Trench systems invariably generated a trench map, without which it would have been difficult to navigate round the maze of trenches in any given sector, an invaluable aid to any new battalion coming into the line. But even with a map it was quite easy to become lost, particularly at night when moving into the line to relieve another battalion. With the men of C Company, Archie would usually spend approximately four days in the firing line before being relieved for a spell in the support and reserve trenches, after which they moved back to the relative safety of a rest area behind the lines. Although difficult to programme, the constant rotation of troops was not only good for morale but it also prevented unnecessary casualties in the firing line by not having too many men exposed at once. However, indiscriminate shelling by the enemy, as B Company had already found to their cost, could deal out instant death and injury at any point and at any time.

By the beginning of May 1916, the men found themselves in yet another sector of the front-line at Festubert. Not only was this sector as notorious as Givenchy for the level of hostile activity, but life was constantly made more difficult by flooding. With the water table only a few feet below ground level, the trenches were necessarily shallow, with a parapet constructed above ground level for protection from enemy fire. Inevitably, in poorer weather the trenches would flood, requiring pumping and draining in an attempt to disperse the water. To combat this, several islands of defence had been constructed at points along the line that were occupied on a rotational basis by the battalion.

With orders to hold out until the last man if attacked, it goes without saying that none of the men welcomed his turn of duty, particularly as the Islands provided a focal point for enemy fire. On 10th May, Island 30A was attacked by a German patrol without causing casualties. The next day they were back again, and this time Sergeant Harriott[3], the battalion sniping expert, was killed by machine gun fire.

Barbed wire was another defensive tool that both sides used to protect their respective trench systems. Well-planned wire entanglements would slow up any attack and funnel attackers into prepared killing zones. Each side had small gaps in the wire to allow the passage of patrols into No Man's Land but, generally, unless the wire was breached by shellfire, it could form an impregnable barrier to advancing troops. During their time at Festubert, the battalion expended a great deal of energy strengthening the existing wire and without doubt, Archie would have been involved in this hazardous activity. Over the two nights of 19th and 20th May, battalion working parties laid over two hundred coils of wire on their frontage. It was while supervising one of these working parties that Second Lieutenant G.E. Elliot,[4] the battalion Signalling Officer, was killed.

After another short period of training and re-equipping, during which time the men of C Company were able to have a bath, the battalion was moved a little further south to Cuinchy, taking over the Cuinchy Left Sector from the 2nd Argyle and Sutherland Highlanders on 28th May. C Company, along with B and A Companies, were in the firing line with D Company in the support trenches. Cuinchy was described as a 'slaughter yard' by the poet Edmund Blunden who was an officer in the 11th Battalion. He remembered the sector as running through an extensive brick field, which was all that remained of the brick factory that once dominated the area. It was the huge brick-stacks that gave this sector of the line an almost surreal atmosphere, one which Robert Graves, the poet and author, also remembered while serving there with the Royal Welsh Fusiliers:

3. Lance Sergeant Gilbert Harriott aged 23. Buried in the Le Touret Military Cemetery. Ref: III.F.9.
4. Second Lieutenant George Edward Elliott aged 20. Buried in the Bethune Town Cemetery. Ref: III.K.13.

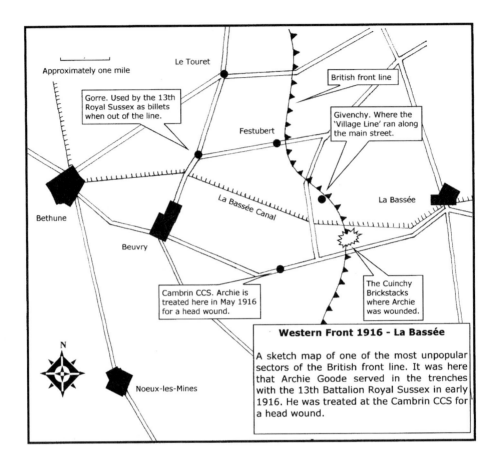

Approximately one mile

Le Touret

British front line

Gorre. Used by the 13th Royal Sussex as billets when out of the line.

Givenchy. Where the 'Village Line' ran along the main street.

Festubert

La Bassée Canal

La Bassée

Bethune

Beuvry

Cambrin CCS. Archie is treated here in May 1916 for a head wound.

The Cuinchy Brickstacks where Archie was wounded.

N

Western Front 1916 - La Bassée

A sketch map of one of the most unpopular sectors of the British front line. It was here that Archie Goode served in the trenches with the 13th Battalion Royal Sussex in early 1916. He was treated at the Cambrin CCS for a head wound.

Noeux-les-Mines

The trenches have made themselves rather than been made, and run inconsequently in and out of the big thirty foot high stacks of bricks; it is most confusing. The parapet of a trench which we don't occupy is built up with ammunition boxes and corpses. Everything here is wet and smelly. The Germans are very close: they have half the brick-stacks, we have the other half. Each side snipes down from the top of its brick-stacks into the other's trenches. This is also a great place for German rifle-grenades and trench-mortars.[5]

5. *Goodbye To all That,* Jonothan Cape..

In the trenches opposite the 13th battalion was a Saxony infantry regiment. Aggressive and professional, they provided a welcome to the Sussex men over the next two days which they would not forget. The war diary:

May 29th
Between 10 and 11am the enemy sent over several HEs [high explosives] and Whizz Bangs [shells from German 77mm Field Guns] blowing in a portion of the Coldstream Lane communication trench. At night an enemy raiding party succeeded in entering a small portion of C Company's front. The raid was preceded by a heavy bombardment on our front and support line trenches. Parapet was damaged in several places. 6 casualties. The raiding party succeeded in capturing an NCO and several rifles. A demonstration was also made by parties of the enemy in front of A and B Company. They were met by rifle and machine gun fire.

The next day there was further activity on C Company's front. This time they were fortunate that the enemy's tunnelling under No Man's Land had ended a little short of the lines. Had the mine exploded directly under the British lines there would have been significantly more casualties:

May 30th
Enemy fairly quiet during the day until he [the Germans] exploded a mine in front of C Company. Considerable damage was done to our parapet...... several men were buried but only one killed.

Archie would not have witnessed the carnage following the exploding of the mine. He was one of the six casualties reported in the war diary on 29th May. Wounded on the right side of his head, he was evacuated to the battalion aid post and later to the casualty clearing station at Cambrin. The process of dealing with casualties at the clearing station was little different from today's accident and emergency departments, albeit a little busier at times!

Upon arrival, the wounded would typically undergo a brief triage, or sorting, by a receiving officer to help determine the nature and severity of their wounds. Individuals with serious wounds were then seen by a doctor more rapidly than those with less severe injuries and those who were clearly beyond help were placed in a separate area. After initial assessment and treatment, patients were either admitted to a ward or evacuated by ambulance train to one of the stationary hospitals. The Cambrin Military Cemetery and the Cambrin Churchyard Extension, with over two thousand war graves, now mark the former site of the casualty clearing station.

His casualty record shows he was back with the battalion within the week, no doubt refreshed and cleaner after a few days of sleeping and eating away from the front. Not all the six C Company men survived that shell burst on 29th May. Private Edward Punch[6] from Worthing died of his wounds later that day.

As June rolled relentlessly on, the battalion, by now well versed in trench warfare, considered themselves to be old hands. The new drafts of officers and men that began arriving in June were steadily bringing the battalion back up to strength. In the middle of June the 13th Battalion left the Cuinchy Brick-Stacks and, while they were without doubt pleased to see their relief arrive, they marched away with some pride. Despite their casualties, the Sussex men had performed well during their time in defence of a notorious sector of the line and now the time was fast approaching for them to show their courage on the offensive.

The build-up for the huge Somme Offensive was now in its final stages; although the 13th Royal Sussex would not be directly involved in the 1st July fighting, they would have a part to play in one of the sideshows further north. Richebourg L'Avoue had already witnessed heavy fighting in 1915 and, like so many of the villages and towns along this part of the front, had been absorbed into the sprawling fortifications that ran like a smear across the battered countryside. The support line trenches and breastworks now cut through the main street, taking advantage of the cellars and derelict buildings that remained, providing some sanctuary from shellfire and trench mortars.

6. SD/3182 Private Edward Punch. Buried in the Cambrin Churchyard Extension. Ref: N.40.

Opposite the British lines was the German salient known as The Boar's Head, a legacy of the Battle of Auber's Ridge, fought a year earlier resulting in over 11,000 British casualties. Divisional staff had decided it was time to remove the offending salient and the 116th Brigade had been selected to make the assault. It was of course part of a much larger plan that would unfold on the morning of 1st July on the Somme. In order to draw attention away from the activity further south, three diversionary attacks would be mounted at other points along the front, the Boar's Head Salient being one of them. In the event these diversions did little to confuse an enemy, who by this time was well aware of what was about to unfold. With no reserves available to support them once they had gained the enemy lines, the troops engaged in these attacks were to all intents and purpose considered expendable. Little wonder, then, that the casualty rate was as large as it was.

Major-General R. Dawson, the newly appointed commander of the 39th Division, intended a two-battalion attack involving men from the 116th Brigade. The choice of battalion for the assault was the decision of the Brigade Commander, Brigadier-General M.L. Hornby[7] DSO, and to him the three Southdowns battalions seemed the most obvious choice. They had built up a good reputation since arriving in France and had the confidence of brigade staff. Initially the 13th Battalion was to be held in reserve, with the 11th and 12th Battalions leading the assault. Sensing disaster in a plan that had given the troops little time to prepare and was to be carried out over difficult ground, Lieutenant-Colonel Harman Grisewood, the commanding officer of the 11th Battalion, expressed his misgivings forcibly to Hornby. Such questioning of command decisions was not to be tolerated. The unfortunate Grisewood was immediately removed from his post and sent home; his battalion was relegated to support the attack. Grisewood may have been sent home in disgrace but he did at least prevent his beloved battalion suffering the heavy casualties that were to be inflicted on the others.

At 2.50am on the morning of 30th June, the noise of the distant artillery bombardment further to the south in the Somme area was joined by the guns of the 39th Divisional Artillery pounding the

7. Brigadier-General Montague Leyland Hornby (1870-1948)

enemy lines in the Boar's Head Salient. To the German troops it was quite obvious an attack was imminent and they retired to their deep dugouts and shelters to wait for the British troops to leave their trench lines and begin their advance across No Man's Land. Eight pages of detailed operational orders made clear the 13th Battalion's part in the attack and, sometime after midnight, the various companies made their way to the jumping-off point in the front-line. The attack was to take place under a smoke screen which, as it turned out, was more of a hindrance than a help. Colonel Draffen recorded the events that followed in the war diary:

> At 3.05am the leading waves of the battalion scaled the parapet, the remainder following at 50 yard intervals. At the same time the flank attack under Lts. Whitely and Ellis gained a footing in the enemy trench. The passage across No Man's Land was accomplished with few casualties except in the left companies [A and B Company] which came under very heavy machine gun fire. The two right companies [C and D Company] succeeded in reaching their objectives but the two left companies only succeeded in penetrating the enemy's wire in one or two places. Just at this moment a smoke cloud which was originally designed to mask our advance drifted right across the front and made it impossible to see more than a few yards ahead. This resulted in all direction being lost and the attack devolving into small bodies of men not knowing which way to go.

Draffen's summary was quite correct: the confusion caused by the smoke and combined with the heavy enemy machine gun fire that had cut down the men of A and B Company had, in effect, broken the momentum of the assault. He continued with:

> Some groups succeeded in entering the support line, engaging the enemy with bombs and bayonet and organising the initial stages of a defence. Other parties swung off to the right and entered the trench where the flank party were operating, causing a great deal of congestion.

On the left the smoke and darkness made the job of penetrating the enemy line so difficult that few, if any, succeeded in reaching the enemy trenches.

Archie was on the right of the attack, with what was left of C Company. Captain Humble-Crofts,[8] his company commander, had been killed. The Company Sergeant Major was wounded and unable to direct operations. This left individual groups to press on alone in an attempt to reach their objectives. It appears that some did. Draffen's account again:

> Some parties of the right company succeeded in reaching the enemy support line where they were subjected to an intense bombardment with H.E. [high explosive] and Whiz Bangs. Captain Hughs who was wounded seeing his company was in danger of being cut off gave the order for the evacuation of the enemy trenches and the remainder of the attacking force returned to our trenches.

It was a similar story with the 12th Battalion. German machine gun fire swept No Man's Land, cutting down the waves of advancing men, while heavy and accurate shellfire turned the already shell-torn ground into a killing field, where it was almost impossible to either advance or retreat. Despite this, the enemy trenches were reached by those who survived that maelstrom of fire, but with many of their officers and senior NCOs now lying dead and wounded behind them. It was only in isolated pockets of resistance that the men of the 12th hung onto their gains. But hang on they did, bravely resisting determined German counter-attacks until early morning when they too were compelled to withdraw in the face of superior odds.

With the survivors now back in their own trenches and No Man's Land littered with their dead, dying and wounded, the battalion's front-line trenches were subjected to a deadly and prolonged artillery bombardment resulting in yet more casualties. It

---

8. Cyril Mitford Humble-Crofts aged 34. Commemorated on the Loos Memorial Panel 69-73.

lasted for two and a half hours and was the final curtain of what can only be described as a fiasco. No ground had been gained and the flower of Sussex youth had been sacrificed in a diversionary attack that Divisional Headquarters referred to in an official communiqué as a 'local raid'. It wasn't until later that day that the full extent of the casualties became apparent. Battalion roll calls soon confirmed what was painfully obvious: very few of those who took part in the attack were answering to their name. The total casualties sustained by the three Southdowns battalions were 15 officers and 364 other ranks killed and 21 officers and 728 other ranks wounded. The 13th Battalion had taken the brunt with nine officers and 169 men killed with a further nine officers wounded. The war diary does not record the number of other ranks wounded or how many later died of their wounds.

Present at the 13th Battalion's roll call parade was Private Archie Goode, no doubt wondering why he had survived and others had not. Relieved by the 14th Hants later that morning, the remnants of both the attacking battalions, now amalgamated into one under the temporary command of Lieutenant-Colonel Draffen, marched away from the front-line with barely enough men to make up two companies. Some fifteen hours later, on an eighteen mile front, a similar story of disaster was about to unfold as the British and French Armies launched the first day of the Somme Offensive which by nightfall on 1st July, would leave over 20,000 dead on the battle-field. As the shockwaves generated by the enormous casualties on the Somme began to echo around the Empire, a similar wave of sorrow struck the Sussex towns and villages which were home to the Southdowners.

An analysis of the casualties from the Boar's Head action has been made by the military historian Paul Reed, using the *Soldiers Died in the Great War 1914-19* database. From this information, which provides the place of birth and enlistment of each individual soldier who died in the Great War, the spread of casualties across the county becomes apparent. *Soldiers Died* shows that some seventy percent of the 349 killed in action were resident in Sussex. The vast majority of the others would also have been Sussex residents but the database does not show place of residence if born outside the county. In total, 77 towns, villages and parishes in the county were affected and with over 700 wounded, some of whom would later die from their wounds.

In West Chiltington, the families of two local soldiers, Norman Ayling and Robert Agate would have undoubtedly been visited and comforted by Ada Goode after the news of their deaths had been received. The village was a small and compact society and Ada was always generous with her time and support for the community. Both men had been serving with Archie in the 13th Battalion and, while Archie was thankfully not on the casualty lists, Ada would have been only too well aware what it was like to have sons serving in the war. Norman Ayling's body was never recovered and he is commemorated on the Loos Memorial, as is Private Arthur Hampshire from the 12th Battalion who was born and raised in neighbouring Pulborough. He too lost his life at Richebourg.

It would have been too much to expect that the 39th Division would not be drawn into the second phase of the Somme Offensive; although the battalion initially found themselves back amid the brick-stacks of Cuinchy and later at Festubert, they were still very much below strength. New arrivals of officers and men were a constant interruption to the now familiar rotation between the trenches, training and rest. Some, like the unfortunate Second Lieutenant Carter,[9] would only last ten days before being killed. Others would last longer.

Along with heavy casualties came the opportunity for others to gain promotion and, as one of the more experienced soldiers in his company, Archie was promoted to Lance Corporal on 8th August. He would now have responsibility for a section or part of a section and be expected to provide leadership under fire. He would soon have the opportunity. On 13th August, the 39th Division received orders to move south to the Beaumont Hamel area in preparation for an offensive north of the River Ancre.

Being infantry, they marched the fifty or so miles to their new sector. Apart from a scheduled stop at Magincourt en Compte, where they underwent further training at Monchy Breton, they were on the road for five days marching as a brigade through the backroads of Artois and Picardy. Although the local population was quite used to

9. Second Lieutenant N.C. Carter aged 22. Killed on 23rd July 1916. Buried in the Bethune Town Cemetery. Ref: III.K.33.

the spectacle of marching troops by now, it must have been an impressive sight as they marched through the small hamlets and villages en route. A brigade of infantry while on the march would take up to two and a quarter miles of road and over two hours to pass a given point. With a whole division on the road, some 15 miles of road would have been taken up with men and transports.

This was no forced march. There were plenty of rest periods and for many it would have been a welcome relief from front-line trench duty. The further south they marched, the more the surrounding countryside would have reminded them of the rolling chalk landscapes of their home counties, something that would not have gone without comment in the ranks of the Sussex and Hampshire men.

On 27th August, they arrived at Mailly-Maillet, a small village to the west of the Ancre Valley. Here the division received its orders for the part it was to play in the general attack along the front from Thiepval to Guillemont. Their task was to capture the three lines of enemy trenches situated on the high ground to the south of Beaumont Hamel. Moving across country from the refuge of the Mailly Mailet Woods, the battalion arrived at the assembly trenches sometime after midnight. Fortified by the rum and coffee ration, they waited impatiently for the dawn. On 3rd September, the 39th Division attacked at five in the morning with all three of its Infantry Brigades. The 13th Battalion war diary takes up the story of C Company:

> About 5.25am C Company left the old British line east of Peche Street and moved forward into a hollow in No Man's Land taking cover behind a ridge north east of Peche Street. When this move was completed D Company moved from West of Peche Street. By this time all the officers of C Company had become casualties and 2nd Lieutenant Story took command of C and D companies.

Clearly it had already gone badly wrong. The advance of the 49th Division on their right had stalled in the face of furious machine gun fire, leaving the Sussex men badly enfiladed from the St. Pierre Divion direction. This machine gun fire had cut down the leading ranks of C Company leaving only two officers unscathed. The 13th Battalion was under orders to provide support for the 11th

Battalion, but they were unsure exactly where the men of the 11th were. The only other officer unwounded was Second Lieutenant Henning, who managed to get in touch with the reserve company of the 11th by sending a runner across to their positions. Their reply was that they had been told to stay put, putting Storey in a quandary as to what he should do next:

> After waiting for some time [presumably for orders which didn't arrive] 2nd Lieutenant Storey took C Company forward [D Company also moved up with them] to support the other companies of the 11th. The company advanced over the ridge to be met by a heavy burst of machine gunfire. 2nd Lieutenant Henning and several men were wounded. 2nd Lieutenant Storey then took forward D Company, part of C Company and a few men of the Rifle Brigade (stragglers). Unfortunately direction was lost and instead of turning to the right to support the 11th battalion [they] swung round too much to the left and entered an enemy trench which was badly knocked about by shell fire. 2nd Lieutenant Storey stayed in this trench for about two hours without being attacked but being heavily shelled the whole time.

Archie and what remained of C Company had been in this situation before and as a Lance Corporal he was now expected to show his mettle. They had reached the enemy trenches but without support they were isolated. Archie and any other NCOs would have been busy organising the trench defences against counter-attack. While this was going on, Storey pushed out patrols to his right and left to try and establish contact with any British troops. No contact was made, but they did see British troops on the right withdrawing. Concerned at being cut off by counter-attack, they eventually withdrew to the ridge in No Man's Land from where Storey was ordered to stay put. The position was untenable and they were soon on the receiving end of an intense enemy bombardment. With their own ammunition running out they had little choice but to retire.

Elsewhere the attack had failed, particularly on the right where the men of the 49th Division had taken over 3000 casualties. In the

116th Brigade, the 11th Battalion had over 100 dead while Archie's battalion, who were only in a supporting role, reported 135 dead, wounded and missing. The 14th Hampshires, who were in their first action as a battalion, lost heavily. Of the 570 men that went into the attack, 17 officers and 440 other ranks were casualties.

The next day the brigade was relieved and marched to bivouacs in Prowse Fort Wood, just west of Mailly-Maillet. Here they spent a wet night huddled under waterproof capes before finally moving to more substantial billets in Bertrancourt. Archie had survived his second major action and he must have wondered how much longer his guardian angel would remain on duty. Five days later they were back in the trenches in the left sub-sector of Beaumont Hamel, with Archie and C Company in the support trenches at White City.

Beaumont Hamel, which would not finally fall until November, was one of a number of villages the German army had turned into a fortress. The enemy positions commanded the valley across which attacking troops would have to cross, a valley still strewn with the dead from the attack on 1st July. It was here that Archie was wounded for a second time. Random shelling from enemy batteries hit the support trenches on 11th September. The war diary does not record any casualties that day only mentioning that, during the four days the battalion was in the trenches, the enemy were fairly active.

Archie's casualty records describe his injuries as gunshot wounds to his face, the left side of his back and left hand. The notes made by the reviewing medical officer on his discharge paperwork give a clearer picture of the extent of his injuries:

> He states that he was wounded in France. He states that when he was in a trench he was hit in the jaw by a piece of shrapnel, this caused a compound fracture of the lower jaw. The soft tissue of the chin was entirely shot away. He was also wounded in the left iliac region [hip] and in the left hand.

Evacuated to the No. 11 Casualty Clearing Station at nearby Gezaincourt, he was admitted to the 13th Stationary Hospital in Boulogne two days later. He had got his Blighty wound that would ensure his eventual evacuation to England, but would remain in France while his condition was stabilised. For some seriously wounded men hospitalised on the French coast relatives were allowed to travel across the channel to visit them. I have no idea if Ada travelled to Bolougne during his stay in hospital, but she would have certainly been informed that he had been seriously wounded. It was probably a mixture of relief and worry that overtook the family in Sussex: relief that he was 'out of it' and alive, but worry regarding the extent of his injuries. In Sussex the war was never very far away. The great artillery bombardments on the Somme and elsewhere could often be heard from the downland summits, providing a constant reminder of loved ones in danger.

Archie had been fortunate that the regimental aid post and the field ambulance were not inundated with casualties on the day he had been wounded. With serious shrapnel wounds to the face and jaw, the primary treatment would have been to maintain his airway and prevent him from choking to death on blood and debris from the wound. It is likely that this help was close at hand and, once he was able to breathe without hindrance, any immediate serious haemorrhage could be dealt with. In many cases such as this, an emergency tracheotomy would be the only way of securing his breathing. Had he been wounded during a period when the field ambulance teams were overstretched he may not have survived. Archie's war was over; ahead lay eighteen months of hospitalisation and convalescence before he would be discharged as no longer fit for war service.

The medical notes only give us an indication of what this young man went through over the subsequent months it took to reconstruct his face and jaw. With a shattered jaw, initial surgery would have focused on wiring the remaining pieces together and grafting bone from the hip. He would have been fed during this time through a tube until the jaw had healed. Plastic surgery was in its infancy in 1916, but there were some remarkable procedures being developed. Archie had a number of plastic operations in Boulogne, where the French medical services had established a plastic surgery unit and later, it appears, he had further operations at the King George Military Hospital in London.

The King George was originally built for His Majesty's

Stationary Office, but on its completion in 1915 it was so admirably suited as an additional medical facility that it was converted to a military hospital. Between 1915 and 1919 some 71,000 patients were treated there. Archie's numerous operations would have involved tube and pedicle grafts from the upper chest and shoulder to replace the lost tissue around the jaw, a ground-breaking procedure in 1916. To replace the lost tissue from his jaw, surgeons would have to graft replacement tissue using a stem or tube of tissue. A tube pedicle is a flap of skin sewn down its long edges, with one end left attached to the site of origin; the other is attached to the site to be grafted. For patients with severe facial disfigurement a tube might be taken from the stomach area and initially attached to the wrist. After a number of weeks the tube would be disconnected from the stomach, the arm raised and the loose end of the tube attached to the site on the face to be repaired. It was a complex and lengthy procedure which accounted for the amount of time Archie spent in hospital.

Staff at the King George also fitted Archie with upper and lower jaw dentures in early 1918. While these seemed to be firmly in place, it was noted he couldn't chew on hard food. On discharge there was still a piece of shrapnel in his fourth lumber vertebrae, but movement of his left hand was normal. Another note records he was complaining of pain in his left diaphragm and that he had a great deal of facial disfigurement.

On 11th March 1918 he was discharged from the army, the reviewing medical officer described him as:

> A respectable and honest man of good character, disabled
> by wounds, who desires employment in Canada as a
> farmer.

Understandably, he wanted to return to Canada but for the foreseeable future he would have to return home to Ada and the girls. By November 1918 a new and more deadly enemy had raised its head, one that would generate a casualty list far in excess of any the Great War had produced in four years of fighting. By November of 1918 a strain of influenza seemingly no different from that of previous years proved to be so deadly, and engendered such a state of panic and chaos across the globe, that many people believed the world was coming to an end. It struck with amazing speed, often killing its victims within just hours of the first signs of infection. So fast did the 1918 strain overwhelm the body's natural defences, that the usual cause of death in influenza patients, a secondary infection of lethal pneumonia, often never had a chance to establish itself. Instead, the virus caused an uncontrollable haemorrhaging that filled the lungs, and patients would drown in their own body fluids.

One of the victims was Archie Goode. He died at home in West Chiltington in the arms of his elder sister, Violet, just before Christmas 1918. He was twenty-two years old. The death certificate recorded influenza compounded by the onset of pneumonia. It was a tragic end to a young life that had survived the battlefield and long months of painful recovery and I can understand why my grand-mother and the family chose to erase the painful memory. He shares a final resting place and gravestone with his father in the West Chiltington Churchyard. His name also appears on the Thakeham War Memorial; beneath it is that of his brother, Lynton Goode.

3

Anzac

Lynton Goode

On the other side of the world, five days after his younger brother enlisted in Chichester, Lynton Goode walked into a Brisbane recruiting office and volunteered for overseas service with the Australian Imperial Force. Lynton emigrated to Australia sometime around 1910, although I have had some difficulty in discovering the exact date. There is a Lynton Goode recorded as sailing from London on the *SS Ophir*, in March 1910, if this was Lynton, he would have been two days short of his sixteenth birthday. There are several other listings in migration records of individuals who might be him, but none that are conclusive enough to be absolutely sure. What exactly he did after he arrived in Australia is not clear. In the 15th Battalion nominal roll of 1915 Lynton is described as a 'tobacco farmer', which would possibly place him in the Stanhope area to the north of Brisbane where the tobacco growing industry was based. He was either working his own land or, possibly, working for another grower.

The army records I received from Australia not only confirmed that 1817 Private Lynton Goode was my great-uncle, but they also included copies of his attestation papers, service record and casualty record. I can't help but wonder why he gave his brother, Charles, as his next of kin, rather than his mother. In fact, in early 1916 Ada had to request information regarding her son and she did not have official confirmation of his death until 9th September 1916, over a year after Lynton had been killed in action. One other unexplained piece of information emerged from Lynton's paperwork; a handwritten note instructs that a final draft of the letter informing the next of kin of his death should also be sent to a Miss Hamilton, giving an address in Alexandria, Egypt. Who was this Miss Hamilton and what was her relationship with Lynton? Leaving the Hamilton question unanswered for the time being, my next step was to determine the part played by Lynton in the Gallipoli campaign.

The Australian Imperial Force was Australia's response to the call to arms; those who enlisted did so for the duration of the war. Notably, the AIF retained its fully volunteer status until the end of the conflict despite two national referendums on conscription. Over the next four years, 331,814 Australians would be sent overseas to serve, and of these some sixty-four percent would be killed or wounded. The 15th Battalion was formed six weeks after the declaration of war in September 1914; three quarters of the battalion were volunteers from Queensland and the remainder from Tasmania. Together with the 13th, 14th and 16th Battalions, the unit formed the 4th Infantry Brigade commanded by Brigadier-General John Monash.[1]

By 1915, the Allied military leadership had no real answer to the impasse of trench warfare in the way of alternative battlefield strategy. In their desperation to find a way around the stalemate, the Allied High Command fixed on the Dardanelles Strait leading from the Mediterranean to Constantinople, the modern day Istanbul. In Australia thousands of young Australians had volunteered for service abroad by Christmas 1914. For some it was a welcome break from the hardships of working the land, for others like Lynton it was a chance to perhaps get home to England again and see the family, but for many it was simply an adventure. The Army could afford to be choosy and many were turned away as unfit for service but, on 23rd January 1915 in Brisbane, 20 year-old Lynton was declared fit for active service and joined the 15th Battalion.

The 4th Brigade left Brisbane for overseas duty just before Christmas 1914; after a short stop in Albany, Western Australia, they

---

1. Brigadier-General (later General Sir) John Monash (1865-1960). After Gallipoli, appointed GOC 3rd Australian Division, and from June 1918, General Officer Commanding Australian Corps.

disembarked in Alexandria in February 1915 where they joined the AIF's 1st Division and became part of the Australian and New Zealand Army Corps[2] commanded by Lieutenant-General William R. Birdwood. Together with some British troops, the Anzac forces had been kept in Egypt because of unsuitable training facilities in England and later helped protect the Suez Canal, following Turkey's entry into the war in October 1914. Now they would be diverted to take part in an amphibious landing on the Gallipoli Peninsula.

The Anzac Divisions were given the task of taking and holding the most northerly landing zone at Gabe Tepe. The aim of the first wave of fifteen hundred Australian troops was to secure the beach and seize the high ground of the third (or Gun) Ridge and the heights of the Sari Bair Ridge. Control of this high ground was vital for success. By the end of the first day the Australians expected to be established on this high ground and linked up with Allied troops, who were landing on the tip of the peninsula. The combined landing forces would then secure the forts guarding the Dardanelles and the Navy would sail through to the Sea of Marmara and take the ultimate prize, Constantinople.

It was at this point that I began to look for information in relation to the role the 15th Battalion played in the campaign. To understand the events that led to Lynton's death, I needed to know more about his battalion and the actions they took part in. Once again I turned to the Internet, my search producing an astonishing number of useful and informative websites relating to Australian forces in both world wars. The size and depth of information these sites held was quite remarkable. One in particular, The *Anzac Research* site, directed me to a message board whose members were specifically interested in the 15th Battalion. Here, I corresponded with other researchers who had relatives who served with the battalion. It was through contact with individuals on this website that I managed to obtain a copy of the 15th Battalion war diary[3]. The war diary gave me a graphic description of the day-to-day actions of

2. 'Anzac' was first used in Gallipoli in 1915, but eventually came to be used as slang to describe any Australian or New Zealand soldier. Today in Australia and New Zealand Anzac Day is celebrated every year on 25th April.
3. The war diary is now available online at: www.awm.gov.au/diaries

the battalion as seen by the commanding officer Lieutenant-Colonel James Cannan. Very few private soldiers were mentioned by name, but it was possible to get a reasonably clear impression of what took place in the nine weeks Lynton served with the battalion by matching the war diary records with other official histories.

I also managed to get a copy of the out-of-print history of the 15th Battalion.[4] This text provided more of the missing details and assisted me greatly in understanding the events that led up to the August Offensive and, in particular, the fighting that Lynton and A Company took part in during the desperate scramble for Hill 971 in early August 1915.

The landing of Allied forces on the Gallipoli Peninsula took place in the early hours of 25th April 1915. Troops were put ashore at Cape Helles and further north at Anzac Cove. By the end of the first day, apart from isolated groups who had penetrated further and encountered stiff opposition from Turkish forces, the Australians had in reality only gained a few hundred metres by nightfall. In effect, they made little further overall progress in the remaining seven months of the campaign. By the middle of May the four hundred acre bridgehead, which was referred to as Anzac, had established a mile and a half frontage along the beach with its front-line extending to the rugged slopes of Sari Bair in the north and to Bolton's Ridge[5] in the south. At the end of Bolton's Ridge was the isolated Chatham's Post which was the most southerly position occupied at Anzac.

So how and when did Lynton Goode arrive on the peninsula? Once again the archive material available online from the Australian War Memorial website proved to be invaluable. Almost every troop movement from Australia to the battlefields of the Great War were recorded in the form of nominal rolls. Each infantry battalion was regularly reinforced with new recruits and these reinforcements were clearly documented. The researcher has little difficulty in tracing the movement of individual soldiers, their personal details and the troop ships they sailed on.

Over the course of the four years of the Great War, the 15th Battalion was reinforced on twenty-three occasions with fresh troops

4. History of the 15th Battalion, Australian Imperial Force by T.P. Chataway (William Brooks. 1948).
5. Named after Lieutenant-Colonel W. K. Bolton, CO of the 8th Battalion.

from Australia. Just over two weeks prior to the Anzac landings on 25th April, the fourth reinforcements for the 15th Battalion left Brisbane on the SS *Star of England*, a Dominion Line ship of some nine thousand tons that had been requisitioned by the Commonwealth government to carry troops of the AIF abroad.

For 1817 Private Lynton Goode, getting himself and his kit aboard the *Star of England* marked the end of initial training and the beginning of his long journey to join A Company. Of the 111 men who embarked on 8th April, only 101 would arrive on the peninsula to join the battalion on 2nd June. Sickness and disease, already becoming a major factor among the troops at Anzac, would claim the remainder either in Egypt or on the final leg of the journey to the Greek Island of Lemnos, the jumping off point for the peninsula.

Enlistment had thrown men together from all walks of life and from all parts of the Commonwealth. Of the men on board the *Star of England*, thirty-four gave their next of kin in the United Kingdom, two in South Africa and two in Canada. One of the Canadians, a Robert Hamilton originally from Brandon City in Manitoba, joined up on the same day in Brisbane as Lynton. Hamilton would survive the war and return to Australia. The Hamilton connection did not go unnoticed. Were Robert Hamilton and the Miss Hamilton, as referred to in Lynton's papers, related?

Yes, it was clutching at straws, but the coincidence was too tempting not to follow up. I got in contact via the internet with Tom Mitchell, the archivist at the University of Brandon in Canada. I explained the background to my enquiry and he very kindly offered to check local material in an attempt to find any reference the Hamilton Family in Brandon around 1915. Tom's reply was a little disappointing but predictable:

> I have checked for Hamilton's buried in the Brandon cemetery. None. I have checked for the Clover Leaf Dairy in Brandon c.1914. No listing. I have checked for a W. Hamilton in Brandon c.1914. No listing. Not sure where to look next.

It looked very much as if that line of research had come to a full stop. Was this mystery lady the sister of Robert and did he introduce her to Lynton while they were in Egypt waiting to move to Gallipoli, or was she a girl he had met and of no relation to Robert? I shall probably never know, but the likelihood of her being a nurse is high. There would be little reason for her to be there otherwise, and she must have been a significant person in his life. The romantic in me would like to believe that this was indeed the case. The fact that he specifically asked the military authorities to inform her if he became a casualty leads me to suspect this was perhaps more than a passing relationship.

Alexandria to Lemnos Island was a three day sea voyage. Lemnos had become the Allied base for operations in the Dardanelles and was home to the Navy and some of the Allied High Command. The island was also becoming increasingly full of wounded and sick troops from the peninsula. The initial planning for the campaign had not for a moment envisaged the stalemate that had brought the advance to a standstill and the sheer numbers of wounded and sick that were overwhelming the already overstretched medical services. Not that this would be immediately apparent to reinforcements from Australia, who invariably found themselves at Lemnos before embarking on the final crossing to the Anzac beaches.

Such was the reputation of the Anzac troops by this time that they were often kept on board ship whilst at Lemnos to avoid the inevitable confrontations with authority. Whether this happened to the fourth reinforcements there is no way of telling, but we do know from the 15th Battalion War Diary that Lynton Goode along with the rest of the fourth reinforcements arrived at Anzac on 2nd June. The battalion was in bivouac in Rest Gully (sometimes known as Reserve Gully) having earned a long promised rest, and there was no doubt that these additional men were badly needed.

In the thirty-seven days since the Battalion had landed in April, the casualties had begun to mount up: 10 officers and 128 other ranks had been killed, 296 had been wounded and a further 103 were officially missing. By the time the battalion was moved out of the front-line, very few of the original officers remained and the battalion was well below strength. To Lynton and the other reinforcements arriving from Egypt, the condition of the battalion must have been something of a shock. Many individuals were in a very poor state and, although the battalion war diary gives little away regarding the welfare of the men, we do know that they had been involved in almost continuous fighting from the moment they landed. If this was not enough to contend with, sickness was reducing the battalion strength on a daily basis.

Approaching from the sea, Lynton would have been aware of the stench that hung over the peninsula even before he set foot on the beach at Anzac Cove. The dreadful smell, generated from the wholly inadequate sanitary arrangements and the unburied dead that were still strewn across much of the fought-over ground, was just one more thing for new arrivals to get used to. The battalion war diary notes a steady stream of men being sent down the line to hospital suffering with Dysenteric Diarrhoea. Known by the troops as the 'Gallipoli Trots', it reduced the already weary troops to a state of almost total physical weakness, rendering them useless as fighting men. By July, well over a 1000 men a week were being evacuated from the peninsula and by August, some eighty percent of men at Anzac were suffering with dysentery. The men of the 4th Brigade were particularly badly hit. On the day before Lynton arrived at Rest Gully, Quarter Master Sergeant Lord and Company Sergeant Major Hanson were sent to hospital, unfit for further active service. Thirty-two men were recorded as sick on 28th May, and over the rest of June a further twenty-five would be recorded as sick and sent to hospital. The majority of these would not return to front-line duties.

Landing at night, Lynton would have to wait until morning to be introduced to the other enemy on the peninsula: flies. The flies, millions of them engorged from corpses and the numerous open latrines, covered everything. By July they had become a plague of almost biblical proportions, the primitive conditions in which the invading army lived did nothing to help combat the problem. Even before food had been half consumed it was black with flies, which the troops swallowed with each mouthful of food and drink of water. They crawled all over the troops in the trenches, were the topic of conversation in every post and trench and they spread dysentery at an alarming rate. Many would argue they were more of a nuisance than the Turks. Chattaway's comments about the state of the battalion at this time were frank and to the point:

> As a health resort, the Gallipoli Peninsula was an utter failure. From the first day of the landing diarrhoea had

become a nightmare to the men. The flies, the continual odour of rotting bodies along with the inadequate and mostly unpalatable food, and at intervals, a marked shortage of water, all helped to aid this dread disease in undermining the health of the men. In this matter our medical staff were faced with a most difficult problem. Any man capable of standing erect, sick though he happened to be, could not be evacuated without seriously weakening the unit. Added to this, loyalty to their mates prevented the men from leaving the peninsular other than on a stretcher.

Lynton's arrival brought the strength of A Company up to 143 and almost daily reinforcements were quickly bringing the battalion up to full strength again. By 7th June, Cannan[6] recorded 622 other ranks and 18 officers on roll. By 27th June, this had increased to 24 officers and 670 other ranks. In another month the battalion would be up to a strength of 717 other ranks and 25 officers. Undoubtedly, there was a reason for this and clearly the 4th Brigade was going to be involved.

To break the deadlock another plan was emerging to move the campaign to a successful conclusion and Lynton had arrived just in time to take part. This time the focus would be to the north of Anzac at Sulva Bay and on the heights of the Sari Bair Ridge. Towards the end of June these plans were well advanced and there was every confidence that this offensive, planned for August, would achieve the much needed breakout. Despite the fact the battalion was at rest, they were worked hard both day and night mainly undertaking that task that every front-line soldier became so familiar with over the four years of the war: digging. They dug trenches, saps, graves and dugouts, unloaded stores and ammunition and did so under shell-fire and continual sniping.

For a brigade about to go into action, one might have assumed that a more balanced programme of rest and activity would have been the order of the day, not a debilitating regime of fatigues that would further weaken already tired troops. Bizarrely, once the rumour of the impending offensive had circulated, the numbers of

6. Later, Major-General James Harold Cannan CB, CMG DSO (1882-1976). He left the 15th Battalion a year later to command the 11th Australian Infantry Brigade.

46

men reporting sick began to decrease; there was a clear desire to be part of whatever was going on and not to let their mates down.

By the end of July, Lynton would have been relatively at home in Rest Gully and adjusted to life at Anzac with all its dangers. The period between June and July was very quiet by Anzac standards, but it proved to be the lull before the storm and the fact that over 500 men of the battalion were now unseasoned troops was not missed by Cannan. It was practically a new unit and one which had not fought together or even trained together and, to Cannan's disquiet, no opportunity was to be provided for the battalion to prepare for its role in the coming offensive. This was particularly worrying, as Monash had intimated to his battalion commanders that night marches in rough country on compass bearings would be involved.

So what was it about the 15th Battalion's role that was the cause of Cannan's uneasiness? It centred on the range of hills that could be observed from most of Anzac, the Sari Bair Ridge, the very ridge that had been included in the objectives for the first day of the landing. This imposing ridge links a number of hills that begin at the northern end of the Anzac bridgehead. The three highest points are Chunuk Bair at 850 feet, Hill Q at 900 feet and Koja Chemen Tepe or Hill 971. From this ridge descend a confusing maze of gullies or deres which merge into three main valleys, Sazli Beit, Chailak Dere and Aghyl Dere. This was to be the battleground for the 4th Brigade in what was to become known as the August Offensive.

The plan involved the capture of outlying Turkish outposts which prevented access to the gullies leading up to the ridge, the storming of Hill 971, Hill Q and Chunuk Bair and finally a link up with the 3rd Light Horse Brigade, now dismounted, who would advance from Russell's Top[7] across the Nek.[8] The light horsemen would be supported by the New Zealanders moving down behind

7. Russell's Top was part of a ridge line that stretched northwest from Anzac Cove and joined the second ridge, along which the Anzac frontline was established, at the large round hill called Baby 700. Russell's Top was joined to Baby 700 by a thin bridge of land called the Nek. The Top was the highest point within the Anzac perimeter and commanded views along most of the Turkish line to the south of Baby 700. On it was sited an artillery battery and at least eight machine guns. It was named after Brigadier-General Andrew Russell, commander of the New Zealand Mounted Rifles Brigade, who established his headquarters on it in May 1915.
8. The Nek is a narrow stretch of ridge which connected the Anzac trenches at Russell's Top to the knoll called Baby 700 on which the Turkish defenders were entrenched. In total area, the Nek is about the size of three tennis courts.

the Turkish lines from the captured Chunuk Bair to meet them at Baby 700. On paper the operation looked and sounded simple, but this was its downfall. It was nothing like simple in operation and was far too ambitious. The 15th Battalion's part in the plan, together with the 16th and 14th Battalions, was to take Abdel Rahman Bair which formed the northern slope of Hill 971, while the 29th Indian Brigade, under Brigadier-General H.V. Cox[9], would storm the summit of 971.

A number of diversionary attacks were to be made to keep the Turks busy in the south of the sector and to prevent the rapid movement of Turkish reinforcements to the north. Of these diversions, the 1st Australian Brigade's charge at Lone Pine was one of only two successful actions of the whole offensive but sadly claimed the life of 32 year old Second Lieutenant Everard Digges La Touche,[10] a County Down man and a great friend of my paternal grandfather. Everard was fighting with the Australian 2nd Battalion and died from his wounds later that day.

British involvement would require the 10th and 11th Divisions, commanded by Major-General Stopford,[11] to land at Suvla Bay, take Kiretch Tepe and occupy the high ground of Chocolate Hill and W Hill. Once the village of Big Anafarta had fallen, they would be on the left flank of Hill 971 and in a position to support the 4th Brigade and Cox's Indian Brigade. To add weight to the Australian assault, the British 40th Brigade would accompany Monash. The stage was set for the final disaster of the campaign.

Monash had been quite correct about the night march element: the Battalion would have to find its way through some very difficult terrain in the darkness and from there onto its objective. On 6th August, the brigade left its bivouac positions in Rest Gully at 9.35pm. Lynton and the 15th Battalion took up their station behind the 13th and 14th Battalions and the 16th Battalion and the Indian brigade brought up the rear of the column. From the start, the unwieldy column moved in fits and starts along the newly-made

9. Later, Major-General Sir Herbert Vaughan Cox (1860-1923).
10. Buried at Lone Pine Cemetery.
11. Major-General Sir Frederick William Stopford was commander of IX Corps. Stopford's long-distance command (from an off-shore battleship) during the Suvla Bay landings was found entirely wanting in direction and focus. In the event Stopford's obvious failure resulted in his being sent home in disgrace to England in mid-August 1915.

road that ran along North Beach. There was no moon and the night was pitch black. As they marched up the beach road they could hear the unmistakable sounds of battle on their right flank.

What they could hear in the darkness above them was the New Zealand Mounted Rifles attacking Turkish positions in the steep foothills of the range. The Mounted Rifles were tasked with clearing the way for the New Zealand Infantry Brigade who were to take Chunuk Bair. This action by the Mounted Rifles received very little recognition and was largely overshadowed by the events that were about to unfold. It was undoubtedly a highly successful feat of arms and described by Charles Bean,[12] the Australian war correspondent, as an operation, '…the brilliance of which was never surpassed, if indeed equalled, during the campaign'.

Meanwhile, the stop-start progress made by Monash's brigade had brought the column to another standstill, this time for fifteen minutes at Number 3 Outpost. The dead of 40 Brigade were testimony to the fight that had taken place to secure it. The difficulties of moving such a large body of men had quickly become apparent, and in order to keep pace the battalion either found themselves at a steady double or at a standstill while yet another delay rippled down through the column. Monash was becoming impatient as the tight timetable he had set for this operation began to slip.

By the time Lynton and the men of the 15th and 16th Battalions had begun their climb up through Taylor's Gap towards the steeper slopes above them they were already dangerously behind schedule. Taylor's Gap was intended as a shortcut but was to lead to a maze of small gullies and washaways. Despite the fact that the battalion was being guided by Major Percy Overton[13] and a local Greek guide who were familiar with the area, the confusion of interconnecting gullies and ravines was now beginning to dramatically slow the battalion down. Adding to these difficulties, they were now being harassed by groups of Turkish troops who were putting up a very effective defensive action.

12. In 1914 Bean was nominated by the Australian Journalists' Association to accompany the AIF as official war correspondent, and he joined the troops on Gallipoli and the Western Front. After the war he was appointed to write the official history of Australia's participation. He subsequently set up the Australian War Records Section and conceived the idea of the Australian War Memorial, to be built in Canberra.

13. Major Percy John Overton of the Canterbury Mounted Rifles was killed later on 7th August 1915. He was mentioned in dispatches.

By 2.30am Cannan was seeking reassurance from Overton that they were proceeding in the right direction His subsequent entry in the battalion war diary gives some impression of the frustration that he was beginning to feel:

> Eventually got in touch with Major Overton and his guiding party about 02.30 in a gully which was at the time temporary Brigade Head Quarters. At this point D Coy [Company] was detailed as advance guard with Battalion HQ in rear of leading platoon of B Coy. Advancing 200 yards across an open clearing fire was opened on us from a gully running parallel to our front, this was assaulted with the bayonet and taken and advance continued. We then advanced across some open ground and enemy opened fire on our front and both flanks which necessitated the deployment of the whole of the advance guard, C and D Coy was sent forward to support B Coy. The assault pushed on and ridges cleared of enemy and advance continued. A Coy was then sent forward on the right to protect the advance. At about 3am again got into personal touch with Major Overton and party. I closely questioned him with regard to our continued advance and asked him to indicate approximately the position of the 200 foot contour of the Abdul Rahman Bair.

Shortly after 3am Cannan was obliged to commit all three companies to engage the Turks. Major D. Cannan,[14] commanding A Company, soon found himself and his men involved in fierce hand-to-hand fighting in the steep broken country that was providing good cover for the Turkish riflemen. As this engagement gathered pace, the 16th Battalion had meanwhile closed up on its sister battalion and together this body of men, mixed together in the confusion of the darkness, fought the enemy in a deadly battle that was to last until the dawn.

So close was the contact that men were firing at their opponents at ranges of less than five yards, inflicting terrible wounds. The

---

14. Major D. H. Cannan was killed on 8th August 1915. He was the brother of Lieutenant-Colonel James Cannan.

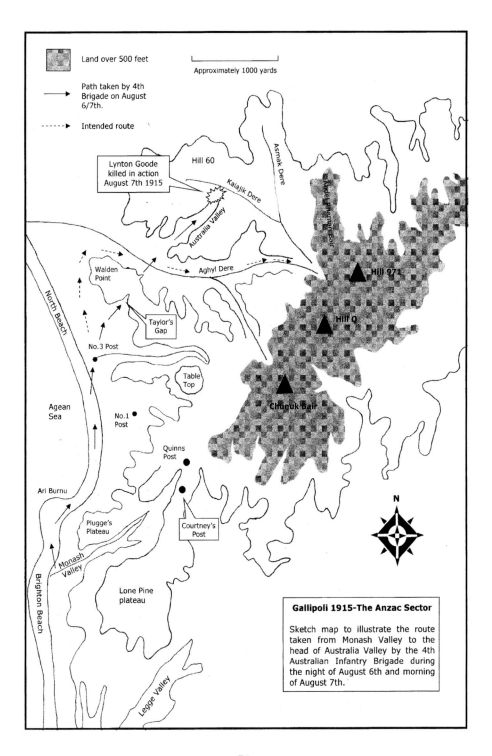

Land over 500 feet

Approximately 1000 yards

Path taken by 4th Brigade on August 6/7th.

Intended route

Lynton Goode killed in action August 7th 1915

Hill 60

Asmak Dere

Kalajik Dere

Australia Valley

Aghyl Dere

Walden Point

Hill 971

Hill Q

Taylor's Gap

No.3 Post

Table Top

Chunuk Bair

Agean Sea

No.1 Post

Quinns Post

Ari Burnu

Plugge's Plateau

Courtney's Post

North Beach

Monash Valley

Lone Pine plateau

Brighton Beach

Legge Valley

N

Gallipoli 1915-The Anzac Sector

Sketch map to illustrate the route taken from Monash Valley to the head of Australia Valley by the 4th Australian Infantry Brigade during the night of August 6th and morning of August 7th.

Australians charged again and again with fixed bayonets in an effort to dislodge stubborn groups of Turks and, although by now retreating in the face of the determined Australian attacks, had successfully brought the advance to a standstill. All around, the living and the dead lay together in a confusion of shallow scrape-holes. The unseasoned Australian reinforcements had fought well but many of them now lay dead or wounded in the scrub. It must have been a shocking introduction to warfare for these young men. When daylight finally broke on the battleground, the Turks had gone and the battalion found itself on a ridge they assumed was a spur of the Abdel Rahman Bair and that the valley they were looking down into was Asmak Dere.

Unfortunately they were not where they thought they were. During the night the advancing troops had become hopelessly lost and were in fact on a ridge looking down on the Kaiajik Dere, below Hill 60. The Asmak Dere lay on the far side of Hill 60. Although several of the battalion's officers, including Cannan, suspected they were off route they had no way of confirming this belief; the maps that had been issued were inaccurate and none of them, apart from Major Overton, had the opportunity to recon-noitre the area before the offensive began. Overton was no longer with them, having left before the close-quarter fighting began. The situation looked bleak.

Surviving the battle was Private Lynton Goode, now digging in with the remnants of A Company along the south western crest of the Kaiajik Dere. They should have been on the summits of the Sari Bair Ridge by now, instead they were exhausted and nowhere near their objective. They were also taking a considerable number of casualties. Cannan's recollections of the morning of 7th August were recorded in the war diary:

> Having reassembled my command I found that I had a frontage of about 100 yards to put in a state of defence with the support and communication trenches and then dug reserve trenches which was done in very quick time and an excellent performance considering the exhausted condition of the troops......we were then informed by our Brigadier General (Monash) that we were to consoli-

date our position and we would not undertake any further offensive movement that day and we then remained in our position…until instructed to report to Brigade HQ at 1945 hrs on 7th August for orders. Our casualties during this period of the operation were 7 officers wounded approx, 30 other ranks killed approx and 75 other ranks wounded.

Cannan acknowledges the tiredness of his men, but what he had failed to record was the pitiful state of the men of his command at this point in the battle. They were in a badly enfiladed position, taking casualties, exhausted, hungry and, above all, thirsty. Along with the initial ration of one full water bottle, was the order to avoid drinking needlessly and to conserve it to the last moment of endurance. To men already dangerously dehydrated this was not good advice. We know from Chattaway's account that there was often a scarcity of water and all water had to be brought up from the beach on a daily basis. It is highly probable that large numbers of troops were suffering from an accumulated dehydration as a result. Clearly this and the question mark over the physical fitness of the majority of the men must have had an impact on the progress of the advance of the 4th Brigade. By dawn of 7th August they were desperately tired and many of them were unable to continue.

The 15th Battalion's position was not a secure one; they were overlooked by Turkish snipers on the next spur to the north and by now Turkish artillery had also found the range. By mid morning the defensive line had been withdrawn to the reverse slope of the ridge which undoubtedly prevented further loss of life. It was a decision that was too late for Lynton. In all probability it was enemy fire or shrapnel from a bursting shell that initially wounded him. His casualty form records he was wounded in action on 7th August 1915 and, on 16th March 1916, some seven months later he is still listed as 'wounded not yet rejoined'. It is not until the Court of Enquiry held at Serapeum, nearly a year after his death, that he is officially listed as killed in action. Testimony at the Court of Enquiry from Sergeant C. Hollamby, Lynton's platoon Sergeant, is plain:

Informant states that on or about 7th August 1916 on the

left of Suvla Bay, Goode was killed. Informant camped
with him for some time but is quite certain Goode is dead.

We will never know the exact circumstances of his death, but it
would appear from the evidence that he was one of the other ranks
whom Cannan recorded in the war diary as being killed and
wounded on that day. His body was never identified and when the
Australian Military Mission arrived on the Peninsula in early 1919,
the remains of many from this action were found where they had
fallen over three years earlier. Lynton joined the hundreds of others
from his battalion who were to remain unidentified and consigned
to a common grave on the battlefield. His name is commemorated at
the Lone Pine Cemetery.

A very much reduced 15th Battalion was withdrawn from the
front-line on 9th September and four days later they embarked for
Lemnos with a complement of 11 officers and 136 other ranks. Their
total casualties during the month long August Offensive numbered
14 officers and 581 other ranks. These were heavy losses, albeit
nothing like the number of casualties the brigade would suffer once
they reached the Western Front in 1916, but enough to render the
battalion ineffective until reinforcements arrived.

After the failure of the August Offensive the writing was on the
wall for the campaign and evacuation became the order of the day.
Over the course of several days, in what must be described as a
brilliant operation involving some extremely creative planning, the
whole force was moved off the peninsula under cover of darkness
without a single casualty. It remains a great irony that the only
totally successful element of the whole campaign at Anzac came in
the final days when the beleaguered troops withdrew from the
positions they had defended so tenaciously for months. Many left in
tears, almost ashamed to be leaving their mates behind in the neatly
tended graveyards that littered Anzac. To those that survived, this
was the final tragedy of the campaign, though not of the Australian
experience in the war.

In September 1916, a year after he was killed, further news of
Lynton reached his mother in England after she had written to
Victoria Barracks in Melbourne asking about the circumstances of
his death.

September 9th 1916

Dear Madam

In answer to your enquiry for No. 1817 Private Lynton Goode, 15th Battalion, A.I.F. We have been informed that he was killed on August 7th 1915 near Suvla Bay. The informant, who was a friend of Private Goode, has no further particulars but is quite certain he is dead. We are very sorry indeed to have to send you such meagre details and will gladly forward to you at once anything that we may hear in future.

Assuring you of our deepest sympathy

Yours faithfully

J. M. Lean (Major)

It was a tragic end to a young life and devastating news for Ada and the children. If Lynton's death was not enough, the news of Archie's wounds in the trenches at Hamel in September 1916 had brought additional worry to the family. As the casualty lists grew longer and 1916 moved towards its conclusion, the family braced themselves for the coming months.

4

Sussex Yeoman

Douglas Allen Watts

On 7th October 1915, almost exactly two months to the day that Lynton was killed in action, my maternal grandfather Douglas Allen Watts landed on Gallipoli as part of the large body of reinforcements that had been requested by Sir Ian Hamilton,[1] Commander-in-Chief of the Gallipoli campaign. Coming ashore on Cape Helles at the already legendary Lancashire Landing, he would not learn until much later that the brother of Margery Goode, the girl he would marry in 1922, was lying with the dead in the northern sector of Anzac.

Douglas' landing was unopposed as his regiment disembarked onto the rickety planking of the pier that at least prevented them from getting their feet wet, a different story from the morning of 25th April when the sea was red with the blood of the 1st Battalion, Lancashire Fusiliers as they fought desperately to establish a beach-head and won six Victoria Crosses 'before breakfast'. The story of how Douglas arrived on Gallipoli is in itself part of the story of the Sussex Yeomanry Regiment and its transition from a territorial cavalry unit to its final days as an infantry battalion in the trenches of the Western Front.

Douglas was a keen photographer and the photograph album he kept of his wartime snaps is a wonderful visual record of his life

---

1. General Sir Ian Standish Monteith Hamilton (1853-1947) was Commander-in-Chief of the Mediterranean Expeditionary Force. Having been made a scapegoat for the failure of the opera-tion, Hamilton was recalled to London on 15th October 1915, effectively ending his military career.

as a private soldier and later, in 1918, as a pilot in the fledgling Royal Air Force. It was through this collection of photographs that I was able to begin piecing together the record of his war service. I knew he had fought at Gallipoli and served in Egypt and I remember my father showing me a picture of an aircraft that Douglas had crashed during flying training. I had always wondered how he had escaped from the mangled heap of wires and spars without serious injury. I also recall playing with his medals as a young child. Alas only one, his British War Medal, survived those childhood games.

However, that medal was enough to provide me with his regimental service number, which was the key to a more detailed research giving me access to his Medal Index Card (MIC). As soon as a member of the armed forces was posted overseas he qualified for a campaign medal which was recorded in the Medal Index; an MIC will usually indicate the regiments the soldier served with, his service number or numbers and what ranks were held. Consequently, the cards helpfully provide the researcher with a record of all medals awarded to an individual and often the theatres of war in which they first served. Four campaign medals were awarded during the Great War: the 1914 Star, the 1914-15 Star, the British War Medal and the Victory Medal. The Medal Index Cards have all survived and are available online through the National Archives website. Unfortunately, the reverse side of the cards, where next of kin addresses were often recorded were not digitalised at the same time and these are currently unavailable to the online researcher.

Douglas' Medal Index Card provided several lines of research to follow. It corroborated the regimental number on his British War Medal and his service as a private in the Sussex Yeomanry. It also established that he served in the Royal Sussex Regiment for a while, which accounted for the Royal Sussex cap badge he had kept. Finally, it noted the date of his commission into the Royal Flying Corps, which soon after became the Royal Air Force on 1st April 1918. The theatre of war that a man served in was specified by a code, in this case the entry '(2B) Balklands 9.10.15', was clear evidence of his embarkation to Gallipoli in 1915. His medals included the 1914-15 Star as well as the Victory and British War Medal.

His army records unfortunately did not survive and several hours of scrolling through reels of both burnt and unburnt records at the National Archives left me with little more than a headache and some amazement at how many soldiers named Watts served in the Great War. With no service record to provide any detail, there was a possibility that the regiment had a history published somewhere and ten minutes on the internet provided me with the title and author of the long out of print volume, *'The Sussex Yeomanry and 16th (Sussex Yeomanry) Battalion, Royal Sussex Regiment 1914-1919'* which had been published in 1921 and written by Lieutenant-Colonel H.I. Powell-Edwards.

It was as I had suspected: the Sussex Yeomanry was re-mustered as an infantry battalion, destined to serve in the trenches as the 16th Battalion of the Royal Sussex Regiment. A copy of the book was available in the West Sussex Records Office at Chichester which provided me with a complete history of the war service of the regiment, a nominal roll of all officers and men who served along with several detailed maps and photographs.

To my surprise, two of the photographs published in the book, attributed to a Harold Smith who was killed at Tel el Sheria in 1917, were also in Douglas' collection. It is uncertain whether Douglas was the photographer of the original prints or whether he obtained copies from Harold Smith. I always understood that the pictures in the album were taken by Douglas; but regardless of who took them, they provided me with a unique record of life on the Gallipoli Peninsula and in the Canal Zone in Egypt. Other photographs were related to his time in the Royal Flying Corps and the Watts family and friends. For a soldier to have a personal camera remained a disciplinary offence, despite the fact that by 1915 Kitchener had relaxed his earlier position of not allowing any reporters or photographers onto the Western Front. Douglas had always been a keen amateur photographer and the pocket Kodak he used at home had obviously found its way into his kitbag.

The other source of information that supplemented the official history was the regimental war diary. This provided the usual day to day account of their activities as seen through the officer responsible for recording events. A copy of the war diary was held at the National Archives and in the Records Office in Chichester. I knew it was unlikely that Douglas would be mentioned by name in the war diary unless he had become a casualty or been decorated, and even then, NCOs and other ranks who became casualties were often only referred to numerically when a unit had suffered particularly heavy losses. The war diary was no different in this respect to the many others I had read. The neatly handwritten pages mentioned very few other ranks by name, and it became clear as I read through the diary entries that the regimental history compiled by Powell-Edwards had relied heavily on these day to day accounts, many of them completed in his own neat handwriting during the regiment's service in the field.

Like so many of the yeomanry regiments that were raised and trained for a cavalry role, the 1/1 Sussex Yeomanry[2] never fought as a mounted regiment during the Great War. The regiment had been in existence in one form or another since 1794 when there were up to fourteen troops of Gentlemen and Yeoman Cavalry in Sussex who were willing to serve as a part-time cavalry regiment in the event of the much-feared invasion by Bonaparte. Many of the other yeomanry regiments were raised at this time throughout Britain. In 1908, The Sussex Yeomanry (Dragoons) became part of the newly formed South East Mounted Brigade[3] territorial force with the regimental HQ at Brighton.

As a territorial unit, the regiment still drew its officers and men from the Sussex area. A territorial unit in 1914 required its officers and men to complete fourteen days training per year. This training was usually carried out on a squadron basis and, in the case of the yeomanry, individuals often provided their own horses. This was certainly the case with the war poet Siegfried Sassoon who, before being commissioned into the Welch Fusiliers, was for a short time a private in the Sussex Yeomanry.

Territorials were governed under a different set of regulations to

2. In August 1914, orders were issued to territorial units to distinguish between the home service men and those who had undertaken to serve overseas. The intention was to form reserves made up of those who had not so volunteered. Consequently authority was given to establish a 2nd-Line Unit (1/2) for each of the 1st-Line units (1/1) where more than 60% of the men had volunteered.

3. The South Eastern Mounted Brigade was a territorial force based at Russell Square, London. Here it remained until September 1915 when it was dismounted and departed for Gallipoli. The Brigade was part of the 42nd Division while on Gallipoli. In January 1916 it was on Mudros and moved to Egypt in February 1916 where it was absorbed by the 3rd Dismounted Brigade.

the regular army, for example the territorial soldier could only enlist between the ages of 17 and 35 and the term of service was for four years. Once enlisted, you were appointed to serve with a regiment or corps of your choice within your county and, as a territorial, the army was unable to transfer you to another regiment without your consent. Territorial units were raised for home service only and eighty percent of the unit were required to volunteer if the unit was to embark for overseas service.

It is clear that the War Office request had failed to understand the potential hardship that overseas service would inflict on many of the men and some units failed to arrive at the required eighty percent. Shortly afterwards the figure was lowered to sixty percent! Territorials who wished to serve overseas had to take up the Imperial Service Obligation, and those who did were allowed to wear the Imperial Service Badge above the right breast pocket on Service Dress uniforms.

Living in Arundel, Douglas was a member of C Squadron based in nearby Chichester. He had joined in 1913, along with many others, in response to the growing international tension in Europe. From all accounts, life as a part-time yeomanry soldier was akin to being a member of a rather select riding club, particularly as most of the regiment rode with the local hunt. Obviously, basic military training took place, but Douglas remembered with some fondness the cavalry rides over the South Downs and the annual yeomanry camps where they honed their military skills and perfected their horsemanship in the regimental riding school. When the order came for mobilisation on 4th August 1914, there were already four squadrons based in Lewes, Brighton, Chichester and Eastbourne, but by the time the regiment arrived at its new quarters near Canterbury this had been reduced to three larger squadrons, with the Lewes-based B Squadron being absorbed by the others.

This early mobilisation caused a number of difficulties for men who were self employed, particularly if the success or failure of their business depended on their presence. As far as Douglas was concerned, the family drapery business in Arundel could manage without him and, being a single man, he had no immediate family to support. For others it was a different story. Many had left their businesses in chaos and it seemed that there was little War Office awareness or sympathy for individuals who had left dependant families without any means of support. This inevitably led to financial ruin and family hardship for some, a particularly bitter pill to swallow when others who had not yet volunteered their services reaped the benefit.

As soon as the regiment arrived at their new quarters in Canterbury, the War Office asked for volunteers to serve abroad. The 1/1 Sussex Yeomanry had little difficulty in obtaining the required sixty percent of volunteers, while those who remained behind transferred to the 2/1 Sussex Yeomanry and were destined initially to provide replacements for casualties sustained by the yeomanry in Gallipoli and the Middle East and later, the infantry battalions of the Royal Sussex Regiment. In July 1915 a third regiment, the 3/1st Sussex Yeomanry, was formed to find drafts and act as a depot for the first and second regiments. Serving in the 2/1st was Lynton's elder brother, Walter. There is no evidence that it was Walter Goode who was instrumental in introducing Douglas to my grandmother Margery's family, but I do remember her once telling me that one of her brothers knew Douglas in the army. Walter is the likely culprit here, particularly as they were for a short time possibly serving together.

In September 1915 the 1/1st were dismounted and required to hand their horses over to the Hampshire Yeomanry. As dismounted cavalry they were now, in effect, temporary infantry soldiers and would fight on foot. A period of infantry training followed and the inevitable embarkation orders to proceed to Liverpool came as no surprise. On 24th September, along with some eight thousand other dismounted yeomanry, they embarked aboard the *SS Olympic*, sister ship to the ill fated *Titanic*. That evening, painted in dazzling colours with bright geometric shapes on a lurid yellow background to confuse enemy submarines, the *Olympic*, designated as HM Transport ship number T2810, slipped her berth and hauled out into the Mersey estuary on what was to be her first trooping voyage.

The *Olympic* spent the entire war ferrying troops, a period which was not without incident. In October of 1914, the battleship *HMS Audacious* had struck a mine and was sinking. The *Olympic* arrived and evacuated all but two hundred and fifty essential crew and along with other attending ships attempted, unsuccessfully, to tow the stricken vessel to safety. The *Audacious* finally sank after the remaining crew had been taken off. Another event later in the war saw the *Olympic* in the sights of Germany's U-103. Escaping a torpedo, the *Olympic* turned and rammed her attacker, eventually sinking it. One of these incidents took place in September 1915 while Douglas was on board and served to remind all that the submarine menace was never too far away.

Following the demise of the *Titanic*, the *Olympic* had undergone an extensive refit in 1913. The White Star Line realised that they needed to do more that just put extra lifeboats on the ship. The bulkheads were extended and the ship was given a double skin, thus increasing her overall width by two feet. Potentially, she could now stay afloat with her first six water-tight compartments flooded, unlike the *Titanic* which floundered after the first four compartments were flooded. The refit also extended the lifeboat row along the entire length of the boat deck. Two boats were installed on the poop deck in the aft of the ship, together with additional collapsibles. When the *Olympic* put to sea on that September evening she had a total of sixty-eight lifeboats and with over 8,000 troops on board they would all be needed in the event of a successful torpedo attack. Ship's officers believed that, at worst, the ship could not sink in less than five hours.

On the morning of 27th September the ship rescued the survivors of the French liner *Provincia* which had been sunk by an enemy submarine. Only four months previously, the *Lusitania* had been sunk off the Irish coast with a loss of over a thousand passengers and crew. As a result of this incident and others, submarine attack was on the mind of many of the troops on board. Their fears were compounded when, later that afternoon, the alarm signal was sounded by a succession of short blasts on the ship's siren and the ship took on an appreciable list. This was followed by a loud explosion towards the rear of the ship. Fearing the worst, the order was given to assemble at boat stations. Douglas, wondering if there were enough lifeboats to go round, assembled on a lower deck and missed the excitement that was taking place topside. An enemy submarine had surfaced almost directly ahead of the ship. The ship's Captain, Bertram F. Hayes, had immediately turned the *Olympic* in order to engage the enemy vessel with the ship's gun, mounted in the stern. The *Olympic* managed to fire one round at the submarine which quickly submerged and, although the ship remained on high alert, to the relief of all on board it was not seen again. Margery had always said that he disliked boats and avoided sea travel whenever possible; I now understood why!

Despite the continual fear of submarines and still unaware of their final destination, life on board ship soon settled down into the daily routine of boat drill, 'physical jerks' and lectures. On board space was cramped but most evenings after dinner there were concerts, with the choirs of the Welsh regiments proving the most popular entertainment. Among the many other regiments on board that shared the overcrowded accommodation was the Norfolk Yeomanry. One private soldier in its ranks would later go on to be commissioned into the Royal Flying Corps (RFC) and, despite having a reputation for crashing aircraft, would see service on the Western Front as a bomber pilot with 55 Squadron. After the war, Captain William Earl Johns would be better known for creating the character of 'Biggles' in the popular series of stories that would become almost a British institution.

On 4th October the *Olympic*[4] steamed into Mudros Harbour, where Douglas' photographs show the troops being taken off the *Olympic* and transferred onto small steamers ready for the short trip across to the peninsula. The war diary records the regiment being accommodated on board the *SS Sarnia* and describes the boat as crowded and the sea extraordinarily calm. The *Sarnia*, previously employed as a cross-channel ferry operating out of Southampton, was one of a number of vessels requisitioned for war service and would eventually be torpedoed off Alexandria in 1918.

Mudros before the Gallipoli campaign was a small port on the Greek Island of Lemnos; now it was packed with all kinds of shipping supporting the allied offensive across the water. Another of Douglas' photographs caught the great bulk of the heavy cruiser *HMS Terrible* at anchor in Mudros harbour. In its time it was one of the most powerful and largest cruisers afloat, but now, with her main armament removed it was relegated to the role of troopship.

---

4. On 21st November 1916, the British hospital ship SS Britannic, the third in the trio of White Star ships, hit a mine and sank in just 50 minutes. It was on its way to pick up 3,500 wounded soldiers from Lemnos.

The landing on W Beach was the Yeomanry's first real action as infantry; their second was a brisk forced march north for some two miles with full kit along the beach and into Gully Ravine where they climbed steadily to their allotted base. Douglas' photographs show the extensive dug-outs that the regiment constructed in Gully Ravine and the preparations they made for improving this accommodation for the winter months, which fortunately they did not have to endure for too long.

The scene of some desperate fighting early in the campaign, Gully Ravine was essentially a highway from the Gully Beach to the Turkish front-line at Border Barricade. It also provided convenient shelter and bivouacs for units who were not up in the firing line. Characterised by a largely flat gully bed, the steep sides provided some protection from hostile fire, providing one kept to the its eastern edge.

There were no landings at Gully Beach on 25th April, but units of the 29th Division reached Gully Beach three days after the initial landings, securing the mouth of Gully Ravine without resistance. By midday on the 28th the advance up the gully had lost its momentum; fatigue and thirst, together with a resolute Turkish opposition, had brought things to a stand still. There followed a determined Turkish counter-attack along the whole of the Helles Front on the night of 1st May which achieved several breakthroughs, one of these being in Gully Ravine. Having breached the first line of trenches, the Turks were only stopped by the fixed bayonets and resolve of the 5th Royal Scots. On 12th May, the 1/6th Gurkha Rifles of Cox's 29th Indian Brigade, the same brigade that would later fight alongside Lynton Goode and the Australian 4th Brigade in the Anzac August Offensive, took the high ground[5] at the head of Y Ravine.

By 28th June, after the so-called Battle of Gully Ravine, the line was more or less stabilised when Fusilier Bluff was taken by the combined efforts of the 2/10th Gurkhas and 2nd Royal Fusiliers. By the time Douglas arrived in October 1915 the front-line was well established and trench warfare was the order of the day. It must have been obvious to all that the campaign had reached a stalemate.

5. Later renamed Gurkha Bluff on 17th May in General Routine Order 160.

The South East Mounted Brigade was now attached to 42nd (East Lancashire) Division, a territorial infantry division that had suffered heavy casualties since the landings in April and in common with every other unit on the peninsula, was ravaged by dysentery. The regiment's first tour of duty in the trenches began on 8th October at Border Barricade and Crawley's Crater,[6] both at the northern end of Gully Ravine. The regimental history recorded those first impressions:

> The trenches themselves were narrow and very good. The wire was no more than a line of knife rests, the wire on which was not good in repair. The two lines were extremely close together and there was a lack of material for dugouts.

Trench life at the Cape Helles front was very similar to the Anzac experience further north. There was the usual continual sniping day and night; men lived and slept on the fire step of their trench with very little shelter from the weather or bursting shrapnel and dysentery was rampant. On 9th October, just two days after landing, the first case of dysentery in the regiment was recorded and thereafter there was a continual stream of cases being sent back to field hospitals on the beach.

The flies were not as bad as they had been in August, when it had been impossible to eat anything between eight in the morning and eight at night; but even in October the clouds of flies made life very uncomfortable during the day, and at night the blankets covering the dugouts would be black with flies. Also, in common with their Anzac counterparts, there was the continual demand for working parties to unload lighters at the beach and bring up supplies. For those units based in Gully Ravine, there was the additional task of removing the debris of excavation from the Cawley's Crater area and Fusilier Bluff where mining and counter-mining operations were underway.

It was not uncommon for men to leave the trenches after a seventy-two hour tour of duty in the firing line and then to be

6. Named after Captain Harold Thomas Cawley, 6th Manchesters. Killed on 24th September 1915.

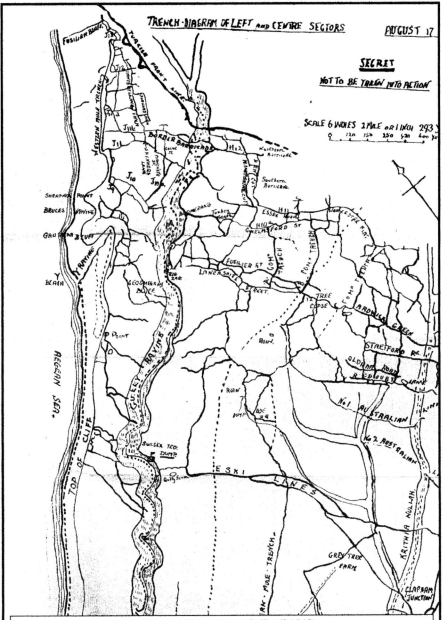

The Sussex Yeomanry at Gallipoli 1915.

A trench map of the Gully Ravine sector showing the location of Fusilier Bluff and Border Barricade in relation to the Sussex Yeomanry Dump. The broken line in Gully Ravine indicates the track up the ravine that Douglas Watts and the Yeomanry would have taken to reach the front line. When not in the front line, the men would be based in dugouts in the ravine.

detailed for a working party on the beach. Understandably, it was not long before the debilitating effects of fatigue combined with dehydration and illness began to impinge on the effectiveness of the yeomanry soldiers. When out of the firing line, they would be in the rest area but even here there was the daily threat of becoming a casualty. On 19th October, RSM Graham was severely wounded by a stray round while sitting in his bivouac; he died later that day, becoming the regiment's first casualty.

At this late stage in the Gallipoli campaign, front-line duty was relatively uneventful; both sides had almost exhausted themselves, the trench lines were well fortified on both sides and frontal attacks had proved to be almost totally unproductive. For the men of the Sussex Yeomanry this meant their time in the front-line was usually comparatively uneventful, although complacency could be shattered by particularly lively episodes of bombing, and occasional small scale attacks. C Squadron had an early experience of Turkish bombers at Border Barricade and found to their cost that:

> The Turks had the upper hand of the garrison in the matter of bombing...C Squadron came down [from the line] with the impression that in their part of the line the Turk needs setting about.

In November the brigade moved to new positions at Fusilier Bluff and again found the Turkish bombers aggressive. On this occasion they were prepared for the Turkish bombers and immediately went on the offensive with a concentrated bombing effort. The war diary records more than six hundred bombs being thrown and catapulted over the Turkish lines in a twenty-four hour period restoring the upper hand, after which things quietened down considerably.

By the middle of November it was the weather that gave the greater cause for concern than the Turks. On 15th November, by way of a prelude, there was a very heavy storm that flooded the trenches and regimental lines; water and mud was channelled down Gully Ravine, flooding bivouacs and burying equipment in a sea of mud. As if this wasn't enough, nine days later another storm of greater ferocity hit the already battered peninsula. For twenty-four hours the rain turned the battle ground into a mire, while the wind rose to hurricane force bringing with it snow and sleet. It was the worst storm for forty years and in a stroke it banished the dysentery and the flies replacing them with knee deep slush and freezing temperatures. At Cape Helles and Anzac there was some protection from the surrounding hills but further north at Suvla, men drowned in the trenches, unable to help themselves:

> At Helles sentries were found in the morning still standing, their rifles in their hands, but they were frozen to death. Blankets and bedding were so congealed with cold they could be stood on end. Everywhere the mud had turned to ice and the roofs of the dugouts were lined with icicles as hard as iron.[7]

Douglas' photographs illustrate what must have been the aftermath of the storm, with blankets and greatcoats hung out in the winter sun to dry, and what looks like a very battered Lancashire Landing with stores being unloaded from a lighter. The yeomanry lines on Fusilier Bluff allowed much of the water to run off and the trenches were spared the worst of the flooding. They were also fortunate in that they had included their greatcoats in their kit, but for many of the men on the peninsula winter clothing was not available, and the struggle to survive took on new dimensions with the weather replacing bombs and bullets.

By 30th November the storm had abated and the beleaguered peninsula forces took stock. Two hundred men had been drowned, with ten thousand suffering from either frostbite or other injuries. Overall, the Allied forces on the peninsula had been reduced by one tenth of their strength. Morale was at its lowest point since the campaign began and there was now talk of evacuation, something many feared would result in enormous casualties.

The first hint of an evacuation came from English newspapers that reached the yeomanry lines in December. This was classic Gallipoli mismanagement of yet another strategic decision being communicated through the press, and only served to fuel the feeling

---

7. Alan Moorhead, Gallipoli (Wordsworth 1997)

that it would be a costly and difficult evacuation. Lieutenant-Colonel Powell-Edwards[8] writing in the regimental history expressed his surprise at the manner in which the news reached them:

> On December 8th [news] papers from England were received which stated that it had been decided that the peninsula must be evacuated. This was news to everyone, though there had been much speculation as to the decision which Lord Kitchener had made after his flying visit some days before when he had gone up to Eski Lines and had at last been able to see things for himself. It was generally felt that the press would have done better to have published nothing definite, for it was obvious that the evacuation must be a ticklish business.

Whether by design or coincidence, the Turkish shelling with their new German guns and ammunition began to increase in intensity after the beginning of December; its effectiveness was illustrated on 19th December when an attack was ordered after a mine was exploded at Cawley's Crater. The Turkish counter-bombardment was much heavier than had been experienced previously and was responsible for a number of casualties. Although the crater was eventually held, the yeomanry had their first real taste of sustained fighting over the five days it took to consolidate the position. The regiment won its first Military Cross[9] in this action and for many it was the point at which the yeomanry soldiers came of age as infantry. It did not become apparent until later that this attack was one of several diversionary actions designed to draw attention away from the evacuations taking place at Anzac and Suvla.

The news that Cape Helles was not to be evacuated came on 20th December in special orders signed by Brigadier-General Harold Street[10]. Having applauded the hugely successful evacuations from Suvla and Anzac, the orders went on to justify keeping a force at Helles:

8. Lieutenant-Colonel H.I. Powell-Edwards was CO of the 16th Battalion from June 1917, taking over from Lieutenant-Colonel G.S. Whitfield, who was evacuated.
9. Captain H. Sayer, MC.
10. Brigadier-General Harold Street (1875-1917). Killed near Hill 60, Ypres, 25th August.

> The position at Cape Helles will not be abandoned, and the Commander-in-Chief has entrusted to the 8th Corps the duty of maintaining the honour of the British Empire against the Turks on the Peninsula and of continuing such action as shall prevent them, as far as possible, from massing their forces to meet our main operations elsewhere

It appeared that they were in for the duration, and many feared they would eventually become prisoners of war of an enemy who was not known for his compassion. At this juncture, seventy-five days after first stepping ashore, the regiment had only 250 officers and men on strength with a disproportionate number of officers to men. During the short time they had been on the peninsula, their strength had been reduced by fifty percent. In other units the story was a similar one. For the most part they were below strength and tired and, to add to their misery, the Turkish artillery bombardment was becoming more accurate.

There was also a very real threat of a sustained Turkish attack reinforced by the divisions released from the north of the peninsula. In fact, the Turkish forces could now assemble some twenty-one divisions. In reply the Allied forces could only muster four divisions across the whole of the Helles front to meet such a threat and even with reinforcements it was highly unlikely any significant advance would be made. The prognosis was not a good one: if the Turks didn't get them, the winter weather probably would. Behind the scenes at strategic command level there was distinct unease at the decision to remain at Helles. Pressure was brought to bear in Whitehall and on 27th December the War Cabinet agreed to the evacuation of Cape Helles.

Christmas Day 1915 was sunny and windless and celebrated by the yeomanry in Y Ravine with the 8th Battalion of the Lancashire Fusiliers, who had been sent down to the beach only to be told on arrival that they were to return to Gully Ravine. The yeomanry would not receive their orders for evacuation until the next day, but clearly the process was underway with units being carefully withdrawn from the lines and sent down to the beaches to embark under the cover of darkness. Powell-Edwards documented the movements of the yeomanry:

> On the 29th orders were received about midday to move
> that night. Transport was to move as soon after 4pm as
> possible.
>
> At 3pm we heard Corps could not provide extra mules
> as promised. Also the Regiment would embark at 'V'
> Beach, with the baggage at 'W' Beach. The baggage was
> at 'V' Beach in accordance with [previous] orders.
>
> At 3.30 twenty men with two officers went down to
> shift the baggage from 'V' to 'W' Beaches.
>
> At 4pm, just as the officers' kits and squadron baggage
> was being moved off, a message was received cancelling
> the move! So everyone sat down to a kitless night and no
> dinner.
>
> On December 30th orders were received to move at
> 3pm to Gully Beach.

The men were fed at Gully Beach while they waited for
darkness and at 9.45pm Douglas and C Squadron marched down
the shoreline to V Beach, under the command of Major H.L.
Kekewich,[11] where they embarked on tenders moored alongside the
beached hull of the *SS River Clyde*. The *River Clyde* was a permanent
monument to the slaughter that took place on V Beach on the
morning of 25th April when the ship was used as a Trojan horse in
the initial landings.

The *River Clyde*, carrying two thousand soldiers from the 1st
Royal Munster Fusiliers, 2nd Hampshires and 2nd Royal Fusiliers,
was run aground at 06.22 beneath the Sedd el Bahr Castle with the
intention of landing its human cargo through sallyport exit doors cut
in its bow. Despite this, the plan failed and the exit gangways, now
targeted by Turkish rifle and machine gun fire, became a death trap
for those attempting to get ashore. After the Helles beachhead was
established, V Beach became the base for the French contingent and
the *River Clyde* remained beached as a dock and breakwater.
Although under constant shell fire from Turkish guns on the Asiatic

11. Later killed in action at Sheria, November 1917.

side of the Dardanelles, the ship's condensers were used to provide fresh water and a field dressing station was established in the hull.

The inside of the hull was pitch dark as the yeomanry clambered through the same exit doors that, seven months previously, had been choked with the dead and dying of the 29th Division.[12] It was with some difficulty that the men and equipment moved onto the tenders that took them out to the waiting *SS Princess Alberta.* Military Landing Officers had resorted to torch signals in an effort to keep noise to a minimum, signals that did much to confuse the anxious men waiting in the darkness. For these Sussex men, their Gallipoli adventure was over. They had not experienced the bloody fighting that took place in the summer of 1915 or suffered the huge numbers of casualties that had devastated other regiments in futile frontal attacks on Turkish positions. The yeomanry were fortunate in only suffering twenty-eight casualties from enemy fire; far more had been invalided out with dysentery than had been killed in action. Some of these men, such as Second Lieutenant Hugh Wyatt, would never recover, dying in a ward of one of the Alexandria military hospitals.

As for the evacuation, not a single life was lost. It is hard to believe that the Turks were unaware of the Helles evacuation, given that troops at Anzac and Suvla had already been withdrawn. Did they prefer to allow the withdrawal to go ahead unopposed in order to prevent a further shedding of blood, or did they genuinely not know what was going on under their noses? Douglas always believed that the Turks were aware of what was going on and let them leave Helles intact; I should like to believe that but, in truth, it is highly unlikely.

Douglas' travels over the next two years are largely based on the few records available that place him with his unit. The regimental history lists four soldiers with the name Watts, none of whom have the initials D.A. or service in Gallipoli and Egypt. The Private B.A. Watts, who is recorded as having served in Gallipoli with the 1/1st Yeomanry, must almost certainly be Douglas. He would have left the island of Lemnos with the regiment on 2nd February 1916, embarking on the *SS Caledonia* for Egypt. Here they

---

12. There were over 1000 casualties at V Beach. A total of nine Victoria Crosses were won in the two days it took to take V Beach and overcome the fortified positions at the head of the beach.

were to discover that the Sussex Yeomanry would, in all probability, cease to exist as a mounted cavalry regiment when they became part of the newly formed 3rd Dismounted Brigade[13] under the command of Brigadier-General H. W. Hodgson[14] CVO. Despite the hope that they might in due course remuster as a cavalry, a year or so later in January 1917 the regiment became the 16th Battalion (Sussex Yeomanry) Royal Sussex Regiment. There was now no going back, their mounted days as cavalry were over.

Douglas' photographs of bathing in the Suez Canal suggest he was still with the regiment during the five months they spent as part of the Canal Defence Force. His Medal Index Card confirms he was issued with a new service number in the 16th Battalion Royal Sussex Regiment in January 1917. On 3rd April, the Dismounted Brigade joined the Egyptian Expeditionary Force. The new Commander-in-Chief of this army group was Sir Edmund Allenby,[15] who replaced Sir James Murray after his disastrously unsuccessful attempts to take Gaza from the Turks.

After that there is a gap in Douglas' records of over a year before the London Gazette Supplement[16] posts a notice of a Lance Corporal Douglas Allen Watts of the Royal Sussex Regiment being promoted to temporary Second Lieutenant in the Royal Flying Corps with effect from 19th March 1918. There is a brief reference in the battalion war diary of some officers and men being allowed home on leave in 1917 and it would appear that Douglas was one of them. Photographs in his photograph album dated Summer 1917, depicting family picnics on the Sussex Downs, swimming parties at Brighton and tennis matches, definitely place him in Sussex for a period over that summer. I remember my grandmother telling me that he had been ill in the army, which could have been another reason for being at home; several officers and men were recorded as having suffered from diphtheria, some of the more serious cases would perhaps have been sent home to recover.

13. Part of the 74th (Yeomanry) Division.
14. Later, Major-General Sir H.W. Hodgson, would command the Imperial Mounted Division in Palestine.
15. Under his command, British armies advanced into Palestine and captured Jerusalem from the Turks, on 10th December 1917. At the decisive battle of Samaria in September 1918, Allenby, by skilful use of his cavalry, defeated a Turkish army of 100,000 under command of Field Marshal Liman von Sanders, capturing more than 75,000 prisoners and 350 guns.
16. 21st August 1918.

The last four months of 1917 were dominated by hard fighting as the new Commander-in-Chief set about reducing the Turkish hold on Palestine. It is unclear if Douglas took part in the Battle of Beersheba[17] in October 1917, or if he was involved in the next phase of the offensive that followed a week later, concluding with the capture of Tel el Sheria. At some point in early 1918, after returning to Egypt, he transferred, along with eight other soldiers from the battalion to the Royal Flying Corps to begin pilot training. There is no mention in the war diary of them leaving the battalion and we don't really know what prompted Douglas to transfer to the RFC; he was a little older than the average recruit, being almost thirty years old, but in all probability it was in response to the ever growing demand for pilots and observers and a desire to try something a little more glamorous. Life in the RFC must have looked far rosier than foot slogging around the arid landscapes of Palestine while being shot at by the Turks.

I was fortunate in finding Douglas' RFC and RAF records at the National Archives. Although his army records had been destroyed, the RAF records were intact and detailed the training squadrons he had flown with, some personal family information and the date of his discharge from the service. There was also a tantalising reference to an injury received as a result of an 'aero accident' in March 1918. Banking on the fact that his injury and flying accident would inevitably have generated a casualty card, I contacted the RAF Museum at Hendon in the hope of finding details of the crash. As usual the museum staff were extremely helpful and went out of their way to help me in searching for the documents I wanted. To my amazement the details of this accident were intact along with some further information of a spell in hospital and the date of leaving Egypt on a troopship to return home.

Together with Douglas' photographs, this additional information enabled me to get a reasonably clear picture of his progress through the flying training programme in Egypt and his movements during the final year of the war. By late 1916 the need for well-trained aircrew was placing a huge pressure on the nation's opera-

17. Sometimes known as the third Battle of Gaza. British and Dominion troops broke through the Gaza-Beersheba line capturing 12,000 Turkish soldiers, paving the way for the fall of Jerusalem in December 1917.

tional and training facilities and, as the need for replacement pilots and observers became critical, additional training programmes were established in other countries, well away from the upheaval of war. Egypt was an ideal location for the training of pilots and an extensive training structure was put in place.

By July 1916 three reserve squadrons had been formed in Egypt, and the Number 3 School of Military Aeronautics was established at Aboukir in November of that year. Initially the cadets were from Britain but, as Britain's home training facilities began keeping pace with demand, the Egyptian flying schools began to recruit locally. This is probably the route that Douglas took when he arrived at the cadet wing some time in early 1918. It would not take him long to realise that flying was a dangerous activity.

By the end of 1916, the lessons being learnt by the RFC on the Western Front in terms of the loss of men and aircraft were beginning to influence the training and preparation of pilots for combat. In the early stages of the war, with military flying in its infancy and the demand for pilots outstripping supply, the training programme was turning out pilots for front-line squadrons sometimes with little more than five hours flying time.

It was also the case that the quality of training received was dependent on untrained instructors, some of whom were reportedly reluctant to allow the pupil full control of an aircraft with only one set of flying controls; consequently, most pupils rarely progressed beyond the fundamentals of flying. Instructors were usually pilots who had survived a tour on the front and had been sent home to 'rest' before being posted back to an operational squadron. These individuals, tired and in many cases suffering from nerves and combat fatigue, were not the best people to teach and mentor novice flyers. It was reasoned at the time that any proficient pilot should be able to pass on his knowledge to another and that a good pilot would also be a good instructor. The result was too often a fatal one for the unfortunate pupil pilots who, if they survived training without a serious crash, were sent to France either to fall to the guns of the enemy Jastas[18] or to crash through inexperience and sheer lack of flying time, sometimes within days of arrival.

18. Jagd-Staffel – German equivalent of the RFC Squadron.

It was largely through the persistence of Robert Smith-Barry that the training of RFC pilots began to improve and, by the time Douglas flew his first solo in 1918, flying training was unrecognisable from the very basic tuition of the early years of the war. Smith-Barry was a veteran pilot who had learnt to fly in 1911 and was one of the original RFC pilots who landed in France with No. 5 Squadron in 1914. In July 1916, he became the CO of 60 Squadron. Required to send men and machines over the lines on a daily basis, Smith-Barry was appalled at the half-trained pilots he was being sent, and on more than one occasion refused to send inexperienced pilots over the lines merely to become what he termed as 'Fokker Fodder'. His views on the inadequacy of the current training programme finally prompted Trenchard to send him home in August 1917 to reorganise flying training at Gosport.

It was at No.1 Reserve Squadron at Gosport under the leadership of Smith-Barry that the quality of instructing improved significantly during 1917. At Gosport, instructors were taught the skills of teaching novice fliers, using a new flying training syllabus designed to prepare pilots to deal with every possible situation that they might find themselves having to cope with in the air. Smith-Barry put his immediate thoughts on paper in 1916 with the publication of *Notes on Teaching Flying for Instructors* and, later in October 1917, a more detailed syllabus appeared with *General Methods of Teaching Scout Pilots*. The Gosport System, as it became known, was to have a huge impact on the training of aircrew and undoubtedly saved lives in the closing stages of the war. Aircraft with dual controls were still not available in large numbers, but as they later became the norm for instructing, Smith-Barry ensured they were fitted with speaking tubes[19] to enable pupil and instructor to communicate in the air effectively.

If Trenchard was the father of the Royal Air Force, then Smith-Barry was certainly the father of flying training. His greatest legacy to future aircrew was the basic Gosport System, a form of which was used to teach my father, Hugh Murland, to fly twenty-five years later during the Second World War. Flying training was now taking up to eight months to complete, with the pupil pilot beginning life in a cadet wing at the School of Aeronautics. Here Douglas would have

19. Called the Gosport Tube.

learnt to send and receive Morse Code messages, understand the basics of the aircraft engine, propeller swinging, map reading, and photo interpretation. He would also have to pass examinations in the theory and practice of aerial gunnery and cross-country navigation. At the end of three months those cadets that passed out of basic training began their flying training.

Joining 21 Training Squadron based at Ismalia, Douglas was issued with a uniform and flying kit and introduced to the Maurice Farman Shorthorn. The Shorthorn aeroplane was an RFC veteran, being the first armed aircraft to engage in aerial combat over the Western Front, and was affectionately known as 'Rumpety' to those who flew it because of the noise it made while travelling over the ground. Made predominantly of wood and fabric, a complex maze of wires and struts held the upper and lower wings in place, preventing them from warping in flight.

Douglas went solo in a Shorthorn[20] in early March but on the 18th of that month, despite his previous successful landings, he crashed on landing. The casualty card recorded the cause of the accident:

> [The aircraft] struck the ground at a great pace, undercarriage crumpled up, machine turned over throwing occupant clear. [The pilot was] Injured with slight concussion and grazed fingers.

He was exceptionally lucky to survive the accident and had discovered the difficulties of achieving the perfect three-point landing. In spite of this mishap, it appears he eventually mastered his landing technique and passed out of his elementary flying school in March 1918. On 1st April he arrived at 195 Training Squadron at Abu Sueir as a newly commissioned temporary Second Lieutenant. 195 Squadron was equipped with the Avro 504J and the single seat Sopwith Pup and Nieuport Scout aircraft.

He must have made some impression on his instructors at his elementary flying school to be posted to a squadron that trained scout pilots. The scout pilot was the glamour boy of the air and, like

20. Serial number A4096.

their fellow fighter pilots in the Second World War, they were expected to have more of an aptitude for air combat as well as the ability to master the finer skills of aerial maneuverability, although this wasn't always the case before the Smith-Barry training revolution. The courageous and legendary exploits of scout aces such as Albert Ball, James McCudden and Billy Bishop had inspired a generation of aspirant pilots, all of whom dreamt of flying the single seat combat aircraft. Unfortunately for Douglas this was not to be: after basic instruction in the two-seater Avro 504, his earlier promise ended dramatically with another crash. His photograph of a sorry looking Avro 504 minus its wings and tail assembly tells the story of another lucky escape that ended this time in hospital.

In July he finished flying the faster single-seat aircraft and returned to Ismalia to join 57 Training Squadron to continue his advanced flying training in two-seater aircraft instead, destined to be a bomber pilot. At Ismalia he flew the Bristol RE8, the BE2c and the improved BE2e. Douglas was now in the Royal Air Force, as the RFC and the RNAS[21] had now been amalgamated into a single service in April. His flying training completed, he left for England from Port Said on 14th October 1918. The war had another twenty-eight days to run before an armistice was declared, ensuring Douglas would never have to fight in the air over the European battlefronts.

After a period of home leave he was then posted to 23 Training Depot Squadron at Baldonnel, which had a nominal establishment of Avro 504, RE8 and BE2c aircraft. Within weeks of the armistice, the RAF began to shed large numbers of unwanted personnel, and Douglas' turn came in February 1919. He had made no application to remain in the RAF and, like so many of his generation who had been caught up in the web of the Great War, he simply wanted to go home and get on with his life.

21. Royal Naval Air Service.

5

Skeletons in the Cupboard

Walter Goode and Charles Herbert Goode

In the early Twentieth Century, family members who disgraced themselves were by and large referred to in hushed tones or, depending on the misdemeanour, completely removed from conversation both inside and outside the family. Where money and occasion permitted, they were dispatched overseas to seek their fortune away from any scandal they had created, perhaps only to return when it had all been forgotten and they had achieved respectability. This would appear to be the case with two of my great-uncles who, as a result of ignominy, had to reinvent themselves in another life. For the family historian, the resulting wall of silence that is often generated by having a so-called 'family skeleton' in the cupboard, can be a significant hurdle to progress, as can the invention of cover stories that lead the researcher down false trails. This was certainly true when it came to delving into the past of Walter Goode and his elder brother Charles Herbert Goode.

It was while I was using the internet to research Lynton and Archie Goode that I stumbled across a Josephine Stoll, who was seeking information about her father, Walter Goode, who had been born in the parish of Thakeham, Sussex. He had died in 1950 and she knew very little about his early life. My first thought was, could this be the same Walter that was listed in the 1901 census as an elder brother of Lynton and Archie? Having got in touch with Josephine, she willingly shared the fruits of her research into the Goode family with me and we were able to compare notes. She had spent some time trying to trace her father and, although I did not realise it at the time, this line of enquiry would later unveil an intriguing family story as we untangled a web of half-truths and identity confusion while trying to establish that her father and my great-uncle were the same person.

My first suspicion that Walter was a bit of a rogue came from Josephine in one of her emails to me:

> My father Walter Goode died when I was a baby, and because he fibbed about his age when he married my mother, nearly thirty years his junior, I did a lot of unsuccessful searching. I have finally obtained his birth certificate after checking his army records and through this have begun to learn something of his family background.

The fact that her father had lied about his age had made it very difficult to find his birth certificate and led to a great deal of wasted time and effort. But once the authentic date of birth had been established and the certificate applied for, the names of his parents were revealed as Charles Henry Goode and Ada Jessie Poole, my maternal great-grandparents. The most impressive aspect of Josephine's research was that it has all been carried out via the internet from her home in southern Spain, and it looked pretty much as if she and I might be related. There was clearly still a doubt in her mind as in a subsequent email it became apparent that she thought there were perhaps two individuals with the name Walter Goode. At the time Walter met Josephine's mother, he was an Air Ministry Inspector and using his retired army rank of Captain to prefix his name.

There was also a difference in forenames. Her father's full name was Walter Henry Eric Newling Goode while my great-uncle was just plain Walter. As far as Josephine knew, her father had originated from Corfe Mullen in Dorset and had served in the Indian Army with the cavalry after completing a cadetship at Sandhurst. None of this could be substantiated. Sandhurst had no record of a W.H.E.N. Goode in their extensive cadet archives, the Corfe Mullen connection drew a blank and I could find no link with any of the Indian Army cavalry regiments.

Her research had located the army service record of a Captain Walter Goode[1] in the National Archives. Being unable to visit Kew herself, another researcher had copied the contents of the file for her. The file had been generated by the War Office in response to a request from the civilian police in Sussex for information about a Captain Walter Goode. What was discovered came as a bit of a shock to Josephine. The file contained details of Walter Goode's arrest for fraud and his subsequent conviction and imprisonment in 1925. Moreover, it seemed there was some doubt at the time of his arrest about his actual identity. In the midst of other paperwork, the file contained details of which units he had served with and particulars of his birth date, address and a copy of a birth certificate. The birth certificate confirmed the subject of the file: Walter Goode, was my great-uncle, born in Pulborough to Ada Jessie Goode née Poole. Other paperwork included a newspaper cutting from the *News of the World*, dated December 1925, reporting Walter's trial and sentence to nine months hard labour at Portsmouth Prison. Apart from his age being reported incorrectly in the *News of the World* (he was 35 years old in 1925 and not 29), I was curious to know why there had been some issue over his identity.

The question of identity was again mentioned in a letter to the Sussex Police from a Major Stacke in the Army Records Office, dated 2nd November, 1925:

Sir,

With reference to your letter of 12th October 1925, relative to Captain Walter Goode, I am directed to furnish, from the records in the department, the following particulars of the military service of Lieutenant Walter Goode, who is presumably identical with the subject of your enquiry:-

Served in the ranks   22.4.1915 to 9.1.1916
Appointed to a commission as 2nd Lieutenant,
4th Battalion, the Buffs (Territorial Force)   10.1.1916.
Appointed Acting Captain   11.5.1917
Relinquished appointment of Acting Captain 18.6.1917

1. National Archives Catalogue reference: WO 374/27921.

Promoted Lieutenant	10.7.1917
Appointed Acting Captain	5.12.1918
Relinquished appointment of Acting Captain	10.4.1919
Appointed to temporary commission,	
Indian Army Reserve of Officers	13.4.1920
Relinquished commission on completion	
of service and retained the rank of Lieutenant.	
(London Gazette 8.2.1922)	30.9.1921.

I am to state that his services were satisfactory and that nothing of an adverse nature is recorded against him.

I am, Sir

Your obedient servant
H. Stacke (Major)

There had clearly been some question as to Walter's identity at the time of his arrest by the police at Petworth. Another report, completed after the trial, made it quite clear that he was now unable to use any rank granted to him on leaving the army and he would also forfeit any war medal entitlement. According to his army records, he was only permitted to use the rank of Lieutenant and had obviously been calling himself Captain Goode unofficially. While there was no doubt the Walter referred to in the service file was my great-uncle, understandably Josephine felt this man was not her father. Her father, she argued, was simply another man with the same name with no connection to the fraud case at the Sussex Assizes. In a later email to me she asked the question, how did a convicted felon stripped of his rank and war medals end up as an Air Ministry Inspector, openly using the rank of Captain in World War II?

To further support this, she had also discovered that there were two Medal Index Cards in existence, one for Walter Goode and a second for a W.H.E.N. Goode. Did this, she asked, support her theory that there were two officers with the name Goode who shared a common Christian name? It was a logical and plausible explanation, but I was still not entirely convinced that these two individuals were not the same person. Having more than one Medal

Index Card was not uncommon and at least two members of the Murland family had three each!

A closer examination of the information on the two Medal Index Cards convinced me that my suspicions were correct. The cards did not contain a great deal of data but there was enough to compare the regiments and units detailed on both cards with Walter's service history, as outlined in Major Stacke's letter.

W.H.E.N. Goode	Walter Goode
Ist Herts Regiment	Sussex Yeomanry
9th Secunderabad Division – Lieut.	L/Cpl 2466
Indian Army Reserve of Officers	The Buffs 2/Lt.
Acting Captain	

To verify the two Walters were the same person, the five pieces of information on the two index cards needed to be linked. The common denominator was the Indian Army connection. The 9th Secunderabad Division was an Indian Army formation which included the 1/5th Battalion of the Royal East Kent Regiment (the Buffs) based at Wellington in southern India. The Indian Army List for 1918 listed Walter Goode as serving with the 1/5th Buffs but I needed to prove he held a commission in the Indian Army Reserve of Officers. If this could be done, we were one step closer to W.H.E.N Goode and Walter Goode being the same person.

The fly in the ointment was the reference on W.H.E.N. Goode's Index Card to the Herts Regiment. Walter it seemed had only served with the Sussex Yeomanry and the Buffs and not with the Herts Regiment. If this was so then the chances of a match were slight. A further detailed search through Walter's service file revealed he had in fact been attached to the 1st Battalion Herts Regiment while in France. In May 1916, he was injured in an incident with a pickaxe while supervising trench digging at night near Rouen; he was invalided home after a toe had been amputated on his left foot. On the authorisation paperwork that accompanied him on the hospital ship, *SS Asturias*, was a note of his regiment. Walter had been with the 3/4th Buffs in the 39th Division but attached to the 1st Herts Regiment. Bingo!

Although I was now sure that there was only one Walter Goode and that the father Josephine was searching for was the same man as my great-uncle, we needed more than a series of conclusions drawn from army records and two Medal Index Cards. To do this, I would have to piece together Walter Goode's army service in both France and India to determine the point at which he added to or changed his name.

Walter Goode enlisted in the 2/1st Sussex Yeomanry at the Drill Hall in Church Street, Brighton on 22nd April 1915, as 2466 Private W. Goode. His attestation papers described him as being six feet two inches tall, recorded his age as 24 years and 4 months and his occupation as farmer. The 2/1st were initially the reserve regiment for the 1/1st and eventually become an independent mounted regiment until it was finally disbanded in March 1919, by which time their horses had been replaced with bicycles. Soon after Walter's enlistment, the regiment moved to Maresfield in East Sussex to take over the horses of the King Edward's Horse[2] and the Canadian Mounted Brigade, who had been dismounted and were on the way to France as infantry. During the five months Walter spent with C Squadron at Maresfield, the regiment underwent some fairly intensive cavalry training, including riding school where all ranks had to pass a stringent test of horsemanship before being passed out. For a competent horseman like Walter there would have been little difficulty.

At the end of September the regiment marched by road to nearby Wrotham, where they were digging trenches for three weeks as part of the defence of London, in case the threat of invasion became a reality. About this time a big draft of replacements was sent to the 1/1st Sussex Yeomanry, which as we know, included Douglas Allen Watts, who was about to embark for Gallipoli on the *SS Olympic*. The regimental history records the eagerness of the men of the 2/1st to join this draft, one of them being Sergeant Ernest Beale. Beale would later be recommended for a commission in 1917 and transferred to the 13th Battalion, Yorkshire Regiment. Second

---

2. A cavalry regiment that had been formed a few weeks after the outbreak of war by Sir John Norton-Griffiths. Norton-Griffiths had personally sponsored the regiment to the tune of forty thousand pounds in order that they might be ready for war and overseas duty when required. In January 1915, Canada's two Permanent Force Cavalry Regiments, Lord Strathcona's Horse (Royal Canadians) and the Royal Canadian Dragoons, along with the 2nd King Edward's Horse and the Royal Canadian Horse Artillery, formed the Canadian Cavalry Brigade for service in France.

Lieutenant Beal[3] was awarded the posthumous VC for conspicuous bravery on 22nd March 1918, at St Leger.

Walter, although eligible for the Gallipoli draft having signed the Imperial and General Service Obligation, remained with the regiment which by now had moved to Hoath Farm near Canterbury, where Douglas and the 1/1st had been since late 1914. The decision for him to remain in England was perhaps strengthened by his apparent suitability for a commission. At the time there was a national shortage of officers to staff and command the New Armies that were being raised in response to Kitchener's appeal for men. Amongst the rank and file of established territorial regiments, such as the Sussex Yeomanry, there were many who had the necessary education and background to be considered for a commission. In the 2/1st between 1915 and 1916, over twenty soldiers were commissioned into a variety of regiments, with many more filling the ranks of a depleted officer corps in 1917. Men like Walter Goode had no difficulty in leaving the ranks to become officers and gentlemen.

On 3rd December 1915, the now Lance Corporal Goode completed his application for a commission with the approval of his commanding officer, Lieutenant-Colonel R.H. Rawson and, on 10th January 1916, following an interview with the commanding officer of the East Kent Regimental Depot, he was commissioned into the 3/4th Reserve Battalion as a Second Lieutenant. The notice of his commission was published in the London Gazette on 15th January 1916. A subsequent search of the London Gazette for a W.H.E.N. Goode produced nothing. No officer of that name with those initials had been commissioned in the two years between 1914 and 1916.

The Royal East Kent Regiment was an old and famous infantry regiment known also as the Buffs; the nickname came from the mid eighteenth century when, as the 3rd Regiment of Foot, they were on campaign in the Low Countries. It was during this time the regiment first used the buff-coloured facings and waistcoats to distinguish itself from those of other regiments. Unlike its more famous regular battalions, the 3/4th Battalion, based at Tonbridge, was never destined to go overseas but filled the important role of providing a constant stream of replacement officers and men for the battalions in

3. Ernest Frederick Beal, aged 35. Commemorated on the Arras Memorial. Ref: Bay 5

the front line. As was the case with most regular army regiments that typically had only two battalions, the demand for men to fill the ranks of the New Army saw the Buffs expanding to sixteen battalions during the period 1914-18.

Some time in early 1916, Walter was included in a draft to France, most likely to continue his training as an infantry officer at the No.2 Infantry Base Depot at Rouen before being posted to an active service unit at the front. For new drafts arriving in France, the divisional infantry base depot would be the first stop before being sent to the front as replacements.

I knew from his records and from the British Army List for January 1917 that he was attached to the 1st Battalion Herts Regiment but I could find no evidence of him actually joining the battalion at the front. A copy of the battalion war diary is available online, courtesy of Steve Fuller's excellent website, *The Bedfordshire Regiment in the Great War*[4]. Though typically, very few other ranks were mentioned during the period January to May 1916, all new officers joining the battalion were noted by name. There is no record of a Second Lieutenant Walter Goode or a W.H.E.N. Goode. Steve Fuller also very kindly searched his own records for me and again came up with the same result.

It was while Walter was at Rouen that he was accidentally injured on 15th May, with a pickaxe, while supervising trench digging: a soldier digging next to him hit his foot in the dark, effectively putting him out of action for several months. Sadly, very few of the infantry base depot war diaries have survived. Up until August 1916, the unit number of the IBD corresponded to the division it supported. Thus, from January 1916, up until the time of Walter's injury in May, the 1st Battalion Herts Regiment was in the Givenchy trenches in the La Bassée sector as part of the 2nd Division where they had been serving alongside the 39th Division. By March the battalion had left the 2nd Division, and had come under the orders of the 39th Division. Unfortunately, the IBD war diaries for the 2nd Division and the 39th Division are among those that have not survived, so there is no further record of Walter's injury.

The injury and resulting septicaemia led to surgery and

4. www.bedfordregiment.org.uk

amputation of the little toe of his left foot, which ironically provided him with a Blighty wound and passage home on a hospital ship. One can only speculate as to the circumstances of the accident, but it did prevent him being posted to the front-line and, from this point on, he managed to avoid all active service until he found himself in Iraq in 1920.

It is interesting to contemplate that had Walter been in the trenches with the 1st Herts, it is likely he would have met his younger brother Archie at some stage, particularly as the 1st Herts and the 13th Royal Sussex shared the same sector for a while at Givenchy and Festubert. Later, the 1st Herts moved south to Mensil and were in reserve during the 39th Division's attack north of the Ancre in early September 1916; they took over the front-line from the remnants of the 116th Brigade after the surviving troops, which included Archie, had been forced back to their own lines by counter-attack and enemy bombardment.

Arriving in Southampton on 6th July, Walter attended numerous medical boards while on sick leave. The address on his medical board paperwork is given as Grove Farm, Thakeham, so he was initially convalescing at home. A medical board held on 29th August, described the wound as having healed perfectly, but Walter insisted he was unable to walk more than two miles without pain and swelling in the ankle. By November 1916 the notes from his medical boards were betraying an impatience on the part of medical staff to return him to general duties and, despite Walter still complaining of pain and swelling in his foot, he was returned to the East Kent Regiment Depot at Tonbridge and placed on light duties. On 22nd January, 1917 he was declared fit for general duties.

In normal circumstances this would have resulted in him being returned with the next available draft to France. Incredibly, he was back before another medical board on 21st February. This time the board found that he was:

> Apparently out of health, he easily tires and has a faint trace of Albumen in the urine and some bladder discomfort lasting several minutes after micturation [urination]. He has an unhealed scar on the back of his left hand of a lupoid character.

Once again he was again declared unfit and recommended for home service. The results of the medical board suggested a long standing urinary tract infection, which was enough to keep him at the regimental depot until he was finally declared fit for general service in June 1917, almost a year since he was invalided home on the *SS Asturias*.

He had managed to miss the fighting on the Somme in 1916 and the Battle of Arras in 1917, however, with the third Battle of Ypres only a month away it looked very much as if he would have to finally get his boots dirty in the front-line. But lady luck intervened again. During his time at Tonbridge, although only a substantive Second Lieutenant, he had been appointed a temporary Captain, a rank he now relinquished on news of his posting to the 1/5th Battalion East Kent Regiment, who were based at Bangalore in southern India as part of the Southern Brigade of the 9th Secunderbad Division.

A visit to the British Library and a search of the India Office records provided more of the evidence I had been looking for. In the Indian Army List for October 1918 two Second Lieutenants: W. Goode and W.H.E.N. Goode, are listed as serving with the 1/5th (Weald of Kent) Battalion of the East Kent Regiment. Both these officers were first commissioned on 10th January 1916 into the 3/4th Battalion. In the 1919 List, both officers are listed as Lieutenants based at Wellington Camp. Two men with identical career histories, both with the same surname and a common christian name: they had to be the same person. Arriving in India, Walter would have, in all probability, initially been posted to the infantry depot, before being attached to Wellington Camp where he began the process of tinkering with his name

Searching the marriage records held in the India Office for Bangalore, I came across the marriage certificate of a twenty-seven year old Captain Walter Herbert Eric Newling-Goode of the 1/5th Buffs and a Mary Love. Was this Walter in one of his guises? The 1919 Indian Army list confirmed that Walter Goode had been promoted acting Captain shortly before the wedding date, so had Walter assumed a double-barrelled name for effect? The India Office records also revealed a service record of a Lieutenant, later Captain, Walter Goode which not only confirmed Walter Goode had served in the 9th Secunderbad Division and the Buffs, but lived with his family in married quarters at Wellington Camp until 1920 when he was commissioned into the Indian Army Reserve of Officers.

The evidence in this document finally drew together the service careers of the two Walters. Evidently Walter had added forenames and double-barrelled his surname for some reason known only to himself. Perhaps this new persona was simply that he wanted to adopt a name that sounded a little grander than plain Walter Goode? It was, and still is, quite common for people to 'upgrade' their names by making them double-barrelled. I am sure there was no dishonesty intended at this stage, although the Captain W.H.E.N. Goode identity became very useful after he was released from prison.

A search of the baptism records for Wellington recorded the birth of Walter's first child, Alan Newling-Goode, on 4th June 1920. But Mary would have given birth to her first child without her husband pacing up and down in the hospital corridor. Walter had embarked on the SS *Varsova* on 15th March, and was in Iraq, serving with No.2 Company Supply and Transport Corps at Baiji near Mosul. Having escaped further service on the Western Front, Walter had finally been drafted for service in Mesopotamia, which by this time had become Iraq.

Although he had managed to avoid front-line service during the war years, in March 1920, he arrived in Basra just as the temperature of both the political situation and the featureless landscape was beginning to warm up considerably. In July, rebellion broke out in the north of the country around Mosul. Fuelled by growing resentment over taxation, the insurrection quickly moved south, down the Euphrates River valley. In the province of Mosul, a British outpost was attacked and three British officers and eighteen soldiers were killed before order was restored; but the worst violence was along the lower Euphrates to the south of Baghdad. In the holy city of Karbala, sacred to Shiite Muslims, a jihad, or holy war, was proclaimed against the British. The southern tribes needed little encouragement to join in the fray and, after a column under the command of the 2nd Manchesters[5] had been ambushed and almost

---

5. Captain George Stuart Henderson won the VC during this action. Henderson, who had already been decorated with the DSO and Bar and the MC, died from his wounds.

entirely destroyed near Hillah, a division of reinforcements was hastily dispatched to Basra from India.

The problem centred upon the growing anger of the nationalists who felt they and the country had been betrayed at being accorded mandate status at the Paris Peace Conference in January 1919. The demand for Arab self-government had been ignored in the general carve-up of the Middle East, with Britain controlling the mandate for Iraq and Palestine and France those of Lebanon and Syria. The mandates were seen as a flimsy guise for colonialism, which of course they were. The country was in an almost total state of anarchy for some three months. The British restored order ruthlessly, although with great difficulty, involving the use of air power in bombing and machine gunning turbulent tribesmen. By the time the Cairo Conference had been convened in March 1921, to settle the political future of the region, Walter's small part in the shaping of a new nation was over. He sailed for England and demobilization on the SS *Hanover* in February 1921.

The final piece of evidence was put into place by Josephine. She had found and made contact with the Newling-Goode family and established that their great grandfather had returned from India in 1921 and later bought West Wantley Farm, which was situated between Storrington and West Chiltington. A visit to the West Sussex Records Office unearthed a letter from the solicitor acting for a Captain Walter Goode in the sale of West Wantley Farm, dated 19th June 1923, and some further correspondence regarding Walter's apparent failure to pay debts and tithe rents. The farm was only a few miles from the family home in West Chiltington. The debt problems continued and led ultimately to fraud and a custodial sentence in 1925. After his release from prison he vanished without trace until his marriage to Alice Northall in November 1943.

—⋙—

Walter's elder brother Charles proved to be equally difficult to research. The family story that surrounded the eldest of the Goode brothers again contained numerous stories that can only be described as far-fetched. All we knew as family was that he had at some time disgraced himself and been sent abroad. Initially, all I had to go on was the London Gazette announcement of his commission in 1915. Fortunately, an online search of the National Archives catalogue revealed a file for a C.H. Goode[6]. It was here I found his application for a commission and the related formalities discharging him from the King Edwards Horse and a wealth of paperwork detailing his court martial and a civil court case for fraud! This was obviously a family skeleton that had been very quickly hidden as none of us knew anything about this.

On 6th September 1914, Charles Herbert Goode enlisted as a trooper in the 2nd King Edwards Horse. He was not destined to remain in the ranks for long. In December, Charles either applied for, or was recommended for, a commission in the Royal Field Artillery. The former Uppingham schoolboy had been a member of the school's Officer Training Corps for two years and obviously had little difficulty in convincing the commissioning board of his pedigree. He was 26 years old when he was gazetted temporary Lieutenant on 13th March 1915, into the Royal Field Artillery.

By the early summer of 1915, Charles had completed his instruction at the Aldershot Training Centre and was based near Camberley at Old Deane Common Camp, where he was the acting Adjutant of the 24th Divisional Ammunition Column. As Adjutant he was the CO's personal staff officer and in charge of all the organisation, administration and discipline for the unit, a job which at the best of times was a demanding one, particularly as the column was under orders to embark for the Western Front at the end of July. All this came to an abrupt end on 27th July, when he was placed under arrest and confined to quarters following a series of dishonored cheques involving local tradesmen and brother officers.

In a letter from Charles' commanding officer to the Staff Captain of the 24th Divisional Artillery, Lieutenant-Colonel Talbot outlined the circumstances that led to Charles being placed under arrest and listed his debts. Not only had he bounced a cheque for £20 at the local garage, presumably for car repairs, but he had committed the cardinal sin of bouncing a cheque in payment of his mess bill and on fellow officers, two of whom were officers senior to him. In total he owed some £60, a considerable sum of money in 1915. As soon as the

---

6. National Archives Catalogue reference: WO 339/16342.

first two cheques had been brought to the notice of Colonel Talbot on 19th June, he had spoken to Charles and requested the outstanding amounts be settled immediately. Charles promised to instruct his bank to do this. By 26th June, the Colonel had two more cases of dishonoured cheques brought to his attention; in addition, the other two debts were still outstanding. Charles was placed under arrest and confined to quarters while Colonel Talbot and the regiment worked to find a solution to the predicament; it seemed as if a posting to some forgotten corner of the Empire was on the cards:

> The C.O. asked Lieut. Goode if he was willing to resign his commission if permitted to do so, and he replied in the affirmative; C.O. therefore recommended that he be permitted to do so; and the G.O.C. Aldershot Training Centre recommended that the officers resignation be accepted "unless it be possible to adopt the measures suggested in the communication of the 27th June 1915" – which had regard to service in selected stations abroad and stopping pay to meet debts etc. It was stated that as regards actual performance of military duty Lieut. Goode was a capable officer.

It was the arrival of Charles' wife and their two children on 5th July, that tipped the balance of any sympathy the regiment may have had for an officer who had got into financial difficulties. Colonel Talbot recorded their arrival at the Officers' Mess:

> A lady claiming to be his wife called at the Cambridge Hotel (where we have our mess) today. She came with 2 children, one a baby in arms; she appeared to be in great distress, she informs me that Lieut. Goode has left her for some time without means of subsistence:- I have advised her to write to her mother-in-law, Lieut. Goode's mother, who is I believe a lady of considerable property in Sussex and explain her position, to communicate with her people in the United States, and consult her lawyer. I have arranged shelter and food for her for the night and arranged an interview with Lieut. Goode tomorrow if he desires one.

This was probably the last straw for Colonel Talbot, especially as he had just heard about three further cheques being bounced on a Captain Palmer. The next day, in the presence of Talbot, Charles acknowledged the lady to be his wife and the children to be his, prompting the Colonel to formally recommend that Charles resign his commission:

> I regret to say that I do not consider he should be allowed
> to continue any longer in his majesty's service.

With a civil court case pending over the latest batch of bounced cheques and his wife turning up and disgracing him, Charles was left to ponder his future. Still confined to his quarters, he further tried the patience of the Colonel by breaking his arrest twice, returning to camp on each occasion having apparently dined out with another officer. He placed him in close arrest on 10th July, which removed him from the comfort of the officer's mess and to a tent on the camp guarded by two sentries. That evening, Charles obviously decided to go absent without leave. In recording the event for the court martial, Colonel Talbot found it difficult to hide his anger at the conduct of his adjutant:

> Lieutenant Goode got away from the two sentries at about 8.10pm on Saturday 10th July, whilst going under their charge to the latrine. There is a wood nearby, into which he escaped, and being a good runner, soon outdistanced the sentries, and though a search was continued for some time, and exits from the wood were watched, Lieutenant Goode managed to escape in the darkness.
>
> Under the above circumstances I would be glad, if the recommendation expressed in my letter of 3rd July, viz., that Lieutenant Goode might be called upon to resign his commission, be now amended to read that this officer be removed from the Army, His Majesty having no further need of his services. I would add that on the occasion of his breaking his arrest for the first time, I personally read to Lieutenant Goode Section 22 of the Army Act.

Section 22 of the Army Act of 1913 is very clear:

> Every person subject to military law who commits the following offence; that is to say, being in arrest or confinement, or in prison or otherwise in lawful custody, escapes, or attempts to escape, shall on conviction by court-martial be liable, if an officer, to be cashiered, or to suffer such less punishment as is in this Act mentioned, and if a soldier, to suffer imprisonment, or such less punishment as is in this Act mentioned.

In going AWOL he had passed the point of no return, where previously there was a glimmer of a chance he may have been able to retain his commission, albeit in some far-flung trench on the other side of the world. He was now a fugitive. Rather than be given the opportunity to resign his commission with some dignity, the Army would see to it that he suffered the dishonour of being cashiered at a general court martial and discharged in disgrace.

The question of his destination once he had escaped was answered by the copy of a telegram found in his service file reporting the arrest of a Charles Goode on 20th July, by the civil police and his remand by Steyning Magistrates Court. With Steyning only ten miles from the family home in West Chiltington, it seems more than likely he had gone home, probably to raise the cash to pay off his debts in an attempt to offset the possibility of criminal charges. In this he was apparently successful. After hearing the case on 26th July, the magistrates considered the offer by counsel of immediate payment and permitted Captain Palmer to accept the £20 owed, thereby withdrawing the charges. Charles was off the hook with regard to a criminal record but was arrested again by the Military Police and detained at Shoreham with the rear party of his unit, the main body of the 24th Divisional Artillery having already embarked for France.

The court martial of Lieutenant Charles Herbert Goode took place at Deepcut Barracks on 13th August 1915. He pleaded guilty to the three charges, none of them relating to the issue of fraudulent cheques but focusing on the two occasions he broke arrest and his escape from custody on 10th July, from Old Dean Common Camp.

The court found him guilty of all the charges and sentenced him to be dismissed from His Majesty's Service. There is a note in the file to say that the sentence was officially communicated to Lieutenant Goode on Wednesday 25th August.

I couldn't help but wonder about the circumstances surrounding Charles' wife and children turning up at the officers' mess in distress, and the note by Colonel Talbot suggesting she contact her family in the United States. Searching through the service file again, I found another reference to the United States written in Colonel Talbot's neat longhand:

> This officer is an intelligent, active and zealous officer, and so far as his military duties are concerned, these have been carried out satisfactorily. He has stated to me, he served in the United States Army as a cavalry officer, and is a graduate of West Point, and has seen service in Mexico.

If this was so, when did Charles first go to the United States? An email from the Uppingham School archivist confirmed he had left in 1908. He enlisted in the Army in 1914 aged 26, so there was an unaccounted period of six years when he could have been out of the country. A search of the passenger list of people leaving the UK between 1908 and 1914 revealed a Charles Goode departing for the USA from Liverpool on 18th March 1911, on the *RMS Megantic*. The *Megantic* was one of the White Star Line luxury liners and the passenger manifest records a 23 year-old Charles as travelling in Third Class as a single man. Unfortunately, there is no further evidence, beyond the age and marital status being correct, that confirms this was Charles Herbert Goode.

But there is a record of a Mrs. Harriet Annie Goode travelling back to New York in March 1916, with two children, Howard Daniel Goode aged 2 years and 11 months and Phyllis Mary Goode aged 1 year and 2 months. They embarked on the *SS St. Paul* at Liverpool on 4th March and arrived in New York nine days later on 13th March. This was almost certainly the lady with the two young children whom Colonel Talbot assisted in July 1915. Luckily, the Ellis Island immigration records in New York documented the arrival of the family in more detail and provided the evidence that this was indeed Charles' family.

Immigration records for March 1916, indicate that Harriet and the children had retained their British citizenship. Howard was born in Detroit in November 1912, and Phyllis it seems was born between late 1914 and early 1915. The family's last place of residence before embarking on the *St. Paul* was an address in Slough, Buckinghamshire. The passage to New York was paid for by a Mrs. Hamilton living in Detroit, described on the passenger manifest as the childrens' grandmother. Harriet had, it seemed, taken Colonel Talbot's advice and contacted her mother to assist her in returning home.

From this evidence, we can realistically assume that Charles did go to the United States where he met and married Phyllis Hamilton and started a family. When they returned to England, the family most likely lived with Ada and the girls at West Chiltington where Phyllis was born. Although there is no official record of the birth of Phyllis in English BMD records, her birthplace is recorded in the Ellis Island documentation as Thakeham, Sussex. So the 1914 Christmas gathering at the Goode family home would have also included Harriet Goode and her son Howard and possibly even Ada's latest granddaughter, Phyllis Mary Goode. This happy state of affairs was destined to be short-lived: by July 1915, Charles had abandoned his young family and left them without any means of support.

Harriet Goode, née Hamilton, had emigrated with her family to the United States in 1908. Her birth date is given as about 1887 and place of residence in the USA as Detroit. A search of the passenger lists for 1908 found the Hamilton family had boarded the *SS Corsican* on 19th March. Harriet, then 21 years old, travelled with her parents, James and Mary. They arrived at Halifax, Canada and were documented by U.S. immigration as crossing the border on 28th March. Their last place of residence in England was given as Slough, which accounted for Harriet's address in Slough in the months before she and the children returned to Detroit. Harriet, according to passenger manifest documentation, had been staying with her grandmother.

United States federal census records give us a little more information about the family over the next few years. The 1920 census has them living in New York State in Erie. By 1930 they had moved south to Lake Maitland in Florida. The family were still together, but there is no record of Charles living with his wife and children.

My next line of enquiry was the West Point Military Academy archives. If Charles had been an officer graduate of West Point then there would be a record of it. An email to the archivist requesting information on Charles drew another blank; they had never heard of him and there had not been a cadet of any description called Charles Herbert Goode between 1908 and 1914. I even asked them to search again in case he had used his mother's name, Poole. The result was the same. He had not been at West Point, so was the claim he had been involved as a cavalry officer in Mexico also untrue?

Since 1910 Mexico had been embroiled in a violent revolution, with opposing political and military forces struggling for control of the country. In 1913 the United States President, William Howard Taft, sent a military force into Texas and stationed them along the Rio Grande to protect Americans in the region. This show of strength caused Mexican militants to redirect their violence from their own countrymen to Americans. In 1913, when Woodrow Wilson became President, he denounced the new revolutionary government in Mexico and refused to recognise it as a legitimate government. As a result of his position, violence toward Americans intensified and there were incidents of murder, robbery, kidnapping for ransom and property destruction. War would probably have been declared but for the more pressing need for the Army in Europe. Even so, the region would not see stability until early 1919. Whether Charles had any part in all this will remain obscured by time. It is possible he was for a time with the American military forces, although I consider this extremely unlikely.

I was also curious as to what happened to this young man after his court martial in 1915. Having been discharged from the Army as unfit to hold a commission, Charles would soon become liable for conscription. New legislation designed to become law in February 1916 would enable the government to impose military service on all single men aged between eighteen and forty-one. Despite the efforts of recruiting campaigns, the numbers of volunteers for the Army was slowly dwindling and it must have been pretty evident that at some stage conscription would become a necessity. The early warnings of a manpower shortage were brought home by the huge casualty lists that the Loos Offensive of September 1915, generated, confirming the Western Front stalemate and heralding the slaughter on the Somme in 1916. If Charles wanted to avoid being conscripted into the ranks, he would have to leave the country, and do so before the act came into force. Unfortunately, I can find no firm evidence of a Charles H. Goode or a Charles H. Poole returning to either the United States or Canada. It is quite possible he returned using a different name or names, in which case it would be almost impossible to track his movements.

Nevertheless, we know that he did return to the United States at some point and, according to the family story, apparently worked as a designer for the Ford Motor Company in Detroit. There was possibly a grain of truth in this, as he already had a Detroit connection through his marriage to Harriet. With this in mind, I contacted the Benson Ford Research Centre who confirmed he had not been in upper management, but they kindly passed my request onto the Ford Motor Company employee records centre. My enquiry was answered by Jamie Myler, the senior research archivist: it had revealed nothing. They had no record of a Charles Herbert Goode working for Ford in any capacity.

The Charles Herbert story remains unfinished. If his children Howard and Phyllis married and had children of their own, then there is a new branch of the family I am so far unaware of. I dimly remember meeting him, I was about eight years old when he visited my grandmother Margery with his Canadian wife. Whether he and his second wife had a family is still unknown and will no doubt keep me digging away until I find out.

I am undecided as to the motives of Walter and Charles. Did they consciously plan to avoid service in the front-line, or did they take advantage of circumstance and opportunity? For Walter, it would have been a simple matter to engineer the pickaxe incident that resulted in his Blighty wound and evacuation home. Having got home again, did he decide to try and remain there for as long as possible? It certainly seems as if the medical board was getting a little impatient with his constant excuses and complaints about a relatively insignificant injury. Then, just when it looked likely he was about to be sent back to France, he conveniently developed a urinary tract infection, which kept him at home for a further five months. I did wonder if his posting to India was engineered by the East Kent Regiment. Did they send Walter to India to avoid the embarrassment of one of their officers being summoned to a court martial to face charges of malingering?

Charles, it would appear, deliberately broke the rules on the eve of his unit embarking for France. He clearly knew the consequences of bouncing cheques on his fellow officers, just as he would have been well aware of the seriousness of absconding from close arrest. It could be argued that he knew full well the penalty of his actions, and used them to escape army service. I confess to having little sympathy with the antics of Walter and Charles, particularly when two of their younger brothers did their duty and paid dearly for it. Reflecting on their motives, I was reminded of the words Charles Bean wrote in 1921: "What these men did, nothing can alter now. The good and the bad, the greatness and the smallness of their story will stand." Although he was referring to the men of the AIF, it seemed an appropriate epitaph for Walter and Charles.

6

Ulster Volunteers

Thomas Stanley Murland and Charles Henry Murland

When the call to arms came in 1914 it would have included my great-uncle Thomas Stanley Murland, had he not finally succumbed to tuberculosis in 1912 while working for the Canadian Survey, in British Columbia. His previous service in South Africa with the 17th Battalion of the Imperial Yeomanry, would have certainly marked him as a useful and experienced officer. Stanley's appointment to the Imperial Yeomanry appeared in the London Gazette of April 1900 where he is described as a 'gent' and granted the rank of temporary Lieutenant. By the time the announcement appeared in the press, he was already two days out of Southampton and beginning the lengthy sea voyage to Beira in Mozambique.

On the *SS Geleka* with Stanley were another 62 officers, 1019 other ranks and 53 horses, all bound for service in Rhodesia and South Africa. The 17th Battalion included the 50th Hampshire Carabiniers, the 60th North Irish, the 61st South Irish and the 65th Leicestershire Yeomanry Squadrons. The North Irish Squadron, which included Stanley and family friend Holt Waring, was commanded by Captain R.L. Moore. Their cap badge was the Red Hand of Ulster on a white shield, the same symbol that would be adopted by the 36th Ulster Division in 1914.

Not a great deal of information on Stanley's activities over the two years he was away is available. We know he landed in Portuguese East Africa on 11th May with his squadron to join the Rhodesian Field Force commanded by Colonel Herbert Plumer, an officer who would go on to distinguish himself as one of the finest army commanders on the Western Front during the Great War.

As far as Stanley was concerned, he spent the next six months marching up, across and down Southern Rhodesia preventing what would have been a dangerous incursion by the Boers into Rhodesia. On more than one occasion they exchanged shots with Boer Commandos before finally moving south from Bulawayo in early December to the Orange River Station and De Aar. A few days before Christmas 1900, they joined the hunt in Cape Colony for the elusive Boer generals Johannes Brand and J.B.M. Hertzog. There is an account in Richard Doherty's *History of the North Irish Horse*, of an action that took place on 22nd December 1900, involving both Irish squadrons, that concluded with Stanley and forty-four men being taken prisoner for a while by the Boers and later released to walk the twenty miles back to De Aar. This must have been their first full-blown confrontation with the enemy, one that would have under-lined the character and resolve of their foe.

The London Times of 11th April 1901, has a list of officers discharged to duty from hospital. Listed with those officers of the Imperial Yeomanry was a Lieutenant T.S. Murland. There is no record of why he was in hospital; possibly it was the first indication of the TB that would eventually kill him before his fortieth birthday. Whatever the reason, he would probably have been admitted to the Imperial Yeomanry Hospital at Deelfontein, situated near De Aar. Sickness amid the British troops was extremely high in South Africa: of the 22,000 dead, some two thirds died of sickness of one kind or another.

The hospital had been funded to look after the yeomen described by the Red Cross as individuals who 'were likely to be drawn from a social class accustomed to greater comforts than the regular soldier'. They were certainly correct in that assumption, as the Imperial Yeomanry officers and men who sailed for Africa in 1900 were all volunteers and of a better quality the regular army was used to dealing with in its ranks. Most of the companies that volun-teered for service were drawn from the lower middle classes and skilled working classes of the time. While the other ranks were sometimes referred to as 'gentleman rankers', the officers were generally recruited from the landed and professional classes who viewed fighting the Boers akin to chasing the fox in the local hunt. Typically, the Irish officers of the 45th Company of the Imperial Yeomanry were drawn largely from the Meath and Kildare Hunts and were referred to as the 'Dublin Hunt Company'. Volunteers such as these, were the first citizen soldiers of the Twentieth Century and the forerunners of the Kitchener New Armies that would fight and emerge victorious on the battlefields of the Great War.

In the 1902 Army List, Stanley is listed as a temporary Captain which would imply he was a senior officer in his company, particularly as the battalion had only one Major who was second-in-command of the battalion. Stanley returned home after two years service, being entitled to wear the Queens Service Medal with clasps for Cape Colony, Orange Free State, Transvaal and Rhodesia. The medals have long since vanished, along with those of two of his brothers, but I still keep looking on internet sites such as e-bay and medaltracker.com, just in case they one day resurface to take their place as family heirlooms.

Home Rule first reared its head in Ireland in 1870 and became one of the dominant issues in domestic British politics up until the start of the Great War. Home Rule was the name given to the process of allowing Ireland more say in how it was governed, releasing them from the rule of London and thus soothing those in Ireland who wanted more devolved power. Standing in the way of Home Rule was the House of Lords who, for decades, had rejected any attempt to push through the necessary legislation. The upper house saw the introduction of Home Rule as the start of a process whereby the power of London would be diluted, arguing that if Ireland was granted Home Rule, then other parts of the empire would want similar treatment. As far as the British government was concerned it was very much a done deal, and despite all the arguments for and against Home Rule, a Home Rule Bill was introduced into Parliament by Asquith's Liberal government in April 1912.

One of the major problems faced by Asquith was the Unionist movement in Ulster who were set against any form of Home Rule, believing it would lead to the break-up of the United Kingdom. In

Parliament, opposition took the form of the Unionist Party, an alliance of parties dominated by the Conservatives.

The Ulster Volunteers, championed by the Unionist MP Sir Edward Carson[1], were founded in 1912 to resist Home Rule for Ireland. On 13th January 1913, the Ulster Volunteer Force was formally established by the Ulster Unionist Council. Recruitment was limited to 100,000 men aged from 17 to 65 who had signed the Ulster Covenant[2] and was placed under the charge of Lieutenant-General Sir George Richardson KCB. During this time the Unionists enjoyed the complete support of the British Conservative Party, even when threatening rebellion against the British government. On 23rd September 1913 the 500 delegates of the Ulster Unionist Council met to discuss the practicalities of setting up a provisional government for Ulster. Ulster was preparing for civil war.

The Murland family was very much involved in the formation of the Ulster Volunteer Force and the subsequent gun running episodes that took place prior to the outbreak of war in 1914. Charlie Murland was secretary of the County Down UVF and commanding officer of the Castlewellan Company of the 1st County Down Volunteers. He also commanded the battalion for a short time in 1914. Jim and Warren Murland were also active Unionists and involved in training the company in the grounds of the Annesley Estate at Castlwellan. Several references to gun running and to drilling the various volunteer units, can be found in grandfather's diaries, and family legend has it, that the guns and ammunition that were distributed to the County Down Volunteers, were stored in the mills at Annsborough.

The most famous of the gun running activities took place in April 1914, when 30,000 German rifles with 3,000,000 rounds of ammunition were landed at Larne, with the authorities effectively blockaded by the motor vehicles of the UVF. At the time my grand-father, Howard Murland, was serving in Burma with his regiment. His diaries betray his increasing feelings of isolation and frustration while all this was taking place at home. If Ulster was to become

1. Sir Edward Henry (later Baron) Carson (1854-1935) First Lord of the Admiralty 1916-17.
2. On 28th September 1912, 237,368 men signed the Ulster Covenant pledging to 'using all means which may be found necessary to defeat the present conspiracy to set up a Home Rule Parliament in Ireland'. 234,046 women also signed.

embroiled in an armed resistance then he wanted to be part of it. He took home leave in April 1914 in order to be with the family if civil war broke out.

On Saturday 21st March 1914, the news that officers of the British Army at the Curragh had effectively mutinied[3] and refused to participate in what they saw as a betrayal of Ulster, put paid to the Government's immediate plans for Home Rule. Directives for military action were withdrawn and tension was defused, if only by Asquith giving in to the rebellious officers. The Curragh Incident demonstrated it would be almost impossible to use the British Army to coerce Ulster into Home Rule from Dublin.

This then, was the turbulent background to the raising and formation of the 36th Ulster Division. By the time war broke out the UVF was in effect a thoroughly disciplined body of men, something the British High Command were well aware of. Kitchener was keen to have the UVF in khaki and, after the guarantees were given that Home Rule would not be pursued until after the war and the UVF would be kept together as a unit, the volunteers signed up for service in an army that a few months previously they had been preparing to fight.

The three infantry regiments of the division all had their territorial base in Ulster. The Royal Irish Rifles, The Royal Irish Fusiliers and the Royal Inniskilling Fusiliers, in common with British regiments raised for the New Armies, were licensed to create additional battalions as required. Here was the blueprint for an Ulster version of the English Pals battalions which in themselves, were an expression of Ulster protestant power and independence, held together by an ethnic protestant solidarity.

Most, if not all, of the men who joined up had signed the Ulster Covenant in September 1912, as had all the Murlands. The Ulster Covenant was signed by just under half a million men and women from Ulster in protest of Home Rule Bill and was in effect the signature of the Ulster Division. All of the 1,350 men from County Down were formed into the 13th Battalion of the Royal Irish Rifles; after

---

3. 57 out of the 70 British Army Officers based in the Curragh Camp, many of them Irish unionists, threatened to resign their commissions in the British Army rather than enforce the Home Rule Act in Ulster. The officers were led by Brigadier-General Hubert Gough. They were not technically guilty of mutiny as they had not, at the time, refused to carry out a direct order.

enlisting at Belfast, they took up residence on the estate belonging to Lady Dufferin at Clandeboye. The wooded demesne at Clandeboye provided the backdrop to the spectacular Helen's Tower, a replica of which, the Ulster Tower, would later stand as a permanent memorial on the Thiepval Ridge to the men of the 36th Division.

As their numbers swelled, they were divided into four companies. The 40 Annsborough and Castlewellan men, along with their officers, Charlie Murland and Bob Matthews, joined men from Downpatrick, Ballynahinch, Dromore and Hillsborough in C Company. The patriotic mood and fervour of the day was captured in the speeches given at a civic send-off in honour of the men of Castlewellan. Addressing the assembled company was Mr. Hugh Armytage-Moore[4], JP and Chairman of the County Down UVF:

> The men of Castlewellan have nobly responded to the call and are ready to play the part of soldiers inspired by a fine sense of patriotic duty. As members of the British Army, you will manifest the characteristics by which it has always been distinguished – valour, skill, resourcefulness and honour. To be a British soldier today is to be a gentleman in arms; to defend a noble cause, and defend it with clean hands and a clear conscience. The relationship between officer and man has always been one of particular pride in the British Army. Self sacrifice and consideration on the one hand have inspired obedience and confidence on the other, and those whom I am privileged to address are singularly fortunate in having an officer, in the person of Lieutenant Charles Murland, who is well fitted to uphold such fine traditions. You have known him well for many years and from first to last, in whatever capacity he has met you, he has been your friend. I am therefore glad that he is with you now and you with him, and I only hope that in times of difficulty and danger he may be there still to lead and to advise[5].

4. Hugh Armytage-Moore was manager of the Annesley estate from 1909 to 1917. He later inherited Rowallane House at Saintfield (now a NT property) and created one of the finest gardens in Ireland. He was awarded the RHS Victoria Medal of Honour in 1942 for his contributions to horticulture.
5. Down Recorder 1914

The vast majority of the Castlewellan men listening to Hugh Armytage-Moore's speech were employees at the Murland mills who would have known Charlie well in his capacity as employer. For some it must have felt little had changed apart from the khaki they had exchanged for their civilian clothing. There had been another, more private, send-off a few days earlier for Charlie and his brother Warren, who was now a Second Lieutenant in the North Irish Horse. At that gathering of family and local dignitaries, Charlie had been presented with an engraved regimental sword and dress scabbard and Warren with a cavalry saddle and bridle. The tone and content of the address on that occasion was a little different; Armytage-Moore reminded them of the importance of the need to replace casualties in the division only with men who were volunteers and covenanters and not to forget why the UVF had been raised in the first place:

> All I can say is go on, go on for your original object, go on for the present struggle, go on for the future dangers, and remember that it is when those dangers are surmounted that we revert mainly to our original object to never forget for one moment, as we never will, that we will never submit to any Home Rule Bill, that this or any other government may wish to place upon the statute book[6].

These strong words barely disguised the fact that these men were part of an oath bound division who were totally committed to the survival of Ulster as part of the United Kingdom. They would fight for their country in time of national need, but when it came to Home Rule they would fight for Ulster.

Life at Clandeboye soon settled down to training and preparation for moving overseas. The question of who would command the 13th Battalion was resolved on 21st September, with the appointment of Lieutenant-Colonel William Henry Savage, a retired Indian Army soldier who came from Cushendun in County Antrim. Savage had a long service record going back to 1882, during which time he had

6. Down Recorder 1914

served with the 3rd Queen Alexandra's Own Gurkha Rifles, before retiring in 1912. William Savage brought an Indian Army discipline with him that did not always fit easily with the officers and men of the battalion but, with a national shortage of officers to take up command of the New Army battalions, many experienced men like Savage were brought out of retirement to fill the gaps. It is not clear if he had signed the Covenant himself or what his political sympathies were, but he did prepare the battalion for its baptism of fire on 1st July 1916.

Soon after Savage arrived, he appointed Major Robert Perceval-Maxwell as his second-in-command, Captain R. Fridlington as his Adjutant and Lieutenant David Bell as Quartermaster. Charlie was appointed temporary Captain at the same time. It would appear that Charlie was commanding C Company at Clandeboye. David Bell in his *Reminiscences*, which he published in 1962, remembered Charlie during an inspection of C Company:

> When the company was taken out on the parade the huts were inspected to see that nothing was left behind. Capt. Murland took C Company on parade and the quarter-master inspected the huts and found rifles and equipment lying about. This was reported to Capt. Murland, who himself stayed behind on the following parade. There was again equipment lying around, so he ordered a fatigue party to put everything into stores. That was alright until the evening when there was a great outcry in the camp about the things that were missing. It was then discovered that no allowance had been made for the clerks and tradesmen who weren't on parade. From that day until the Battle of the Somme, any shortage of equipment was blamed on Capt. Murland.

He recalled another occasion when the battalion was making preparations to leave Clandeboye for their move to Seaford in Sussex. Charlie and the company officers were instructing the men how to position themselves and their equipment in an orderly fashion to enable them to get into a railway carriage without causing chaos. By using benches to represent the seats in a railway carriage, and with the men marching along an imaginary platform, they were given the order 'left wheel' by the Company Sergeant Major, marched into the 'train' and ordered to sit down:

> Captain Murland had given the order to entrain when he met Arthur Burns from Dromore who had lost his place in the ranks. "Where are you going?" bellowed the Captain, "Are you the ticket collector or what?"
> "No sir," replied Arthur.
> "Then find your seat or the train will be away without you."

The move to Seaford was a popular one. The Ulster Division continued their training on the South Downs. The local population, who had initially wondered how these wild men from Ulster would behave, soon accepted the Irishmen as their own. Sussex also brought the war a little closer; from the peace and tranquility of the Downs the occasional distant crash of gunfire could be heard from the Western Front battlefields. Armageddon was not far away.

For some of the 13th Battalion officers, their new location provided an opportunity to get away from camp and relax a little. London was not far away and Brighton and Eastbourne were even closer. Charlie had teamed up with an old friend, Captain James Davidson of Bangor. James was a director of the family linen firm and from all accounts attempted to escape the confines of military life at every opportunity. In a letter home dated 16th July 1915, James grumbled about the weather and Colonel Savage:

> We are having the most abominable weather at present, rain almost every day and quite cold. I should quite enjoy a fire today for everything is so damp and miserable. The little car is going all right but I have had little opportunity of using it so far, as weather has been so bad. Hope it will clear for the week-end. I expect Charlie and I will go for a run to Brighton or Eastbourne on Sunday. It is now very hard to get leave to be away from camp for a night, we have to put our names in a book and this has to go before the C.O. for approval, who is not a bit liberal in this or indeed anything for that matter.

The letters that James Davidson wrote home have been preserved in the Public Records Office of Northern Ireland in Belfast. In another short letter dated 20th July, it is evident that Charlie and James did manage to get away from camp and out in the car:

> Chas. M. [Charlie Murland] and I went over to Eastbourne on Sunday afternoon and stayed there for dinner. We had a run in the car first through a very quaint old village called Alfriston where there is a celebrated old inn absolutely crammed with beautiful old furniture, you would have enjoyed seeing it. The weather was lovely and we greatly enjoyed the run.

A week later, they dined with two friends from County Down who were visiting Seaford:

> Jessie Smyth and Miss Hall are in Seaford for a few days. Chas. M. and I are to dine with them and Teddy Smyth tomorrow.

The Smyth family was another of the well-to-do Ulster linen families and cousins of the Murlands. Captain Edmund Fitzgerald Smyth, better known as 'Teddy' to his friends, was an officer with the 11th Battalion and well known as an Irish international rugby player, having been capped on four occasions. Teddy owned the Lisburn Weaving Company and, after being commissioned had shared the Officer's Mess with Charlie and James Davidson. Jessie Smyth and Charlie also had a romantic attachment and, at one stage, it was thought they might marry. Another of the Smyth family, and particular friend of my grandfather, was William Haughton Smyth. Haughton was a Managing Director of the family firm, William Smyth and Co. Ltd at Banbridge, and was now serving as a Captain in C Company with Charlie.

In September 1915, the Ulster Division moved to Bordon and Bramshott, in Hampshire, for musketry and machine gun training. At Bordon they were joined by the Divisional Artillery and the new Divisional Commander, Major-General O.S.W. Nugent[7], an Ulsterman

---

7. Major-General (later Sir) Oliver, Stewart Wood Nugent. DSO (1860-1926)

from County Cavan who had previously commanded the 41st Brigade in France.

It was around this time that Charlie became ill. From the evidence in Charlie' service file it is unclear exactly when, but from James Davidson's letters and medical board reports it looks very much as though he initially became ill in September 1915. James wrote home from Guadaloupe Barracks at Bordon on 26th September:

> Poor Charlie Murland has got a bad throat which the Dr. thinks looks rather diptheretic and he has gone off to hospital. I hope this won't turn out to be the case, it would be such bad luck for him to get laid up now when we are almost on the point of leaving.

In actual fact, Charlie had a little more than just a bad throat: the medical reports in his service file had diagnosed syphillis and he was sent home on three months sick leave. Evidently sightseeing was not all that was on the agenda during his visits to Brighton and London! The Army has always had difficulty in deciding whether VD was a self-inflicted wound, and therefore subject to military punishment, or was purely a medical condition and treated like any other disease. What they did do was issue a general order that warrant officers and NCOs could be reduced in rank if they became infected and officers could be asked to resign their commissions, however, Charlie avoided this penalty. He was more concerned about being left behind and being unable to leave for France with his battalion, particularly as the infection was slow to clear up. In November 1915 he was given another three months sick leave by a medical board. James Davidson wrote home on 12th November from France:

> We heard yesterday that Charlie M. has been granted another 3 months leave so he must be a great deal worse than he imagined. It is unfortunate for him and also the battalion, but he will at least miss most of the winter out here, which is something to be thankful for.

The battalion arrived in France on 4th October 1915, disembarking at

Bolougne with a full complement of 30 officers and 995 other ranks. After a short spell in billets at Rainneville and St. Gratien, they began their probationary period with the 7th and 8th Battalions of the Royal Warwicks in the 12th Division's Fonquevillers sector, opposite the heavily fortified German strongpoint of Gommecourt. This was a similar period of instruction that Archie Goode and the 13th Royal Sussex received with the 8th Division when they arrived in March 1916.

It was a relatively quiet introduction to the trenches for the Irishmen. Between Fonquevillers and Gommecourt the ground was flat, but with a slight rise behind the German front-line. To get to the British forward trenches, long and tortuous journeys had to be made along communication trenches stretching back through the village. Originally dug by the French, they were in poor condition, often blocked by debris and prone to easy flooding. The battalion had its first casualty here: Rifleman Thomas Quinn was wounded with a grenade fragment. Further periods of attachment with the 12th Division continued, interspersed with brigade training exercises. Casualties during this period were light, the battalion war diary records four men wounded by sniper fire and shrapnel.

Winter 1915 was a cold one in the trenches of Picardy, and the men of the Ulster Division soon came to realise that life in the trenches was not an easy one. Often they were knee deep in water, and when temperatures dropped below freezing the misery increased considerably with the inevitable thaw. Fortunately, the usual rotation between the front-line trenches and the comparative luxury of rest areas, where they were at least sheltered from the elements, did provide some relief.

By February 1916, with the coming Somme Offensive in mind, the 36th Division was allocated its own sector opposite the formidable German Schwaben Redoubt. The three infantry brigades of the division occupied a frontage which essentially straddled the River Ancre and neatly divided itself into two sub-sectors: Hamel to the north and Thiepval Wood in the south.

In April, Charlie was declared fit for active service again and in May he returned to the battalion. James Davidson recorded his delight in seeing him again in a letter home on 21st May:

Charles Murland arrived out here on Friday and has joined the 13th again. He stayed with us till today and as you can guess we were all very delighted to have him.

Albert Uprichard would also have been glad to see him back in the 13th Battalion. Albert, by now a Major, was commanding D Company and had been a friend of Charlie's since boyhood. The Uprichards, like their friends the Murlands, were another family who were part of the linenocracy of Northern Ireland and owned the Springvale Bleachworks at Banbridge. Both families shared a love of horses and racing, and one of Albert's brothers, Forster Uprichard, was serving as a Lieutenant in the North Irish Horse with Charlie's brother Warren.

Charlie had arrived just as the weather was improving. It was Spring, and the battalion, as part of 108th Brigade, was taking its turn in the front-line trenches in Thiepval Wood. The wood was a dangerous place for troops, with German gunners continually randomly shelling the Irish positions. A narrow gauge tramway that was built through the wood to aid the evacuation of wounded to the casualty clearing stations in the rear was frequently hit and in a constant state of repair. Behind the scenes, well away from the prying eyes of the German forward positions, the preparations for the coming offensive continued. To the ordinary soldier going about his daily duties it would not have been missed that there was considerable movement going on, with huge stockpiles of ammunition, medical supplies and other resources being established behind the lines.

To even the most simple of minds, it must have been obvious that something big was being planned and it would almost certainly involve them, particularly as they had been busy attacking dummy trenches that had been laid out in the rear at Clairfaye Farm, which were an exact replica of those that faced them on the other side of No Man's Land. They were, of course, quite right. Haig's ambitious Somme Offensive was planned for 29th June and the Ulstermen were only weeks away from the biggest British offensive action of the war so far – a fight that would secure their place in Irish legend.

The battle plan for the 36th Division on the opening day of the Somme Offensive, or the 'Big Push' as it was referred to by those involved, focused on the heavily fortified Schwaben Redoubt. The Redoubt was a network of well-dug trenches and deep dugouts situated on the high ground overlooking the Ancre. Between the Ulstermen and the first line of the German trenches there were reported to be sixteen rows of wire and a further five protecting the second line. If you stand at the edge of Thiepval Wood with Mill Road in front of you, the ground rises quite steeply for 250 feet over the 1000 yards of ground between the bottom of Thiepval Wood and the German third line. Modern infantry with lightweight equipment would think twice before assaulting fortified positions over such terrain. I have often wondered what the regimental officers of the Ulster Division thought, in the days preceding the battle, of their chances of making it to the German fifth line at Grandcourt. At a distance of over three kilometres, this was the division's ultimate objective.

A veritable library has been generated by the Somme Offensive and its aftermath and I don't propose to go into great detail as regards the Ulster Division's role on 1st July, beyond placing in context Charlie's activities on the day. The 13th Battalion, together with the 11th Battalion, were tasked with attacking the northern slopes of the Schwaben Redoubt and clearing the northernmost trenches towards the Ancre river valley and those on the road between St. Pierre Divion and Grandcourt. It was a small part of the much larger plan, a plan that looked good on paper, but relied heavily on the successful advance of the divisions on each flank of the attack. If the attack by the 29th Division north of the Ancre and that of the 32nd Division at Thiepval failed, then the Ulstermen would be cut to pieces by enfiladed fire on both their flanks. It didn't bear thinking about.

The other key to a successful offensive action in 1916 was good co-ordinated artillery support to reduce the enemy trenches and dugouts to a morass and cut the protecting wire. Saturday 24th June was the first day of a six day long bombardment that opened along the whole of the eighteen mile front. The noise produced by this storm of fire could be heard in London and the southern counties. Ada Goode and the family could hear it in West Chiltington, as could Archie in the trenches of La Bassée further north. In Thiepval Wood and Hamel it must have sounded as if the Horsemen of the

Apocalypse had begun their ride from Hell. Watching the rain of shellfire fall on the enemy positions it was little wonder that the British and Empire troops believed their attack would be a pushover, after all who could possibly survive such an onslaught?

On the fourth day of the bombardment, the 13th Battalion were moving up through Martinsart in the pouring rain to relieve the 11th Battalion in the front-line trenches, when an enemy shell exploded in the midst of No.11 Platoon and the Headquarters staff. Fourteen men were killed outright and almost sixty wounded, including Major Perceval-Maxwell who was second-in-command of the battalion. Robert Perceval-Maxwell was a wealthy landowner and member of a family who, since 1628, had lived at Finnebrogue, a magnificent manor house which stood at the centre of a large estate bordered by the Quoile River and Strangford Lough in County Down. A great field sportsman, Robert was Master of East Down Harriers and had the reputation in the County of being one of the best harrier huntsmen. Although wounded again on a later occasion, he survived the war but would tragically lose both his sons and a nephew in the conflict.

Unexpected rain postponed the attack until 1st July, which extended the artillery bombardment of the enemy lines but also allowed the German batteries to continue pounding the Ulster front line at Thiepval Wood and Hamel. By the night of 30th June, even though the trenches were in a very poor state and there had been numerous casualties, the men were keen to get going. July was the Orangemen's month and 1st July was associated with the Battle of the Boyne, a protestant victory won by William of Orange over 200 years earlier. Now the Ulstermen of the Twentieth Century were poised to fight another battle, a battle that despite the casualties and errors of judgement would mark the beginning of the end for the German Army in the Great War.

The final bombardment of enemy lines at 6.25am began under a clear blue sky. The barrage would lift at 7.30am as it had done on all the preceding mornings, but this time it would be followed by waves of attacking troops taking what was left of the Germans by surprise, or so it was hoped. General Nugent was under no such illusions – the Germans were not stupid and had been alerted for weeks that the British were planning an offensive, the build-up of men in the forward areas had hardly gone unnoticed. Nugent's plan was to use the dead ground in front of him to allow his troops to lie out on No Man's Land unseen by the German forward positions and, as soon as the artillery barrage had ceased, to move quickly into the enemy trenches before they had time to climb out of their dugouts and man machine guns.

At 7.15am the first wave of men moved out of their trenches and lay down to await their officers' orders, their places in the vacated trenches being taken by the next wave. All along the front, soldiers had been told to walk across No Man's Land towards the German trenches as there would be little or no opposition. The great tragedy was that the plan had not been as effective as originally thought, and the wire still presented a considerable hurdle in some places to the attacking troops. Nor had the week-long barrage been entirely successful against the deep dugouts that sheltered the German troops. As soon as the barrage lifted, the German troops were manning their weapons and firing on the advancing troops walking towards them. The vision of long lines of men, with their rifles held high, being cut down in their hundreds is sealed into the imagery of 1st July. Had more run across No Man's Land, as the men of the Ulster Division had done in their initial charge, then the enormous casualty figures of the day may have been greatly reduced.

Lying out in No Man's Land, Charlie and the men of C Company would have heard and felt the aftershock of the huge explosion of the Hawthorn Ridge Mine at Beaumont Hamel, which was detonated at 7.20am. If the Germans had needed any further indication that the assault was about to begin, they now had confirmation.

Minutes after the barrage lifted at 7.30am, the Ulstermen's furious charge had overwhelmed the first and second line trenches and had opened the door for one of the most successful actions of the day. The 36th Division, south of the Ancre, would achieve all its objectives and make the furthest advance on the day by a major unit. But there was a huge human cost in taking the Schwaben Redoubt, and this was partly due to the failure of the 29th Division's attack north of the Ancre and of the 32nd Division on their right flank. Their failure allowed the German machine gunners on both flanks an uninterrupted view of the advancing troops and contributed significantly to the enormous casualties and their eventual withdrawal.

As the 13th Battalion men pushed forward, they became very exposed to machine gun fire on their left flank from St. Pierre Divion and the Beaucourt Redoubt. The hail of bullets was so intense that a large number of the battalion's officers and men were casualties before they reached the German positions. Undeterred, the survivors pressed on. On their right, the Belfast men of the 107th Brigade famously took the Schwaben Redoubt trench by trench, dugout by dugout, in some of the fiercest hand-to-hand combat of the day. By 9am they had even taken the German fourth line and were consolidating their position.

From letters written by Charlie and the events described in the battalion war diary, I am reasonably sure Charlie was wounded at the German first line, which was south of the present day Mill Road Cemetery and close to the Ulster Tower. The war diary recorded C Company's progress:

> [They] crossed the first line and almost reached the wire of the second line trench when they were held up by a strongpoint on their left [machine gun at St. Pierre Divion] which appeared to be a bomb store and machine gun post. Just about this time Lieut Rogers was mortally wounded after having given the order for bombers to go to the left flank. The platoon Sergt, Sergt Love was also killed and the platoon was commanded by Sergt Burns who got them into the 2nd line up the communication trench to the right. Here they met Captain Davidson who took command of this section of trench until wounded for the second time.

Also in the German second line were the remnants of A and B Company, who had been raked with fire from the St. Pierre Divion stronghold. Charlie by this time had been hit by machine gun fire, almost certainly from the St. Pierre Divion direction, and was lying somewhere in front of the wire of the first line. In a letter dated 19th August written to my grandfather, who was serving at the front in Mesopotamia, his sister Florence passed on the bad news:

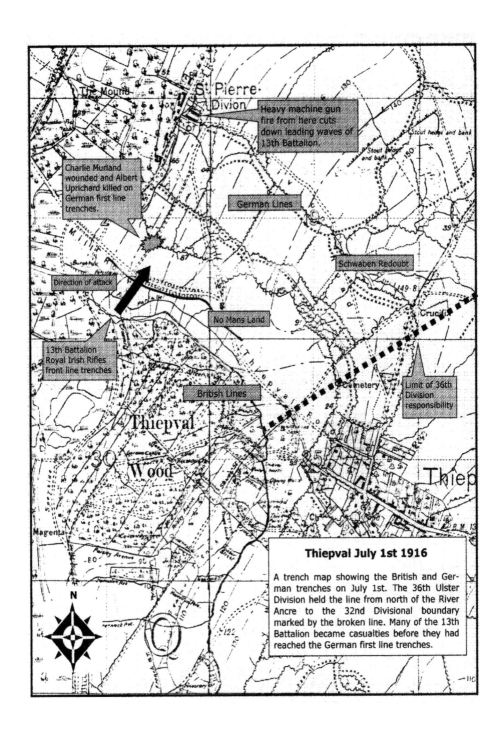

Heavy machine gun fire from here cuts down leading waves of 13th Battalion.

Charlie Murland wounded and Albert Uprichard killed on German first line trenches.

German Lines

Schwaben Redoubt

Direction of attack

No Mans Land

13th Battalion Royal Irish Rifles front line trenches

British Lines

Limit of 36th Division responsibility

Thiepval July 1st 1916

A trench map showing the British and German trenches on July 1st. The 36th Ulster Division held the line from north of the River Ancre to the 32nd Divisional boundary marked by the broken line. Many of the 13th Battalion became casualties before they had reached the German first line trenches.

We have heard from Charlie who is now at the Endsleigh Place Hospital for officers in London. The division did splendidly but we have lost a lot of friends, poor Albert and Haughton are among the dead, Teddy is wounded and Clarence is still missing. Charlie has had a bad time and was hit in the left shoulder sometime after 7.30am on July 1st, he tells us he was there until 9pm when soldiers from his regiment found him and brought him back to safety, one of them was Will Gilmour who had gone out with others to look for him. Charlie saw Albert [Uprichard] killed but could not reach him, Jim has been to Bannvale to see them [Uprichard family] and as you may imagine they are all deeply upset and much concerned for Forster.

Charlie had been severely wounded and was fortunate not to have been killed. It must have been an appalling experience to have witnessed his boyhood friends Albert Uprichard and Haughton Smyth killed. Haughton had fallen as he led his platoon of C Company towards the first German line. Albert, who was leading D Company, died close to Charlie. His death was also witnessed by Rifleman Edmund Kerr, a note in Albert's service file[8] confirms that Kerr saw him killed in front of the German first line trench. Clarence Craig, the South Antrim Member of Parliament serving with the 11th Battalion, was wounded and taken prisoner. Charlie, weak through loss of blood and unable to move, was planning to try and get back towards his own lines after dark. Fortunately, he was found by one of the Annsborough mill workers who eventually brought him in as parties of men were sent out to find the wounded.

The Ulster Division's position was now an exposed salient in the German line a few hundred yards wide and raked by German fire. The German artillery barrage was, by now, so effective that it prevented reinforcements from reaching them. At dusk a deter-mined counter-attack by fresh German troops, who had arrived by rail at Grandcourt, pushed them back to the second German line, a line which they held all the next day until relieved at night by the

8. National Archives Catalogue reference: WO 339/14235

troops of the 49th Division.

The County Down officers were a close-knit group, many of whom had grown up together and mixed socially in the years before the war. They had friends and acquaintances in the other battalions and knew each other's family members. The casualty lists of 1st July echoed through the Ulster provinces, as it did throughout the Empire. Almost everyone knew someone in the long casualty lists. Total British losses for that day amounted to a horrific 19,240 dead, 35,493 wounded, 2152 missing, and 585 prisoners. In two days of fighting, the Ulster Division had lost 5,104 officers and men, killed, wounded or missing. The 13th Battalion had 595 casualties including 8 officers and 219 other ranks killed. Of the 729 men and 23 officers from County Down that began the assault, only 134 answered their names at the battalion roll call on 3rd July. The list of officer casualties included many of the names of the prominent families of Northern Ireland. Charlie would not hear for several days that James Davidson had been killed: after being wounded for the second time, this courageous officer was being carried back by two men and was shot in the head between them. He is buried in the Serre Road Cemetery No.2

Even on 2nd July, it was still difficult to determine who had survived and who had not. Writing from the Peterhead Sap trench at the edge of Thiepval Wood, Lieutenant Herdman, one of the few 13th Battalion officers not to have become a casualty, wrote to his mother to let her know he was safe. He was under the impression that Charlie had been killed:

> Just a note to tell you in spite of all I am alright, not a touch, also to say I have gone through hell with the finest division the British Army has ever seen. As we all said, they would do the right thing when the time came and yesterday, they did a feat that will go down in history. I don't know if you have heard but poor Murland, Uprichard, Smyth, Rogers and many others have branded forever their names in Britain's roll of heroes, oh! Thank God Matthew, Findlay and Moore are only slightly wounded but no news of Ewart and Haughton. But you will see plenty of this when the lists come out. I

don't really think I can write anymore at present, everyone in spite of all are cheery, will write later when I get some sleep.

On 6th July, he wrote again from Martinsart after the brigade had been withdrawn from the front-line:

The calm after the storm, the whole brigade, or what is left, are here. I went to my battalion the other day, Murland was wounded but no hope of Dermot and the others. No word of Rex Neill, nobody seems to have seen him and I'm sorry. I went to the hospital with Col. Packenham to see a Sergt of Rex's company but he had just been evacuated. I must say the hospital nearly did for me after all the stories I heard about their wonderful deeds. Up to the night of the 4th we were sending out parties to bring in wounded, some we got after 3 days. But they came in smiling, hard chaps. I'm afraid the 13th had the worst casualties.

Herdman's letters may possibly have arrived home before the official casualty lists were published. They would have given those awaiting news of loved ones the first hint of the extent of the casualties in Charlie's circle of friends and acquaintances. Lieutenant Rex Neill was an officer in the 11th Battalion; the body of the 21 year-old from Craigavad in County Down was never found and his name is on the Thiepval Memorial to the missing, as is the name of 28 year-old Captain Cecil Ewart of the 11th Battalion. Henry Albert Uprichard is buried close to where he fell in the Mill Road Cemetery which overlooks the site of the Schwaben Redoubt. Here also is Lieutenant George Rogers, another C Company officer from Banbridge, who died between the first and second German lines. Like so many who fought that day, the body of Captain William Haughton Smyth was never recovered and his name is commemorated along with the other officers and men of the Royal Irish Rifles on panel 15A and 15B of the Thiepval Memorial.

Today the site of that remarkable battle is commemorated by a replica of the Helen's Tower that stands in the demesne at

Clandeboye where the division was first assembled in 1914. If you visit Thiepval in late Autumn, from the top of the Ulster Tower the trench lines of the Schwaben Redoubt on the Thiepval Ridge are still visible as chalky smudges, forever imprinted on the landscape.

In September 1916, Colonel Savage was replaced by Lieutenant-Colonel Holt Waring who had transferred from the North Irish Horse. This was a welcome appointment as he was well known to many of the officers and men of the battalion and, more importantly, a County Down man. Savage returned home to retirement.

Charlie's wound had rendered his left arm useless and for a time it was thought he might lose it. Although he eventually regained almost full use of his arm again, it was to trouble him for the rest of his life. By late October he was out of hospital and convalescing at home where he remained until 20th February 1917. It was clear to his next medical board that it would be some time before any return to active duty could even be considered and he was granted further leave until November 1917.

Back at home, he moved into Warren's house at Greenvale and had begun to get involved temporarily in the family business again when he was approached by the Air Board to transfer to the Royal Flying Corps staff. His expertise and knowledge of the linen trade it seemed would be of great value in connection with the production and purchase of aeroplane yarns and linens. In 1917, aircraft production had dramatically increased from the handful of machines available in 1914. By 1918 the number in service was 3,300 and in the intervening years some 55,000 had been built. All of these aircraft had the majority of the fuselage covered in fabric which was manufactured in large quantities in Ulster. For the remainder of the war, Charlie was based in Belfast as the resident RFC Procurement Officer in Ireland.

As for the Schwaben Redoubt, it would not be until October 1916 that British forces would be back in the trenches that the Ulstermen had fought so hard for. The trench lines they had overrun and then reluctantly retreated from, were finally retaken by the 18th and 39th Divisions during the Battle for the Ancre Heights.

7

Irish Horsemen

Warren Murland, James Gerald Murland and William Sydney Murland

Warren Murland was one of Charlie's two elder brothers and a director of the family firm. Like my grandfather he was passionate about horses and riding to hounds, riding regularly with the Iveagh Harriers and the County Down Staghounds. At the outbreak of war in 1914, aged 35, along with a number of other County Down notables, he was invited to join the North Irish Horse. The North Irish Horse owed its heritage to the creation of a volunteer force to defend the country in the absence of a regular garrison of troops. The raising of volunteer units had first been prompted by the actions of the privateer John Paul Jones and his audacious raid into Belfast Lough during April 1778. After a chequered history, the Irish yeomanry regiments finally came of age in 1900 in response to the war in South Africa.

After Stanley Murland and his comrades-in-arms had returned in 1902 from South Africa, the 60th North Irish Squadron of the Imperial Yeomanry became known as the North of Ireland Imperial Yeomanry and eventually, in 1912, simply as the North Irish Horse. Their new role as a Special Reserve regiment gave them precedence over the territorial force regiments and included a commitment for overseas duty in time of national emergency. This was soon to come.

In June 1914, the officers and men of the North Irish Horse were at their annual camp at Murlough Bay in County Antrim. They were visited by my grandfather, Howard, and Warren, who had driven up from Annsborough in Warren's new Belsize car. Grandfather recorded the occasion in his diary:

> Warren and I drove to Murlough with a cargo of ammunition, then went out on the sand hills and watched the North Irish Horse. Saw Masserene, Farnhan, young Maude, Bobby Jocelyn and had a great chat with Holt Waring and Barrie Combe. After lunch drove over to Bryansford and saw Margaret Waring, Holt arrived before we left.

Warren and Howard had been taking ammunition to the UVF companies in County Antrim and afterwards paid a social call on the officers of the North Irish Horse exercising in the sand dunes. The backgrounds of the officers present were representative of many county yeomanry cavalry regiments in the United Kingdom at the time. Galloping across the Murlough Sands were three peers of the realm: Robert 'Bobby' Jocelyn (the 8th Earl of Roden), Major Algernon Skeffington (the 12th Viscount Massereene) and Major Arthur Maxwell (the 11th Baron Farnham). Major Holt Waring was the head of an old and highly respected County Down family and had fought in the Boer War with the Imperial Yeomanry, and Lieutenant Samuel Barbour 'Barrie' Combe was Holt Waring's brother-in-law. Barrie[1] was Master of the County Down Staghounds, the meets of which appeared high on the social calendar of the well-to-do and, from all accounts, these hunt meetings were always well attended by the North Irish Horse officers.

Membership of the leading hunts in the counties of the North was almost an unofficial requirement of any officer of the Irish Horse. Being a regular huntsman was testament to the personal riding skills required as a cavalry officer. Grandfather's diaries are full of references to riding with both the County Staghounds and the Iveagh Harriers, meticulously recording who attended and in what capacity!

As a special reserve regiment, the North Irish Horse was committed to maintaining an expeditionary squadron to be

---

1. I have used the spelling of 'Barrie' as recorded in grandfather's diaries. However on the Ballynahinch War Memorial it is spelt Barry.

mobilised with the British Expeditionary Force in the event of war. On Sunday, 4th August 1914, orders were issued for the BEF to be mobilised, and pre-written telegrams were quickly despatched from Belfast ordering officers and men to report to their respective squadrons. As part of the BEF, A Squadron, under the command of Major Lord John Henry Cole, left Belfast on 7th August and sailed from Dublin's North Wall Quay on 17th August. They were the first non-regular unit to land in France.

There is unfortunately a lack of personal information regarding Warren and his service in the Irish Horse. The usual sources such as the London Gazette record his promotions and the occasion he was mentioned in despatches, but the various squadron war diaries are either incomplete or lacking in detail. His Medal Index Card gives very little away apart from his promotions and the date he landed in France with the regiment. However, there is a service file for Warren in the National Archives[2] and my grandfather's diaries have several references to Warren over the four years of the war which help to fill in some of the gaps.

By the time war was declared, grandfather had returned to his regiment in India and was reliant on information in the newspapers and letters from home to keep him informed of events in Europe. In October he remarked that:

> Warren has been told by Colonel Maude he will get a commission in the North Irish Horse. He has sold his horses.

In November, Warren wrote to him from the regimental depot at Antrim to tell him he was moving to England to join D Squadron at Bedford. Holt Waring, it seems, was also at Bedford at the time and with all this activity going on at home grandfather was clearly getting impatient with sitting around, as he saw it, in Burma, doing very little to further the war effort.

During the first year of the war, each army division had a squadron of cavalry at its disposal; D Squadron had joined the units of the 51st Highland Division who were billeted near Cople in

2. National Archives Catalogue reference: WO 339/28083

Bedfordshire prior to moving to France on 30th April 1915. The squadron was under the overall command of Major Hamilton Russell and embarked at Southampton on 1st May for Le Harve. The D Squadron war diary is intact up until the time the squadron left the 51st Division in May 1916 and became part of the 1st Regiment North Irish Horse. Fortunately, the sometimes illegible pages of the D Squadron diary, that I first looked at in the National Archives, have now been transcribed by Phillip Tardif in Australia and made available online, ensuring that this valuable and unique document is preserved and available to a wider audience. The diary records the six officers, 141 NCOs and men and 158 horses arriving in France at 7am on 2nd May. That evening the squadron entrained for the 23-hour journey to Berguette where, arriving in pouring rain, they immediately began the march to Busnes, finally arriving at 5am on 4th May.

In the first months of the war when the two sides were jockeying for position before they dug themselves in, there was considerable movement of both infantry and cavalry. In a mobile war, the cavalry would be deployed to act as a screen, covering the flanks and gaps between infantry formations and providing a reconnaissance role. In the static Western Front scenario of fortified trenches they were held in reserve until such time as the infantry and artillery had broken the line and had pushed past the gun lines behind the enemy trenches. They would then, in theory, pour through the break to harass any troops preparing to counter-attack, preventing any new defence lines from being established[3].

Before Warren arrived in France with D Squadron in April 1915, the Irish Horse was initially attached to Sir John French's[4] Headquarters at Le Cateau and had seen action while attached to the 4th Division in the retreat from Mons. Later, during the September advance from the Marne to the Aisne, grandfather's friend Barrie Combe, was killed. Barrie[5] was scouting with C Squadron near

3. This in fact never happened, although it came close at the Battle of Cambrai in 1917 when a break in the German line was not exploited in time, largely because of poor communication.
4. Field Marshal Sir John Denton Pinkstone French (1st Earl of Ypres) (1852-1935) Commander-in-Chief BEF 1914-15. Commander-in-Chief Home Forces 1915-18.
5. Lieutenant Samuel Barbour Combe aged 35. Killed on 30th September 1914. Commemorated on the Le Touret Memorial, Festubert and on the Ballynahinch War Memorial, Co. Down.

Conde-sur-Aisne in support of the 5th Division. He was buried by the Germans at Conde Castle but his body was never recovered.

Across the water in the Northamptonshire town of Daventry, the envelope containing the order to mobilise was opened by Second Lieutenant James Martin Gerald Murland on 4th August 1914. His regiment, the Northamptonshire Yeomanry, were a territorial cavalry unit that drew the majority of its officers and other ranks from the surrounding county. Gerry had been commissioned in March 1912 and, like Douglas Watts in the Sussex Yeomanry, had attended annual yeomanry camps and cavalry training school with the other part-time soldiers of the unit. At the outbreak of war, the Northamptonshire Yeomanry officers included, among others, Lieutenant Lord Spencer Compton[6] and Second Lieutenant James Brudenell-Bruce,[7] who was one of the four sons of Lord Charles, the 9th Earl of Cardigan. The Brudenell family were direct descendents of James, the 7th Earl of Cardigan, who commanded the Light Brigade at Balaclava in 1854, a connection that I'm sure had not gone unnoticed with his brother officers! Two of the senior officers were Major John Brooke Cuncliffe of Petton Hall, Shropshire and Major Sir Charles Bingham Lowther, a former regular officer in the 8th Hussars.

The Northamptonshire men were no different to the North Irish Horse in their involvement with hunting; many of the officers and men were members of the well-known Pytchley and Grafton Hunts and, war permitting, continued with their passion for hunting while in France. Sir Charles Lowther was master of the Pytchley in 1914 and took his dogs with him to France and Italy. The Northamptonshire Yeomanry in particular hunted with a pack of hounds behind Arras in 1916 while based at Habarcq and once killed a fox within yards of the British second line trenches. Without doubt it was the close association with hunting that made the yeomanry

6. Lieutenant Lord Spencer Compton, aged 22. His name is commemorated on Panel 3 of the Menin Gate, Ypres.
7. Lieutenant James Ernest John Brudenell-Bruce. Died of wounds on 11th April 1917. Buried at Duisans British Cemetery, Etrun.

cavalry regiments masters of their trade. Once in France, when the opportunity allowed, it soon became apparent that the British cavalry was superior to the French and German cavalry units.

On 10th August the Northamptonshire Yeomanry were moved first by rail to Derby and then, a week later, to Houghton Regis near Luton. As with the officers and men of the Irish Horse at Bedford, an intense period of training followed to prepare them for war. Moving again to Hursley Park, Winchester, the yeomanry were under the orders of Major-General F. Davies[8] commanding the 8th Division. The British 8th Division was a regular army division that was formed by combining battalions returning from outposts in the British Empire at the outbreak of the war to provide a much needed reinforcement to the BEF. It was also the division that Archie Goode had served with when first arriving in France with the Royal Sussex.

A month later, in their role as divisional mounted troops, the regiment paraded at midnight on 4th November 1914 and marched to Southampton, arriving at about 4am. The war diary records an uneventful crossing to Le Harve on *SS Thesbis* with all ranks disembarking on 6th November and proceeding to No 6 Camp on the cliff tops above Le Harve. The regiment was under canvas there until 10th November, when they left for the Merville-Estairs sector.

———

Gerry's younger brother, Bill Murland, was a regular army officer and was commissioned into the 10th Royal Hussars on 22nd February 1913 after a two year probationary period that began in March 1911. The 10th Hussars were a cavalry regiment that my grandfather described in his diary as being 'frightful snobs', having come across them on several occasions while they were stationed in India close to his regiment at Bangalore. Not only were they branded as snobs, but they had the reputation of being, with the possible exception of the Household Cavalry, the most aristocratic and expensive regiment in the British Army. They also upheld the reputation of being the smartest regiment in the British Army. The Shiny 10th, as they were known, had a history dating back to the

8. Major-General (later Lieutenant-General Sir) Francis John Davies. (1864-1968)

early 18th Century, a history that included the magnificent and decisive charge at Waterloo that scattered the French Cuirassiers and the Imperial Guard.

At the outbreak of war in 1914, the 10th Hussars were stationed at Potchefstroom in South Africa, a small township on the banks of the Mooi River that, twenty-eight years later, would be a temporary home to my father while he learnt to fly at No. 6 Air School in 1942. Disturbed from their colonial routine, the 10th embarked at Capetown on 5th August and arrived at Southampton on 19th September. They were immediately sent to Salisbury Plain to join the 3rd Cavalry Division. Leave was scarce and Bill only managed to snatch a few days at home before the regiment landed at Ostend on 8th October. On 13th October, as part of the 3rd Cavalry Division, the regiment fired their first shots in anger. Deployed initially in supporting the retreating Belgian Army, they were forced back with the rest of the BEF to the Ypres Salient which had been formed as a defensive semi-circle around the eastern approaches to the town. The resulting bulge in the front-line was one that British, French and Belgian troops clung onto with a stubborn resolve over the four years of war, despite determined German attempts to break through. The original perimeter line of 1914 was gradually reduced by offensive action during the first two Battles of Ypres and was the scene of some of the most desperate fighting of the Great War. In April 1918, during the last battle of Ypres, the town itself was practically on the front-line.

The first Battle of Ypres, in October and November of 1914, saw the 10th Hussars fighting as dismounted troops, first at Zandvoorde on 25th October, and then at Klein Zillebeke on the 26th. This was their first taste of trench warfare and despite their heavy casualties, they held their line against overwhelming odds. It was at Zandvoorde that they lost Captain Sir Frank Rose and Lieutenant Turnor during the attack by the German 39th Division, which pushed the forward British forces back onto the line being held by the 10th Hussars and other units of the 6th Cavalry Brigade. Here the German advance was checked. The Hussars were withdrawn the next day but not before they had shown the value of cavalry as a mobile reserve. The cavalrymen had demonstrated they could fight equally well dismounted with bayonet and bomb and take their

Gerry Murland's call up notice of August 1914

place in the line when the situation demanded it and, in the case of the Shiny 10th, could hold the line as well.

They had another chance to show their courage during the second Battle of Ypres. By 1915, Ypres, with its ramparts and magnificent buildings, was slowly and methodically being reduced to rubble by German artillery and it was against the background of a burning town that they moved into the trenches west of the Potijze-Verlorenhoek Road, on the edge of the Potijze Chateau grounds. The situation was once again desperate and the Germans were on the threshold of breaking through and entering Ypres. At dawn on 13th May, a German attack began in the sector that was being held by the 6th and 7th Cavalry Brigades. After suffering very heavy casualties during a three-hour artillery barrage, the remnants of the 1st and 2nd Life Guards were forced to retire to the lines being held by the

8th Brigade cavalrymen. The 10th Hussars, now part of the 8th Cavalry Brigade, were serving alongside the Essex Yeomanry and the Royal Horse Guards. The order to retake the trenches, now occupied by the Germans, was received at lunch time. On receipt of his orders and pointing to the offending trench, Lieutenant-Colonel Shearman, the commanding officer of the 10th Hussars, famously turned to his second-in-command, Major Buxton and said:

> That is the trench I am going to take. I shall do it with the greatest ease, there is no doubt about it whatever.[9]

He did exactly that. Leading his regiment from the front in the company of the Essex Yeomanry and Horse Guards, they overwhelmed the enemy and regained the front-line which they held until relieved. The human cost of this counter-attack was a heavy one. The total number of casualties in the three regiments amounted to over 388 killed, missing and wounded. Shearman was killed, as was Lieutenant-Colonel Deacon of the Essex Yeomanry along with 12 other officers. Bill must have been leading a charmed life as he was one of only four officers and 98 other ranks of the 10th Hussars left standing. Sadly, a fellow Pytchley Hunt member from Castle Ashby in Northamptonshire, Lord Spencer Compton, was killed with the Horse Guards. He had been commissioned into the Northamptonshire Yeomanry on 10th February 1912 after completing his officer training course with Gerry and transferred in 1914 to the Horse Guards.

In September 1915, the 10th Hussars, along with the rest of the 3rd Cavalry Division, were again in the trenches and embroiled in the Battle of Loos, moving in early October to the small villages of Humbert and St. Michel where they spent Christmas. 1916 saw the 10th back in the Loos area, manning the trenches around the Hohenzollern Redoubt sector along with the Essex Yeomanry and the Royal Horse Guards. Wondering if they would ever be in action as mounted cavalry again, it was with some relief when the division was pulled out of the line in February for training with the

9. The 10th PWO Royal Hussars and Essex Yeomanry during the European War, 1914-1918. Lt.-Col. H.D.C.Whitmore.

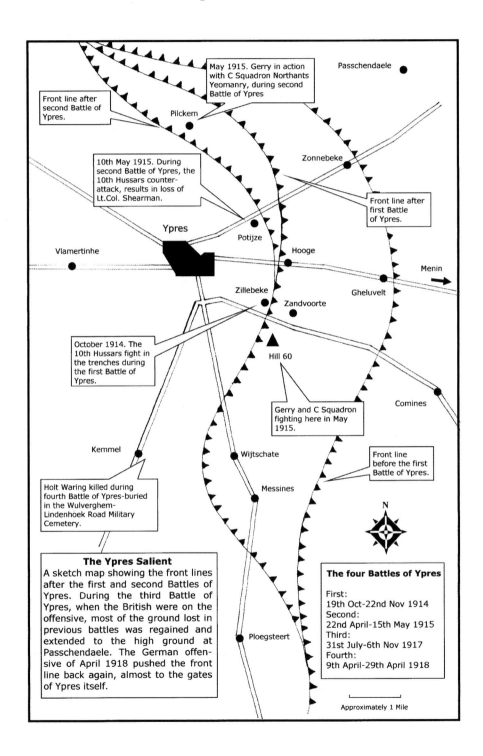

May 1915. Gerry in action with C Squadron Northants Yeomanry, during second Battle of Ypres

Passchendaele

Front line after second Battle of Ypres.

Pilckem

Zonnebeke

10th May 1915. During second Battle of Ypres, the 10th Hussars counter-attack, results in loss of Lt.Col. Shearman.

Front line after first Battle of Ypres.

Ypres

Potijze

Vlamertinhe

Hooge

Menin

Zillebeke

Gheluvelt

Zandvoorte

October 1914. The 10th Hussars fight in the trenches during the first Battle of Ypres.

Hill 60

Gerry and C Squadron fighting here in May 1915.

Comines

Kemmel

Wijtschate

Front line before the first Battle of Ypres.

Messines

Holt Waring killed during fourth Battle of Ypres-buried in the Wulverghem-Lindenhoek Road Military Cemetery.

N

The Ypres Salient

A sketch map showing the front lines after the first and second Battles of Ypres. During the third Battle of Ypres, when the British were on the offensive, most of the ground lost in previous battles was regained and extended to the high ground at Passchendaele. The German offensive of April 1918 pushed the front line back again, almost to the gates of Ypres itself.

Ploegsteert

The four Battles of Ypres

First:
19th Oct-22nd Nov 1914
Second:
22nd April-15th May 1915
Third:
31st July-6th Nov 1917
Fourth:
9th April-29th April 1918

Approximately 1 Mile

Hotchkiss Rifle at St. Riquier, near Abbeville. At the beginning of 1917, they found themselves billeted by the sea at Merlimont, just south of Etaples. Their commanding officer at this time was Lieutenant-Colonel P. Hardwick DSO. Hardwick was to oversee the specialised cavalry training that the regiment carried out over the winter of 1916-17 and lead them during the Battle of Arras in what was possibly one of their finest actions of the war.

In the meantime, Warren and D Squadron of the North Irish Horse continued in their role as Divisional Cavalry to the 51st Highland Division, but were not involved in the second Battle of Ypres. Four months later the Squadron was held in reserve at the Battle of Loos but were again not deployed. It was a frustrating time for the cavalry on the Western Front and was the principal reason why so many cavalry officers and men sought transfers to other regiments such as the Machine Gun Corps and the Royal Flying Corps. The inactivity and the seemingly endless working parties were beginning to have an effect on morale. Over the course of 1915 the Irish troopers dug and repaired trenches, laid telephone wires, cut wood for the trenches, and occasionally relieved the infantry in the front-line while building their winter quarters at Behencourt. Casualties were thankfully small in number.

In December, the 51st Division were withdrawn from the front-line and moved to a rest area at Septenville. The Squadron moved to Septenville after they were relieved by the South Irish Horse, who, much to their annoyance, took over their winter accommodation. Fortunately the weather in December and January was quite mild and, although there was shelter for the horses, some troops were sleeping out in the open. They were on the move again at the end of February, trailing in the wake of the Highland Division as it was moved to a new sector at Roclincourt, just north of Arras. The Highlanders were taking over a vital sector of the line and would be playing an important part in the forthcoming Battle of Arras.

May 1916 saw D Squadron, along with A and E Squadrons, formed into the 1st Regiment North Irish Horse and attached to VII Corps. The war diary for the regiment over the next twenty-two months gives little away in terms of detail. Not only does it fail to mention Warren's promotion to Captain in May, but it gives no detail of the regiment's deployment during that period. The war diary was generally the responsibility of the commanding officer and, in the case of the 1st North Irish Horse, was Lieutenant-Colonel Lord Cole. Cole was clearly a man of few words and content to summarise a month's activity with a single sentence. He mentions very few individuals by name and it would appear from his record that the regiment was principally engaged in providing working parties. Judging by the numbers of officers and men that transferred to other units around this time, the mundane corps cavalry duties had begun to lose their appeal. As the war moved into 1917 and towards the Battle of Arras, the lack of detail in the war diary becomes frustrating. Warren was mentioned in despatches[10] in the London Gazette of 15th May 1917, together with Holt Waring, Captain T.W. Hughes and Major A.H. Russell. There is no record of these officers in the war diary so I can only guess the mentions might have been related to the Arras offensive, although there is no evidence from the diary that the Irish Horse were in action during this battle. Little more is known of Warren's service in France, but there is an interesting comment in grandfather's diary dated 27th May 1917:

The North Irish Horse are very annoyed with their C.O. Lord Cole. Warren was offered second-in-command of the 1/1st Somerset Yeomanry but Cole won't let him go.

For Warren, a move to the Somerset Yeomanry would have meant promotion to Major. The Somerset Yeomanry were also one of the few yeomanry cavalry regiments to remain mounted until the end of the war, something Warren would have been very aware of in February 1918, when the Irish Horse handed over their mounts to the 2nd Cavalry Division remount depot and were permanently dismounted.

10. The lowest form of recognition that was announced in the London Gazette. Originally there was no actual award, the very fact that an individual was mentioned in the Commander-in-Chief's despatch was deemed sufficient. However after the Great War an oak leaf emblem was allowed to be worn with the ribbon of the Victory Medal indicating the individual had been mentioned. The mentioned individual also received a scroll carrying service details and a reference to the despatch in which they were mentioned.

—∞—

The Northamptonshire Yeomanry seemed to have been more fortunate in their deployment as divisional mounted troops and were
certainly fortunate in keeping their horses for the duration of the
war. Once they had arrived at Lestrem in November 1914, the
regiment was chiefly employed at night in digging trenches and
repairing damage to the front-line and support trenches.
Occasionally they relieved the infantry and took over a sector of the
front-line.

1915 saw the yeomanry involved in some heavy fighting at the
Battle of Neuve Chapelle in March, losing eleven men killed and
eighteen wounded. After Neuve Chapelle, the regiment moved
north and the various squadrons dispersed to take up divisional
cavalry roles. Gerry and C Squadron moved to join the 5th Division,
where they were involved in the heavy fighting during the second
battle of Ypres along with the 10th Hussars. In late May 1915, C
Squadron rejoined the regiment who by now had reformed at
Habarcq as VI Corps cavalry.

Habarcq was a small village some seven miles west of Arras
which had suffered very little from the ravages of war, and the
French farmers were still working the fields around the village.
Although it was considered to be a quiet sector, the continual
background noise from artillery exchanges was a constant reminder
of how quickly this could change. Nevertheless, the village seemed
happy to ignore this and certainly the local estaminet and the small
shops in the village benefited from the brisk trade generated by the
yeomanry and other troops billeted in the area. The yeomanry
themselves were very popular in the village and, as almost permanent residents, involved themselves in village life as much as
possible. For many of the men this rural setting was a comforting
reminder of their homes in Northamptonshire and offered a
welcome escape from the drudgery of the front-line.

For the Northamptonshire Yeomanry and the units of the 3rd
Cavalry Division, all this was about to change. In 1917 it had become
increasingly clear that a 'push' was being planned and this became
immediately apparent to the yeomanry when, a few weeks before
Easter 1917, they were relieved of the usual corps cavalry routine of

providing working parties and ordered to undergo specialist cavalry training in preparation for what had become generally called 'the great advance'; an advance that would later become known as the Battle of Arras.

Typically, the Germans had anticipated such an offensive and they began building substantial alternate defences in the Arras area. The Hindenburg Line was constructed about a mile or so behind the original front-line, with its starting point opposite Arras at Railway Triangle, going south. The original front-line was only lightly held and the area between it and the Hindenburg Line destroyed. This destructive decision was central to the German defensive strategy, as it made movement for advancing troops extremely difficult at a time when speed was essential. Bearing this in mind, the Allied plan was modified to include a massive attack to bypass the northern end of the Hindenburg Line as well as a frontal assault to head for Monchy-le-Preux. Once again the Germans anticipated this flanking action and built another defensive line, about five miles to the rear of the Hindenburg Line, called the Drocourt-Queant Switch, pivoted at Queant. The idea was that if the Hindenburg Line fell, the Germans could retire to their new defensive line. These two buffers were intended to prevent the Allied attack gaining the momentum it would need for a decisive drive, and in this they were very successful.

Despite this, the Battle of Arras had considerable initial success. The battle plan involved the British 1st Army capturing the Vimy Ridge and the 3rd Army delivering the main attack on a wide front extending from the Vimy Ridge to Beaurains, just south of Arras. The first day's objectives included taking Vimy Ridge and advancing as far east as the village of Monchy-le-Preux. On the second day, the Drocourt-Queant Switch line was to be taken, thereby outflanking the new German defences.

The main assault began at 5.30am on Easter Monday, 9th April 1917, a day remembered for its appalling weather and bitingly cold wind. The attack went well and in less than an hour the whole German front-line had fallen and Vimy Ridge was in the possession of the 1st Army. On the opening morning of the battle, the Northamptonshire Yeomanry, under the command of Lieutenant-Colonel A.G. Seymour, received orders to assemble on the Racecourse at the western entrance to Arras. Here they joined the

3rd Cavalry Division, which included Bill and the 10th Hussars in the 8th Cavalry Brigade. I do not know for certain, but I feel sure the two brothers must have met up here and exchanged news and wished each other luck in the forthcoming battle. The yeomanry were under the orders of the 37th Division and, accordingly, moved first to Blangy and then through Arras along the south bank of the River Scarpe. At 5pm the regiment passed through the leading units of infantry about half a mile east of Feuchy. Here B Squadron, under Major Sam Benyon, was sent forward to make contact with the enemy, which they did at the Fampoux crossroads. At the same time, Gerry and C Squadron had been sent over the Arras–Douai railway line to protect the right flank. In the process of doing this, they captured four artillery pieces and a number of prisoners. That night the regiment bivouacked in the marshes east of Feuchy, which was not too uncomfortable until it began to snow!

The next day the yeomanry suffered their first casualties of the battle while being shelled in the Scarpe Valley. Lieutenant Andy Chaplin was killed, along with Private David, Captain Jock Lowther and two other ranks were wounded. At the nearby Feuchy Chapel near the Arras–Cambrai Road, the 10th Hussars had also suffered from harassing shellfire, losing ten men and fifty horses. At dawn on Wednesday, 11th April, the regiment received orders to assemble on the reverse slope of Orange Hill to cover the left flank of the 45th Infantry Brigade. The scene that met them was later described by Sir Charles Lowther in a letter to his wife:

> Next morning we moved to the West of Monchy-le-Preux, where there was a sight which I shall never see again – guns in action in the open, infantry attacking, and the cavalry all lined up behind. One could see the whole thing which was more like a field day on Salisbury Plain than anything else.

Trooper Jack Townsend[11] who served with A Squadron also recorded his impressions of the scene before him:

11. In Action as Cavalry. Unpublished manuscript held at the Northamptonshire Records Office. Ref. NY3/3.

From our high position we were able to see for miles around us. To the left, the country beyond the Scarpe could be clearly seen, and to our right the boundary of our vision reached the Arras-Cambrai Road. From the top of Orange Hill, the real height of the Monchy plateau did not stand out in true perspective. To me it appeared we were looking down upon it. Yet the highest ground in Monchy was twenty-five feet above the level of Orange Hill. The centre of the village which was composed of the Square, and the streets leading off to the south of it and the Manor House grounds, was the highest part – beyond that, the streets leading eastwards from the Square fell away at a sharp decline.

Assembled in the snow on Orange Hill that morning were over two thousand mounted cavalrymen waiting for the order to advance. It must have been quite a spectacle. I can't help but wonder if Gerry managed to meet up briefly again with his younger brother before the battle. They were drawn up quite close to each other and must have both been hoping their respective regiments would be involved in the advance.

The infantry attack on Monchy, which began at 5am, was allocated to the 37th Division with the Northamptonshire Yeomanry and elements of the 8th Cavalry Brigade in support. The infantry attack would also have the support of C Battalion of the 1st Tank Brigade. Communication between infantry and cavalry was maintained by one of the Northamptonshire officers, Second Lieutenant Francis Brooke, who advanced with the infantry and, at great risk to himself, made numerous return journeys under heavy fire. At 7.30am information was received that the two brigades of the 37th Division were in possession of the village. The order to advance was given to the Essex Yeomanry and 10th Hussars at 8.00am.

As the leading elements of the Essex Yeomanry and 10th Hussars advanced over the southern edge of Orange Hill, they were immediately met by heavy and accurate shellfire suffering numerous casualties. Entering the village at the north-western entrance, accurate machine gun fire was responsible for further casualties as both regiments galloped through the streets to the central square. Here their advance towards Pelves was halted by German units dug in beyond the village. According to the Northamptonshire Yeomanry war diary, as soon as the 8th Cavalry Brigade had passed through them, they were given the order to advance through the village and clear two woods to the north-east. Trooper Townsend again:

> That ride from Orange Hill will never be forgotten by the men that took part in it. To run the gauntlet of German shellfire, especially now that the enemy was so aware of our intentions, made one wonder how many would reach the village.........Mr. Bristow, on his chestnut, led the way with great courage. Our troop leader did not care much for ground work but put him on a horse and I believe he would have gone anywhere. He even tally-ho'd us in true Pytchley Hunt style as he increased the speed to a gallop. Nearing the bottom of the hill, we sensed an additional danger to the shellfire. Numerous whistling pings signified that machine guns were now firing on us.

Sergeant Cyril Day[12] in B Squadron also had vivid recollections of the ride from Orange Hill:

> We went on at a gallop, the enemy simply pouring shells at us. It was a wonderful sight, the ground was covered with snow, the air keen and frosty and the sun shining making the breath of hundreds of horses look like smoke pouring from machine guns.......Field guns and machine guns were sweeping the country and cutting horses and men down everywhere. It was like being shot at in a trap.

By now it had become clear that the village was obviously not completely in the hands of the infantry and the 37th Division troops were under heavy shellfire and at risk of counter-attack. The situation was not a good one and possession of Monchy hung in the

12. Private diary account held in the Northamptonshire Records Office.

balance. It is clear from the Essex Yeomanry reports of the action that upon their arrival in the village the 37th Division infantry were in isolated and scattered positions. These remnants were collected together by Lieutenant-Colonel Whitmore of the Essex Yeomanry and together they consolidated the positions on the northern and eastern perimeter of the village.

The Northamptonshire men had also by now entered the village and suffered badly from the effects of heavy shellfire impacting on hard surfaces as they rode for the town square. Passing the high walls of the Manor House on his left, Jack Townsend's horse, Fantail, was hit by machine gun fire as the narrow road turned sharply to the left:

> I must have been half-way past this exposed position [the corner of the Manor House grounds] when I felt, and heard, something strike the inner side of my left field boot, and I looked down expecting that I had been wounded. While I was looking down Fantail suddenly collapsed on to his knees and his hind legs bent under him. He had been riddled with machine gun bullets. It was no doubt that it was a spent bullet that had hit my left boot after passing through Fantail's stomach. Luckily for me my horse did not fall [completely] until we had reached the cover of the first house beyond the corner. As we went down, both my feet came flat to the ground, but still in the stirrup irons. My hands, holding the reins, fell on Fantail's neck. With a loud snorting groan, poor Fantail struggled to rise. Blood sprouted several feet from his nostrils and I became smothered with his gore around the neck.

At this point in the battle, although the town was now firmly in British hands, the German box barrage was inflicting heavy casualties on both man and horse. The streets of Monchy were littered with dead men and horses. It was said that in several places the horses were lying so thickly that it was necessary to climb over them in order to make progress. Many of the wounded horses were suffering terribly and had to be destroyed where they lay.

Having secured another horse, Jack Townsend arrived in the

142

square to join what was left of his troop. He described the scene before him:

> Dead lay all around, but chiefly at the street corners, especially at the corners of the streets that declined with steep gradients eastwards from the square. At one of these a dead young infantryman of a British battalion was poised kneeling on one knee, to all appearances as having been killed when assuming the kneeling firing position.

In order to prevent further needless casualties in the, by now, choked-up streets of the village, the Northamptonshire Yeomanry was ordered to retire. It was during this retirement that Gerry won his Military Cross. The citation read:

> For conspicuous gallantry and devotion to duty. When his squadron retired to a fresh position he remained behind under heavy shell fire to attend to two wounded men. He then collected several men whose horses were killed, mounted them on others, and led them safely back through the enemy barrage.

Gerry had been promoted to Captain in July 1916 and had entered Monchy with C Squadron. As the regiment retired to the comparative shelter of Orange Hill he had gathered together wounded and shell-shocked troopers and led them to safety. It was an extraordinary act of courage and would have been witnessed by all those who were still on Orange Hill. There was one other Military Cross awarded to a Northamptonshire officer that day, Second Lieutenant Brooke's bravery had also been recognised. His citation read:

> For conspicuous gallantry and devotion to duty. He was sent up to the firing line to observe the situation, and when the infantry advanced, he went with it, and was able to send and bring back most valuable information, crossing time after time under heavy fire.

Remaining in Monchy defending the northern outskirts of the village, Bill was wounded on four occasions before he was finally taken to the regimental aid post at the Chateau. By the time they were relieved by the 6th Battalion, Royal West Kent Regiment at midnight, the Shiny 10th had suffered 180 casualties of which two officers and 25 other ranks were killed. The Essex Yeomanry suffered 122 casualties, losing one officer and 18 other ranks killed. The Northamptonshire men, having reformed in the safety of Happy Valley, had got away relatively lightly. Of the 356 Officers and men who charged across the mile and a half of shell-torn ground, 14 were killed and 61 wounded. The dead included Lieutenant Brudenel-Bruce and Rugby-born Lieutenant James Goodman.[13] Of the regiment's horses, over 170 were either killed or wounded. An entry in grandfather's diary told of 525 of the 10th Hussar's horses being killed.

It was not until the morning of the 12th that the last of the 10th Hussars finally left the shell-torn rubble that had once been Monchy village. Bill, badly wounded in the left leg, was evacuated first to No. 8 General Hospital at Rouen for treatment and then home. His subsequent treatment and convalescence in England kept him from returning to the regiment until September 1917.

———

Soon after Bill's return, there was a considerable shake-up and reorganisation of cavalry regiments. With the need for more and more infantry replacements, demand was beginning to outstrip supply. Since the beginning of the war the cavalry had always taken a turn in the trenches to relieve the long suffering infantry and when not dismounted in the front-line, they frequently found themselves digging and repairing trenches during the hours of darkness or escorting prisoners. Many of the yeomanry regiments were now being dismounted and reformed as infantry, machine gun battalions or cyclist companies. The fate of the North Irish Horse was already sealed. I can imagine Warren's horror as he discovered he was to ride

13. Lieutenant James Goodman, aged 36, is commemorated on the Arras Memorial to the Missing. Bay 1.

a bicycle instead of a horse! Once again there is little evidence to accurately place him from February 1918 until July 1918, when he was posted to the Royal Garrison Artillery to serve with 17th Brigade Horse Lines. The conversion into the 5th Cyclist Regiment (Royal Irish Horse) was completed by 19th March, just in time for the launch of the German offensive two days later. When the blow struck they were with the British Third Army. Assuming Warren was still with the regiment, I searched the war diary for any reference to him without success. Presumably, he fought with the regiment during the March retreat of the Third Army until his posting four months later, but there is no record of this. It was very frustrating not to be able to get a clearer picture of his activities during the final months of the war.

The German offensives of 1918 began in late March with the opening thrust in the Somme area south of Arras resulting in the British being forced into retreat along a front of 50 miles. German troop strengths had been increased considerably between November 1917 and March 1918. The Treaty of Brest-Litovsk had released German divisions from the Russian Front and now some 177 German divisions were in France, of which 110 were in the front-line. The German High Command was well aware that the arrival of American forces on the Western Front would ultimately spell defeat for Germany unless they could defeat the French and British before the Americans were ready to fight in any great numbers.

It was with this in mind, the German commander in the field, Erich Ludendorff, launched the first of his offensives on 21st March. On the front held by the British Fifth Army, 43 German divisions attacked 12 British divisions. The Fifth Army Front had always been vulnerable as it was only lightly defended and had recently been taken over from the French. I don't propose to go into detailed description of the retreat that Gough's Fifth Army undertook in the face of such overwhelming odds. Suffice to say that, apart from the initial disorganisation and panic, it was enough to slow the speed of the German advance thus enabling others to muster their forces sufficiently to ultimately turn a potential defeat into victory. Many units fought until overwhelmed[14] and sold their positions dearly.

---

14. The most famous of these was the action on 21st March at Manchester Hill, held by D Company of the 16th Manchesters. Lieutenant-Colonel Elstob refused a German call to surrender. Elstob received a posthumous Victoria Cross.

Typical of this determination to stem the advance was the action of the 10th Hussars at Collezy, where Bill and a very under-strength regiment, counter-attacked on horseback and swept through the German lines, cutting down over a hundred of the enemy at the point of the sword. In the face of this fighting retreat, the German advance finally ground to a halt on 6th April. They had lost the essential momentum to maintain such an offensive, exacerbated by heavy casualties and a lack of mobility over a battleground that had been torn to shreds in 1916.

The first attack may have run out of steam but a second thrust took place on 9th April along the Lys in Flanders. This was aimed at taking the Channel Ports and also enjoyed an initial success in terms of territorial gains along a twenty-mile front running south from Ypres. It was checked at Hazebrouck and Ypres with the forward units of the German army only thirty miles from the coast.

Three more attempts at smashing the Allied line along the Aisne and Marne were held principally by the French and American forces and, as Ludendorff decided to withdraw his forces from what had become a dangerous salient at St. Miheil, Foch[15] with the French and the Americans under General John Pershing[16], successfully counter-attacked. Now on the offensive themselves, the British Fourth Army sliced through the German lines on 8th August at Amiens, advancing fourteen miles and taking 30,000 prisoners. Ludendorff later described this as a black day for the German Army.[17] The tide had turned at last.

It was against these events that the 10th Hussars played out their last actions of the war. Bill by this time had been promoted to Captain and had also been mentioned in despatches on 8th November 1917. His dash and courage had obviously been noted as the war diary refers to him as commanding C Squadron. The follow-up to Amiens continued east of Arras, over the familiar ground near Monchy-le-Preux and the capture of the Drocourt-Queant Line which was denied to them in 1917. Casualties remained heavy in all

---

15. Ferdinand Foch was given overall control of the Allied forces in March 1918, serving as Allied Supreme Commander, in which role he frequently conflicted with Pershing over the disposition of U.S. forces.
16. General John Joseph ('Black Jack') Pershing. (1860-1948) Commander-in-Chief American Expeditionary Force, 1917-19.
17. My War Memories, 1914-1918 (1920).

of the Allied fighting units as well as in the retreating German Army.

By early October the regiment was deployed to Honnechy, a small town some five miles south west of Le Cateau. It was here that Bill's war ended. Commanding his squadron, he was acting as right flank guard to the division when they came under heavy machine gun fire from the direction of La Sabliere Wood, south of Maretz. Whether he was wounded at this point in the battle or later during the advance and capture of the town is unclear, but he is listed as among the 70 casualties the regiment suffered that day, together with 106 horses. His wounds were serious and, apart from lesser injuries, he had been hit on the left side of his face and right forearm, which five months later led to the loss of sight in the left eye. He was evacuated to England where he spent several months recovering at Lady Carnarvon's Hospital for Officers in London.

Gerry and the Northamptonshire Yeomanry were destined not to play a part in the 1918 finale on the Western Front. Instead, they would see their war concluded on the Italian Front as part of XIV Corps under the command of the Earl of Cavan[18]. In October 1917, French and British troops were sent to Italy after Austro-Hungarian forces in company with their German allies broke through the Italian front-line at Caporetto. The demoralised Italian troops asked for assistance in their counter-offensive. The yeomanry left for Italy by train on 6th November 1917, arriving at Ventimiglia on the morning of the 10th. On arrival, the regiment was ordered to move to Borcon where they eventually arrived on 25th November.

Italy was in complete contrast to the ravages and destruction of the Western Front. The yeomanry winter quarters were situated on the Venetian plain near Treviso and only 30 miles north of Venice itself. For the troops it must have felt as if they were on holiday, although any thoughts that Gerry may have had in this direction were quickly dispelled when he contracted jaundice just after Christmas. He was admitted to the 62nd British General Hospital in

18. Field Marshal Earl of Cavan (1865-1946) Commanding XIV Corps 1916-18, Commander-in-Chief British Forces in Italy 1918-19.

Genoa on 29th December. The Regiment's war diary recorded his return to duty on 15th February 1918. I could find no further reference to him after this date, and it was only after I had sent for his service records from the Historical Disclosures Department at the Army Personnel Centre that I realised he had been sent home on leave on 18th February.

By early 1918 the first signs of the Flu Pandemic had begun to make itself apparent and was already scything through the ranks of the British Army in Italy and France. On arrival in England, Gerry became ill with the flu virus and did not return to duty in Italy until 9th October 1918, after his medical board had passed him fit for active service. He was just in time, as five days later the regiment moved east, with Gerry now in command of A Squadron, to cross the Piave River and take part in the final offensive of the Italian campaign.

On 26th October, they were at Casa Postioma, moving the next morning to cross the Piave using the pontoon bridge at Salettuol. Cyril Day recorded their advance once they were across the river:

> Moved off at 10pm [on the 28th October]. The roads were packed with traffic and it took until 4am next day to cross the pontoon bridges over the river. Enemy aeroplanes were bombing and firing with machine guns onto the bridges nearly all night. Just as we crossed a number of planes following the course of the river, bombed the bridges on either side of us but for some unknown reason missed the one we were on. I couldn't help but see the hand of God protecting us and gave him thanks. Went onto a village called St. Michells where we baited our horses and had a bit of food ourselves.

The village in which they had halted was San Michele di Piave. The yeomanry were now the advance unit of XIV Corps and, although there was evidence that Austrian resistance was crumbling, there were still isolated pockets of resistance. On 29th October they were ordered to advance through Vazzola and over the Monticano River. The war diary recorded the events when B Squadron reached the Monticano:

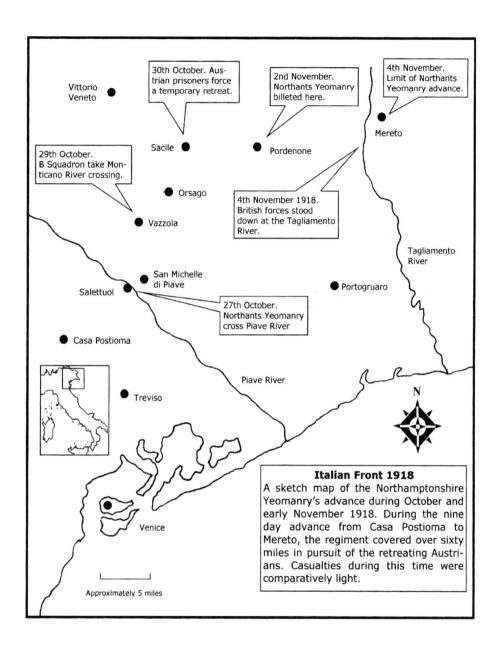

30th October. Austrian prisoners force a temporary retreat.

2nd November. Northants Yeomanry billeted here.

4th November. Limit of Northants Yeomanry advance.

Vittorio Veneto

29th October. B Squadron take Monticano River crossing.

Sacile

Pordenone

Mereto

Orsago

4th November 1918. British forces stood down at the Tagliamento River.

Vazzola

Tagliamento River

San Michelle di Piave

Salettuol

27th October. Northants Yeomanry cross Piave River

Portogruaro

Casa Postioma

Piave River

Treviso

N

Venice

Italian Front 1918
A sketch map of the Northamptonshire Yeomanry's advance during October and early November 1918. During the nine day advance from Casa Postioma to Mereto, the regiment covered over sixty miles in pursuit of the retreating Austrians. Casualties during this time were comparatively light.

Approximately 5 miles

The leading troop leader, with great gallantry charged and captured a machine gun holding the bridge, which enabled the squadron to come into action dismounted, who by Hotchkiss and rifle fire, forced the enemy garrison, 500 to 600 strong, to the right and left of the bridge to surrender and also shot or made prisoners, an enemy party who advanced to blow up the bridge.

The troop officer was Lieutenant G.A. Gillespie, who was later awarded the MC for his part in the action, and Cyril Day, the Squadron Sergeant Major, received the DCM.

Lieutenant-Colonel Lowther and the yeomanry were accompanied by a unit of the Motor Machine Gun Corps and some Cyclists. The next day the forward patrols were in sight of Sacile, a strategic crossing-point over the River Livenza. Based on what little intelligence was available, Lowther judged the town to be largely unoccupied. With A Squadron as advance guard, he deployed his forces to take control of the town recording the day's events in the war diary:

> I attempted a surprise attack on SACILE, which inhabitants said was held, sending 1 Coy [company] Cyclists, 2 machine guns down the main road, 1 Sqdn [A Squadron] to the right and 3 troops to left of town. Only one enemy machine gun opened to begin with and a lot of prisoners were secured, but after half an hour, the enemy – quite a 1000 strong- got organised and advanced in column to within 30 yds of my men, so I had to withdraw, after inflicting heavy casualties on the enemy and taking away 350 prisoners.

Initially, the Austrians had surrendered; however, taking note of the small force they had surrendered to, they changed their minds and turned on their captors. George Dixon's account gives a little more detail:

> The next morning we continued towards our objective on the route marked Cadogne and then off the map. We were

capturing Austrians all along the way – they had dropped their rifles, tin hats etc in their hurried retreat. We also captured a few Austrian cavalry. Joe Albright [C Squadron] was killed when acting as first point on a patrol. We were held up at a place called Sacile. My patrol was sent out to find the CO, Colonel Sir Charles Lowther, to deliver a message when we reached him. He had just had to beat a hurried retreat as the Austrians had hemmed them in on three sides. They had sent a patrol in the place marked Sacile on the map. They had got into the town, and then the Austrians swarmed out in thousands. Prisoners had taken up arms and were attacking them in the rear. The Motor Gun Corps and the Cyclists had to leave their machines and run for their lives. They managed to get back with few casualties. Our regiment had thirteen casualties.

This was to be the last action of the Northamptonshire Yeomanry in the war. Lowther had clearly underestimated the strength of the Austrians in the town who were in no mood to be taken prisoner. Gerry lost three of his men, who were killed in Sacile, and the fact that the regiment got away so lightly in terms of casual-ties is astonishing. It could have been a complete disaster. The next morning the 9th Battalion, York and Lancaster Regiment took the town and the yeomanry continued to pursue the retreating Austrians over the Tagliamento River to Mereto. By this late stage in the war, the Austrian forces had been trying desperately to organise a separate armistice. On 4th November the Northamptonshire men were stood down and ordered to retire to the west bank of the Tagliamento River. For the British forces in Italy, the war was over. For those still fighting on the Western Front, there would be another week before the last shot was fired.

Top left: Germany 1945. 74 Squadron Pilots at Drope. L-R Johnny Bennett, Geoff Lambert, Griff Griffin, Hugh and Laurie Turner.

Bottom left: July 23rd 1945. St. Mary's Church Woodbridge. Hugh and Adrienne Watts on their wedding day. Note the top button of Hugh's tunic undone-the fighter pilot's signature.

Top right: Sicily 1943. Hugh in the cockpit of a Spitfire Mark V during his short stay with 81 Squadron.

Middle right: Drope 1945. Hugh with 74 Squadron pictured with his Mark XIV Spitfire and ground crew, Paddy Flynn and Brooky Brooks. Without his ground crew he wouldn't get into the air.

Bottom right: Martlesham Heath 1944. Hugh shortly before he was commissioned in 1944. At Martlesham the Squadron flew Mark IX Spitfires.

Departed Warriors

Top left: South Africa, December 1943. Hugh receiving his pilot's wings at 27 Air School, Bloemfontein.

Bottom left: Hull 1939. Owen Clarke pictured with Geoffrey Crawford in the garden of 33 Maytree Avenue. The two boys had just been called up and were about to begin their advanced flying training.

Top right: Sergeant Pilot Charles Owen Clarke, taken a few months before his death. This photograph was consigned to a drawer after his death.

Bottom right: Egypt 1918. The Avro 504 that Douglas Watts crashed at Abu Suier. After this accident he was returned to Ismalia to continue his training in two seater aircraft.

Departed Warriors

Top left: Gallipoli 1915. Sussex Yeomanry troops in their dugout positions in Gully Ravine. This photograph was probably taken in November after the storms that struck the peninsula.

Top right: Egypt 1918. The wreckage of the Maurice Farman Shorthorn, serial number A 4096, that Douglas Watts crashed in March.

Bottom: Newcastle, County Down. May 1914. The Volunteer's Parade Colour Party. Warren is carrying the King's Colour second from left. The King's Colour now resides in the Down County Museum. The Murland family were staunch supporters of Ulster Unionism and very active in the U.V.F. Note the German Mauser rifles.

Departed Warriors

Top left: Ballygowan 1960. 13th R.I.F. Old Comrades. Charles Henry Murland pictured at the front of the group. Note the absence of the 1914-15 Star from Charlie's medals. He did not arrive in France until 1916.

Top right: Gallipoli 1915. Sussex Yeomanry troops in the front line at Border Barricade. Note the absence of steel helmets, they were not introduced until 1916.

Bottom left: Egypt 1918. My maternal Grandfather, Douglas Allen Watts in the uniform of a Second Lieutenant, Royal Air Force. The Royal Flying Corps became the Royal Air Force in April 1918.

Bottom right: My great Grandmother, Ada Jessie Goode. Probably taken around 1925.

Departed Warriors

Top left: Warren somewhere in France with the North Irish Horse.

Bottom left: County Down, 1920. Howard and my grandmother Marion. Taken at Edenderry with Howard Ferguson seated with dog.

Top right: Charles Henry Murland, taken probably in 1914.

Bottom right: Worthing 1949. The author with his grandmother, Margery Watts.

Departed Warriors

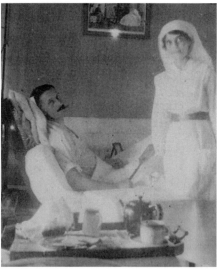

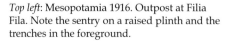

Top left: Mesopotamia 1916. Outpost at Filia Fila. Note the sentry on a raised plinth and the trenches in the foreground.

Middle left: Tigris River 1916. River transport taking troops upriver.

Bottom left: Karachi 1917. Howard in the hospital ward where he spent 9 months recovering from his wounds.

Top right: Ardnabannon 1910. My great aunts Florence and Evelyn with my great uncle Stanley. Pictured two years before his death in 1912.

Bottom right: My grandfather, Howard Ferguson Murland. Taken in India shortly after his return to active duty.

Departed Warriors

Above: William 'Bill' Sydney Murland. Taken probably before he joined the 10th Royal Hussars in March 1911. Bill was a first class horseman and spent much of his later life training and breeding racehorses.

Below: Captain James Gerald Martin Murland in the uniform of the Northamptonshire Yeomanry. Note the MC ribbon above his left breast pocket. The photograph was taken in late 1918 at Contrabissara, Italy.

Top right: The marriage of my grandfather, Howard Ferguson Murland, at Kew on 3rd June, 1920. Howard, in uniform, is standing centre with Marion on his right. Sir David Prain, Marion's Uncle, is standing centre left.

Bottom right: Gentleman Cadet George Osbert Stirling Smyth taken at the RMA Woolwich in September 1908.

Departed Warriors

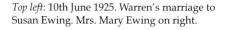

Major G. O. S. Smyth, brother of Police Commissioner Smyth (inset), who was murdered in a Cork club last July, has now lost his life at Drumcondra during the raid on Professor Carolan's house. He resigned an important post in Egypt to serve in Ireland. (See news page.)

Top left: 10th June 1925. Warren's marriage to Susan Ewing. Mrs. Mary Ewing on right.

Bottom left: October 1920. Newspaper cutting recording the death of Osbert in Dublin, with an inset picture of Gerald. The deaths of both Aunt Helen's boys were widely reported in both Irish and English newspapers.

Top right: West Chiltington 1910. The photograph that began the whole project. L-R Lynton, Margery and Archibald.

Bottom right: Warrington 1949. Walter Goode with his daughter Josephine, aged about 18 months.

8

Mesopotamia

Howard Ferguson Murland

My paternal grandfather, Howard Ferguson Murland, was born in County Down on 20th December 1882. The youngest of the five Murland brothers, he was only 13 years old when his mother Sarah died in July 1895. At the age of 14 he attended King William's College on the Isle of Man for a year, before returning home to complete his schooling at Lurgan College in County Armagh, where he remained until December 1900. The 1901 Census for England and Wales records him as resident at 9, Nightingale Road in Portsmouth. Nightingale Road was a private Army Tutor School run by William F. Pearce which specialised in tutoring candidates for the Civil Service Examination. Howard passed the examination, and entered the Royal Military College, Sandhurst in September 1901 as a gentleman cadet. His godfather, Howard Ferguson of Edenderry House, Banbridge, sponsored him and paid the candidate's contribution of £150. He was commissioned on 26th August 1902 into the Essex Regiment before finally sailing to India to join the 64th Madras Pioneers.

Fortunately for us, Howard kept copious diaries from 1906 until his death in 1958. They provide a tantalising glimpse into life in County Down before the outbreak of war, of the political situation in Ulster prior to 1914 and his life as an officer in the Indian Army. The effect of the Great War on him, and the family friends he had grown up with, is reflected in the casualty figures which he records in detail. His diaries of those war years present a remarkable journal of the life of a regimental officer in Mesopotamia and later in a war hospital, recovering from serious wounds.

Howard was very much a County Down man and was brought up at Ardnabannon, the family home at Annsborough. He inherited the family preoccupation with horses and racing and was himself an accomplished cross country rider. He also developed an enthusiasm for collecting stamps, eventually becoming a fellow of the Royal Philatelic Society in 1916. Among his boyhood friends were his cousins Gerald, Osbert, Haughton and Teddy Smyth, the Uprichard brothers Emile and Forster and Barrie Combe. On this group of friends the Great War and its aftermath in Ireland would soon leave its indelible mark.

In April 1914 he arrived home on leave from Burma, having written in his diary something of the turmoil he was going through at the time:

> ***February 14th.***
> I am very much below par these days, and lately have been thinking I had better go home, infernally expensive of course, but what with Ulster and the state I am in, I think it would be best. Jim and Charlie are on the Ulster Union Council and they and Warren command companies in the UVF. So I feel rather out of it.

In 1914 Ulster was heading for civil war and he did not want to be left out. If there was going to be a fight he wanted to be there with the family. Fortunately the onset of war directed these energies elsewhere and Howard narrowly avoided being held back for service in Europe before he embarked for India again. Many Indian Army British officers and NCOs who were on leave at the outbreak of war were refused leave to return to their regiments and redirected to train and lead Kitchener's New Armies. Many of those who were in India when war was declared, including Howard, sooner or later found themselves taking part in the punishing Mesopotamian campaign.

—···—

Mesopotamia

The Mesopotamian Front was one of the so-called forgotten theatres of the Great War. There was no strategic plan in place to conduct extensive operations in Mesopotamia on the outbreak of war, but there was anxiety about protecting the Anglo-Persian oilfields and the pipeline that fed the refinery at Aberdan. On 25th August 1914 the India Office was requested to prepare a ground force to guard the scattered refineries of the Anglo-Persian Oil Company from Abadan Island and gunboats to secure the Shatt-al-Arab estuary. Although the primary aim of the invasion of Mesopotamia was centred on the oil wells, it was also to show support for the Gulf Sheikhs and to impress the Mesopotamian Arabs, who respected only material victory, and to ensure that the Arabs did not join the Turks in jihad.

With these limited objectives in mind, the 16th Indian Brigade under Brigadier-General W.S. Delamain reached Bahrain on 23rd October 1914, and landed successfully at Fao on 6th November 1914. A week later the remainder of the 6th Indian Division began to disembark at Sanila, just upstream from the oil pipe terminal, while Delamain continued to attack the Turks in their positions at Saihan.

Two days later the 6th Division, now under the command of Lieutenant-General Sir Arthur Barrett, defeated a large force of Turks at Sahil. This victory, though not realised at the time, prompted the Turks to abandon Basra but not before they attempted to block the waterway by scuttling ships in the channel below Basra. This failed, but only just, and the successful arrival of the Naval sloops *Odin* and *Espiegle* not only announced this failure, but began the British occupation of Basra.

With the occupation of Basra concluded, the British military incursion had been successful in achieving its aims with very few casualties and the oilfields had been saved from falling into Turkish hands. In hindsight there it should have ended. But it was not to be. The personal ambition of individuals such as the chief political officer Sir Percy Cox,[1] was destined to escalate a relatively minor military expedition into a full-blown campaign. It began with Cox

---

1. He served in the army in India 1884-1890, when he joined the Indian Political Service. From 1893-1914 he held various political posts in the Persian Gulf area and Persia. He was knighted in 1911. During the Great War, as chief political officer of the Indian Expeditionary Force, Cox was responsible for all relations with local authorities in British-occupied Iraq. From 1918-1920 he acted as British minister to Persia.

telegraphing the Viceroy of India urging further advance and the capture of Baghdad.

Baghdad was some five hundred miles up the Tigris, which was the only highway available to the 6th Division. Mesopotamia had no road system or rail communication south of Baghdad and already there was proving to be a chronic shortage of river boats capable of navigating the shallow meandering Tigris. More importantly medical support and stationary hospital facilities were poor and unable to cope with heavy casualties. In addition, Basra as a port of entry for troops and equipment would require extensive development to handle any increase in traffic. In fact it could be argued that the inadequacy of Basra in 1915 as a base for operations in Mesopotamia contributed directly to the fall of Kut-al-Amara. However, the die was cast and so began the gradual reinforcement that culminated in the arrival of Lieutenant-General Sir John Nixon[2] as commander of the II Indian Army Corps. The expedition to secure the oil had become a campaign to take Baghdad.

Not long after Nixon's arrival, the expected Turkish offensive from Nasiriyeh took place at Shaiba which, after some fierce fighting, again saw the Turks retreating. Lured by the prospect of capturing the legendary Baghdad, Nixon sent forces under Major-General Charles Townshend[3] up the Tigris. After overwhelming a Turkish outpost near Qurna in an amphibious assault on May 31st 1915, Townshend began to move inland. By September 1915 the British had taken Kut-al-Amara. Refusing to stop there, Nixon ordered the reluctant Townshend to continue northward.

Arriving at Ctesiphon, some twenty miles short of Baghdad, Townshend came up against a larger, better armed and better supplied, force which had had plenty of time to dig extensive fortifications. Townshend mustered approximately 10,000 infantry, 1000 cavalry, and 30 guns. He attacked Ctesiphon on 22nd November, driving out the Turkish troops but at the cost of some forty percent casualties to his own forces. Unable to withstand a determined counter-attack, let alone advance further, he withdrew back down the Tigris. Short of both supplies and river transport, Townshend

2. Lieutenant-General Sir John Nixon (1857–1921)
3. Major-General Charles Vere Ferrers Townshend (1861–1924)

and the 6th Division made their stand at Kut at the beginning of December 1915 to await relief.

By the time Captain Howard Murland arrived with the 64th Madras Pioneers on 28th February 1916, there was already a considerable build-up of troops and supplies arriving through Basra. In the fifteen months since the original landing, a substantial dockside development had taken place to cope with the ever increasing build-up of troops and supplies. Along the river at Basra, a mile of landing stages had been constructed and further upstream wharfing facilities had been installed along the river frontage. With Mesopotamia mostly devoid of natural building resources, all construction material had to be brought in from India including materials for road making and the railway that eventually connected Basra with Baghdad.

Command had also changed. Nixon, having become ill, was replaced by Sir Perceval Lake[4] in January 1916. Lake arrived to take over as Commander-in-Chief and was immediately ordered to launch an offensive to relieve Townshend and the besieged garrison at Kut. The Indian pioneer regiments were now part of a concerted push north to relieve Kut, providing road and rail communications to supply the relieving Tigris Corps as it advanced towards Kut.

Howard's diary is quite detailed and I have used it extensively in this account of his service in Mesopotamia. His daily entries are a behind the scenes look into the shortcomings of the campaign from the point of view of a company commander. He had already met a number of friends who had been wounded and returned to India when he was in Bombay in early 1916:

Feb 5th.
Bombay. Hotel full of wounded officers[5]. Met Blakeston (Norfolks) and then McPherson (6th Jats) on crutches,

4. Lieutenant-General Sir P.H.N. Lake, KCB, KCMG Chief-of-Staff in London to Sir Beauchamp Duff, Commander-in-Chief of the Indian Army.
5. Probably some of the wounded from Aylmer's advance on Kut and the Umm el Hanna action of Jan 21st where the total losses were 2741 including 78 British officers.

then met Cloete (92nd) who has a bullet at the back of one eye. McPherson is hit through one leg and the other foot. Lewis (Leics), hit in the shoulder says the cavalry in Mesopotamia is useless. Nearly all the 2nd Black Watch are here.

The 64th were initially employed in maintaining and repairing the raised banks or bunds of the River Tigris, vital work as the river was the main supply route for the forces moving north. Later, in June 1916, the regiment was heavily engaged in building the Basra to Baghdad railway, in addition to the standard pioneer work of road building and digging front-line trenches and fortifications.

Leaving Bombay on 22nd February 1916 on the *SS Edavana*, the 64th Pioneers reached the Shatt-al-Arab waterway four days later:

Feb 27th

Lying off Bushehr when we woke up, but about 6 miles out. Two cruisers and a gunboat here. Wireless station, some boats came out but we got no news. Shah and some of the Mountain Battery went off. The 11th Rajputs[6] and 96th Berar[7] are here. Icy cold wind and snow in the hills. In the evening we reached the Shat-al-Arab lightship, two other troopships here, one with the Devons[8] and another with a lot of British troops from the Dardanelles.[9] We were allowed to go on as our skipper had a pilot's certificate for the river.

Feb 28th

In the river. Rather like going up to Rangoon. Passed Fas Fort which we cleared the Turks from at the beginning, passed one German and two Turkish ships which fortu-nately the Turks sank in the wrong place trying to block the channel. The river front at Basra crowded with shipping and stores, lots of Hospitals. The animals were taken off

6. 11th Rajputana Rifles
7. 96th Berar Infantry Regiment
8. Probably the 4th Battalion of the Devonshire Regiment.
9. By December 1915 the British, Australian and French troops had been evacuated from Gallipoli.

Mesopotamia

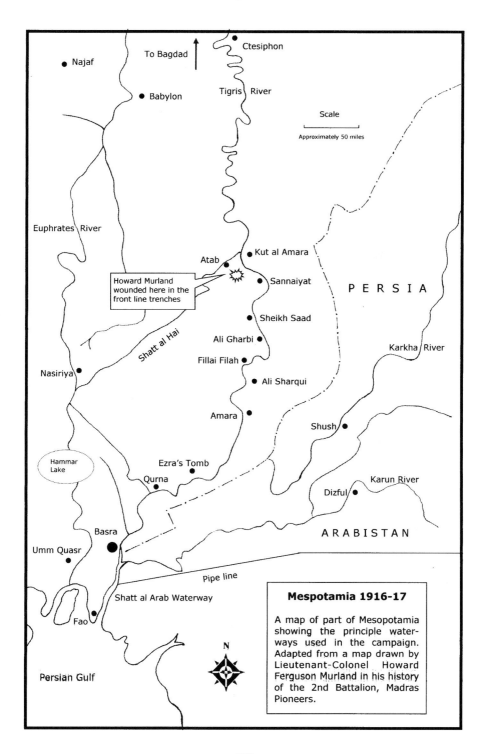

Najaf

To Bagdad

Ctesiphon

Babylon

Tigris River

Scale

Approximately 50 miles

Euphrates River

Atab

Kut al Amara

Howard Murland wounded here in the front line trenches

Sannaiyat

PERSIA

Sheikh Saad

Ali Gharbi

Karkha River

Fillai Filah

Nasiriya

Ali Sharqui

Amara

Shush

Hammar Lake

Ezra's Tomb

Qurna

Karun River

Dizful

Basra

ARABISTAN

Umm Quasr

Pipe line

Shatt al Arab Waterway

Fao

N

Persian Gulf

Mespotamia 1916-17

A map of part of Mesopotamia showing the principle waterways used in the campaign. Adapted from a map drawn by Lieutenant-Colonel Howard Ferguson Murland in his history of the 2nd Battalion, Madras Pioneers.

Shatt al Hai

159

first, then baggage – Number 3 Coy [Company] did the latter and we were at it until 8pm when they decided we should spend the night on board. No-one has a good word to say for the country or the Arabs. Heard I have been elected a fellow of the Philatic Society so am now addressed as FRPSL!

March 2nd
A lot of new transports in today, *Toronto, Elephanta, Clan MacCorquadale, Baimora*. The *Edavana* left at 11am for Kuwait to bring up British troops. The C.O. heard we are to send a company (100 men) to Filai Filah, 40 miles away, north of Amara and 40 miles south of Sheikh Saad, where General Aylmer is. I am to go with No.3 Company which is tophole! I am pleased to be leaving this hole but possibly moving into a worse one, but I should see something of the bally show.

Howard's regiment was commanded by Lieutenant-Colonel Swan. The four company commanders were: Major Bliss, Captain Skinner, Captain Murland and Major Mackie. Other officers included the Medical Officer, Major Godkin, of the Indian Medical Service, Lieutenant Burne, the Adjutant and Lieutenant Urmson, the Quarter-Master. Howard, who commanded Number 3 Company, was assisted by Second Lieutenant Aylward, as second in command.

March 8th
Work again, feeling rather seedy. At 1.20pm Mackie came along with a message from the Wharf asking why I had not embarked with 100 men at 1pm. Rode back to camp and found I was to embark at once for Filai Filah. Embarkation people had not thought to let us know, everybody else apparently had been told bar us. Marched about 5.15 with pack mules and carts, Burne came down with me. Embarked on a sort of Irawaddy boat with 2 barges lashed alongside. Men are very crowded but lots of room for officers.

March 9th

We left Basra about 2am, nothing to do but see that the men get fed. The Tigris winds in the most extraordinary way. Camps all along the banks of men working on the road, got to Qurna about noon – tied up there for some time. Rumour that Kut has been relieved, but nobody believes rumours now. Qurna, the alleged site of the Garden of Eden, is just a collection of mud huts with some politicals and a lot of troops here. The country is rather less interesting than the Suez Canal. Our transport is *P4* (Paddle Steamer). The men seem to be quite happy. We passed a working party of the 7th, 110th and 120th Pioneers who had 'Bloody Roads' tarred up on a bit of corrugated iron, which produced great applause.

March 11th

It rained in the morning. We got to Amara about 9am, two other transports are here. A bridge of boats (Turkish) enables one to cross the river, they are swung back for steamers. This is not a bad looking place. Went to find O.C. Defences and saw General Austin[10] and Ogle, his Brigade Major. General Austin was horrified to find I had only a [single] company and not a double company and I had not been told what I was coming for! The work is apparently to repair a breach in the river bund at Filai Filah and I must cross the river every day. We have no boats which are an absolute necessity.

March 12th

We got to Filai Filah about 7am. A deluge of rain as we were about to disembark and we were all wet through. We landed in a sea of mud, but the men were very cheery. The 20th Pioneers kindly pitched our tents for us. Irwin,[11] the post commander, seems a very good chap and also gave me breakfast which was very good of him. Floods of

10. Brigadier-General H.H. Austin, General Aylmer's senior general staff officer.
11. Major Eric Conway Irwin, MC. He was later killed in East Africa on 19th July 1917. Buried at the Dar Es Salaam War Cemetery.

rain in the afternoon. Gave all the men quinine. We could hear the guns at Sheikh Saad and there is a rumour that we beat the Turks badly 2 days ago. There is a mound here about 20 feet high from which one can see an enormous distance. The post is entrenched and wired. Irwin is to give me covering parties. I now have 2 bellums [long narrow boats used locally by the Arabs] brought up from Amara to cross the river.

March 13th
Marched at 7am. Took in addition 20 men of the 20th Pioneers. It was after 8am when we started to cross, the last party got over at 12.30 – 4 hours! I had to start them back at 2pm. It only took 1? hours the next time – 12 men in each bellum, paddling with shovels. There is a devil of a flood in the river and the breach is about as big as the Thames! Wired to Amara for more bellums and rations. Terrific thunderstorm in the evening.

March 17th
A new monitor went upstream, the *Stonefly. P7, P8* and *T2* went downstream. A small tug brought up 2 barges with mules but had to leave one here to make better progress. Later another tug came down from Ali Gherbi to haul it up. Got a wire that another company is being sent, I hope it is Aylward with the rest of my company. They left Basra on the 16th and have to march from Amara. We only have rations till tomorrow.

March 20th
Wired the Field Park for some reed matting, rained all night and the whole place is flooded again. Sir Percy Lake went up on the *Mejidiyeh* and I put a man on board who has dislocated his shoulder for Ali Gharbi Hospital. The men killed a sheep and I got the kidneys etc, so am well off! The *Mayfly* went up later and we got our letters sent down at last on the *S2* (stern wheeled). There are about 60 boats on the river now

March 21st
Laid out and started digging an entrenched camp for the company. Kirby went down with a fleet of 21 mahelas [larger sailing boats]. Crossed the river in one of these with Cunningham (21st Pioneers) who was in charge. The last attack on the 8th was a hopeless fiasco and General Aylmer has been relieved by Gorringe[12] – another reputation gone. The Russians are said to be within 70 miles of Baghdad. When I got back found Kirby with C.C.J. Barrett who was at Sandhurst with me and is now political officer at Ali Gherbi, we had a great chat. Got a Basra Times from Burne, I wonder where the regiment has gone?

March 24th
River in flood and at 3pm higher than it has ever been. Alarm in the night with a lot of firing, about 50 Arabs had swum the river and rushed the post. Devil of a do and we killed 3 of them.

On 25th March the remainder of the double company arrived after marching from Amara. Four days later a substantial bund had been completed which finally contained the Filia Fila breach. Orders were then received to move south again to contain several breaches in the river bank at Amara. With the Tigris at dangerously high levels, the flood waters were delaying the movement of troops marching up river. Howard began to move downriver on 31st March but would not reach Amara until 1st May! Apart from the distance to be covered he had great difficulty in getting rations for the company. Marching was often delayed by the company's equipment, which accompanied them by river on a mahela. If the wind was unfavourable then progress was slow.

March 31st
Wired Brigade that I was moving and to expedite rations.

12. Major-General George Frederick Gorringe KCB, KCMG, DSO. In 1911, at the age of 43, he became one of the youngest major-generals in the British Army. In March 1916 he became GOC Tigris Corps, charged with the thankless task of relieving Major-General CVF. Townshend's army besieged by the Turks at Kut-al-Amara.

Marched at 7.30, when we got to our destination found a gunner Major with an echelon, an ammunition column, a field ambulance and men of the 1st and 3rd Gurkhas. They have had a devil of a time getting up to Amara which is still 8 days march away for us. Made a perimeter camp in quite a nice place on grass near the river. Mahela arrived at 5pm. Aylward got 2 black partridges and a hare. Thunderstorms after dinner. Lots of excitement in the night, I was awakened by 5 or 6 shots and a sentry shouting 'sahib, sahib'. Ran out and the men lined the trenches. The sentry had seen a man crawling under one of the tents, he challenged him and the man threw a handful of earth right in his face and ran. He fired at three men then seen escaping, but it was very dark. We turned in but had hardly settled down when more shots turned us out again. I think the sentry had mistaken the bushes blowing in the wind for men running – which was quite easy to do. They must have been Arab thieves, following the echelon, from which they had already got some stuff.

April 2nd
Quite fine. Regular procession of boats up the river and at 4pm the *Malainir* came alongside with our rations which I was getting quite worried about. On board were General Sir Percy Lake, General Money,[13] Colonel Beach, Major Hopwood, Wilkie Dent (at Sandhurst with me). The General asked various questions and said an echelon was coming up which was having a very bad time of it. I told him it was already here! Had a talk with Wilkie and the others and arranged for a 'stinker' to the supply people about rations. On the boat I managed to buy some tobacco and biscuits.

April 5th
Terrific bombardment from 4–6am. Must be something

13. Major-General A.W. Money, Chief of the General Staff in Mesopotamia.

big going on. Decided to move tomorrow, the mahela making two trips if necessary. Sent off letters on *P32* going down. Got some letters in the evening off the *Kazimir* which whistled and stopped. I got some tobacco and cigarettes but no home letters for me. Took the men out in the evening with pick helves, to chase hares, which caused great amusement, they got one.

Rations it seemed were not the only factor working against them. As they marched south they were delayed continually by new breaches in the banks of the Tigris, forcing them to stop and repair the earthworks.

April 6th

Marched at 7am. And we got everything into the mahela. Aylward, with the advance guard, got 2 partridges. Hoped to get to Ali Sharqui but found the bunds breaching at Um-as-Samsan, so had to stop there and entrench a camp. At 5.30 a terrific storm came up, with enormous hailstones, which flooded the camp, it was over by 6.30. Heavy gunfire all night, wish we knew what is happening. Lots of wounded going down river.

The wounded they had seen being evacuated downstream were the battle casualties from the last desperate attempt to reach Kut. Gorringe was attacking Hanna with the 13th Division. On the morning of 5th April, they assaulted the Turkish trenches only to find the bulk of the enemy had withdrawn to Fallahiyeh, and that evening the attacking troops took the Turkish positions with the loss of 1,885 casualties. Across the river on the right bank of the Tigris, the 3rd Division were moving up to attack the Turkish positions at Abu Rumman. On 6th April, at first light, the 7th Division stormed the Turkish trenches at Sannaiyat with considerable loss. The 1st Battalion, Oxford and Buckinghamshire Light Infantry lost all their officers and 220 other ranks, leaving just 46 men of the battalion able to bear arms. The 51st Sikhs and the 2nd Battalion, Leicestershire Regiment lost nearly fifty percent of their effective strength, resulting in the remnants being pinned down some 500 yards from the Turkish line unable to advance or retreat. It was only the arrival of the artillery from Fallahiyeh and the subsequent bombardment of Turkish positions that enabled the survivors to dig in and consolidate their precarious position.

If the fierce Turkish resistance was not enough, the weather now also conspired against further progress. Rising waters on the Tigris and waters from the nearby Suwacha Marsh accompanied by high winds began to flood the British forward positions, forcing the Leicestershires and Sikhs to withdraw during the afternoon of 6th April. Gorringe was now under great pressure; if he was to relieve Kut in time he needed to overrun the trench system at Sannaiyet and quickly. But time and a stubborn Turkish defence was against him. A further attack by the 28th and 19th Brigades failed after a costly 300 yard advance. A later effort by the 13th Division ended with the few gallant individuals who did reach the Turkish line, leaving 1,807 casualties strewn across the battlefield.

In the garrison at Kut, Townshend cut rations even further in an attempt to hold out until the end of April. The relieving British and Indian forces were meanwhile battling against floods and storms that added to the sheet of water that was already impeding any significant advance.

Operations now turned again to the right bank and the Turkish positions at Bait Isa, where the Turks had been breaching the bund to add to the already extensive floodwaters. The British attack on 16th and 17th April was entirely successful, inflicting heavy casualties on the Turkish reinforcements. However, what appeared to be a victory for Gorringe's troops had effectively halted the British advance on the right bank.

The last chance to break though to Kut now lay on the left bank. If the Turkish positions at Sannaiyat could be overwhelmed then the way was clear for Gorringe to advance on Kut from the north. Sannaiyat was heavily defended with three lines of trenches. To the north was the Suwaikiya Marsh and to the south the Tigris. Gorringe must have been aware that to attack these defences head-on would in normal circumstances be inadvisable, but the desperate situation at Kut called for desperate measures. Sadly, they were doomed to failure. Of the two brigades ordered to attack only one, the 19th Brigade, left the jumping-off point at 07.00 hours on 22nd April.

They reached the Turkish second line before counter-attacks forced them to retire over ground that had become a morass of mud and water-filled shell holes. By dawn on the 23rd it was over. The Turks had again sacrificed huge numbers of their troops in defending their positions and once again had brought the British advance to a halt.

April 7th
Started a new bund. Edmunds the political officer came along, returning to Amara. He told us the Hanna position was captured the day he left Sheikh Saad. In the afternoon Watkins, F Troop 2nd Sappers, came along and we directed him to Shafi. They told us an echelon of 400 vehicles was behind them and a Brigade of the RFA with 1000 vehicles behind that! Aylward got 4 partridges with 4 shots – I leave him to do the shooting to economise cartridges, he being a better shot than I am.

April 9th
Moved early. Halted at Ali-es-Sharqui to wait for the mahela, big mosque there, with dome ornamented with blue tiles. Got 3 or 4 miles further before finding any work – a pretty bad place. Echelons 15 & 16 went up, including a whole brigade RFA, but they passed inland of us. Saw one officer who had it from a wounded officer that we are 6 miles from Kut and should capture it tomorrow – Seaforths and Manchesters practically wiped out. Swarms of duck here but very wild, Alyward got one. Terrific gale in the night, hung onto my tent pole and Alyward, dripping with water, his tent having gone, crept in at the back of mine and hung onto the other pole. I never remember such a wind – My topee, papers, clothes – everything – blew straight out and I thought it had gone forever. There was a lull and Alyward got his tent up again and then it settled down to a steady downpour. The trenches caved in, being full of water.

April 12th
The *Shihab* called on her way down with some mail – got

some tobacco also 24 plugs of Murray's tobacco from some unknown friend at home – gave 22 to the men. Also a letter from Ned Wright (Company QMS) thanking me for sending him tobacco. At 5pm another hailstorm – stones fully an inch in diameter. The Assistant Surgeon at Filai Filah was on the *Shihab* and said that we had retreated 3 more miles from Kut.

The ration situation continued to be a problem and the company were now working a full day on short rations which were only supplemented with local game and the occasional sheep they were able to buy from passing Arabs. Howard's diary records the seemingly endless succession of breaches they had to deal with. Passing river traffic was also buzzing with rumour of the situation at Kut.

April 17th
Feeling a bit seedy. A passing ship told us our troops within 10 miles of Kut. *S1* went down and shouted there was good news – Aylward thinks he said Kut was relieved last night. The flies are simply bloodsome here.

April 20th
Ration position is serious – we are 30 miles from Amara and only on short rations until midday tomorrow. I think the Assistant Surgeon has given me the wrong medicine – terrific headaches and cough all night. *P19* went up in the evening, full of sympathy but no rations! Said he would report that we had no food.

April 21st
We will hang on until tomorrow, when I shall go up to Amara with the mahela. We had given up hope when, after dark, *P14* arrived and shouted that they had our rations but could not come alongside till moon-rise.

April 22nd
Got our rations at 5.30am. After *P14* had gone, found that

we only had British rations for one day – some cursing! Signalled the *Mayfly* coming down and he not only stopped but came alongside, offered us some of their grub, though very short themselves, had some pleasant chat and took my chit to Amara. Dammed decent.

April 23rd

We always seem to move on a Sunday. A lot of Arabs came to see us and pick up what they could get. Nothing serious along the river till we got to Kumait where there was a very thin bund with a large breach in it. Sent the mahela skipper over to Kumait to see if he could buy anything for the men to eat. Aylward shot 3 partridges and we were very pleased as we thought we had passed out of the partridge belt. Got a box of medical comforts off a ship in the evening – address to O.C. Medical Store Depot, Kumait and as there was no such person or depot they will come in very useful for us! Saw the *Julnar* going up – rumour they are going to run the blockade.

April 24th

A jackal got 2 of our partridges in the night, fortunately our rations came on *P55* – they have sent us biscuits instead of flour and a 5lb tin of butter instead of bacon. Sent 3 men sick and our mail down on the *Mosul*. Lot of work here as there is a long bund 3ft to 4ft high and only 3 to 6 inches thick! Went some miles down river to look ahead. Hundreds of tortoises along the Tigris here. Barumayya and the other boatmen got about 40 large fish. The regiment is at Sheik Saad and very busy with building blockhouses, wiring and building the embankment for a light railway. They are sniped at night by Turkish cavalry. No casualties.

April 26th

P12 left a letter for me from the supply depot. Got a ward orderly and lots of medicines. The *Hunza* which is now the mail boat instead of *S1.* called and got stuck ashore.

> All ships today told us that the *Julnar* had been captured
> by the Turks. We saw her go up river covered with
> armour plate and sandbags & piles of food. They were
> obviously going to run her through to Kut. Supposed to
> be a dead secret but the whole river knew.

The Julnar episode was destined to failure before it began. On
24th April the *SS Julnar* under the command of Lieutenant
Humphrey Firmin RN, with Lieutenant-Commander Charles
Cowley as second-in-command, attempted to run the blockade with
270 tons of supplies. They came under sustained machine gun and
rifle fire at Sannaiyat but continued upstream against the swollen
current. At Magasis, steel hawsers stretching across the river halted
the journey. The enemy opened fire at point-blank range, hitting
Julnar's Bridge. Lieutenant Firman and several of his crew were
killed, the survivors and supplies being captured. Cowley was
almost certainly later shot by the Turks. Both Firmin and Cowley
were awarded posthumous Victoria Crosses.

This was the final agony of the siege of Kut before the inevitable
surrender on 29th April, an agony that was one of the greatest military
disasters ever to have been inflicted on the British Army. The campaign
to relieve Kut had cost the British over 23,000 casualties, not including
the 2000 that died in the garrison during the siege. But worse was still
to come. British and Indians alike left a trail of bleached bones along
that dreadful road from Kut to captivity and slavery. Never, until the
disaster at Singapore in 1941, in the whole history of the British Army,
had there been surrender on the same scale.

Of the Officers and men who surrendered at Kut, it was the
rank and file that received the harshest treatment. From a complement of 2,592 British ranks, more than seventy percent died in
captivity, and as many as 3000 Indian troops suffered a similar fate.
Those who survived were little more than skeletons when they were
released or exchanged two years later. Unaware of the tragedy that
was about to unfold at Kut, Howard was more immediately
concerned with supplementing their rations:

April 28th
Crossed the river in the evening with Aylward who shot

6 partridges. *S2* dropped a mail bag from the regiment, they are working on a huge 180 foot breach. The ladies of Calcutta have sent them 102 parcels of comforts. According to my interpreter the literal meaning of this district in Arabic is, 'land teeming with partridges'. It should be 'land teeming with flies'.

April 29th
A passing monitor told us that Kut had surrendered at 10.45 this morning. Very depressing. Both Subadars plunged in gloom and evidently think the end of the British Raj is at hand. There will now be a devil of a row at home no doubt which may do some good. Only have rations till today but hope to get them tomorrow, having sent a man to Amara.

April 30th
Moved again, before we marched off N'sami made me a little speech – that all ranks were greatly distressed about Kut but, whatever happened, it would make no differ-ence to them. We only got 4 miles before finding more breaches – what a life! Four ships went up but no rations. Said to have been 2700 Brits and 6000 Indians plus followers in Kut.

Arriving in Amara the company rejoined the regiment, only to hear they would be marching back north again almost immediately to begin work on the light railway that was planned to run between Sheikh Saad and Atab on the Hai waterway.

May 1st
Got our rations at 6am. from the *Otago (P24)*. They had not heard Kut had fallen. A patrol of 16th Cavalry went up – to see if the road was fit for horses, later two compa-nies of Mahrattas[14], who camped a mile or two above us. Visited them and saw Prideaux (attached 103rd) and Hill

---

14. There were six regiments of Mahratta Light Infantry. Most of the 117th was captured at Kut.

(attached 117th). They both thought Kut had been relieved. Later all back to our camp, they are to start making a track to Sheik Saad – hope we don't get caught for that. Amara is full of rifle thieves – they have hanged a few Arabs.

May 5th
Marched at 6.30. Delayed by mahela and only did 8 miles. Camped at Qabu-al-Ulwiyah near the 1st. Sappers who were going back to Amara under orders for Nasiryh. Message from a monitor in the evening, "There has been serious trouble in Ireland"[15] – results of a cold footed government.

May 7th
Mahela got a wind so was more rapid. We found a party of the 104th at our camp with Odell (123rd) and Honeybun (IAR 120th). They told us the 67th have a wired post opposite the Dujailah Canal and a Turkish raiding party is reported to be coming to attack Kumait, so must take precautions with the mahela. Odell told me something of the fighting in Ireland. The Es Suin position before Kut is said to be impregnable, with a lake in front of it. *P35* turned up in the evening. Showers of bugs at dinner so no lamps.

May 8th
Rather a long day. Met a convoy of about 80 mahelas with the 6th Jats on board – had a few words with Hailes at a distance. They were en-route for Basra, probably to go to Nasiriyh, where a new division is said to be forming. General Austin and Ogle went down last night so have missed them. The Arabs have made rather a mess of some of our bunds. We camped 3 miles off Ali-es-Sharqui and were eaten alive by sandflies. On the march we were nearly suffocated at one place by incredible

15. This was the first news of the Easter Rising of 24th April 1916 in Dublin.

swarms of small things like mayflies. We ran to get away from them. Subr.[16] N'saumi is bad with dysentery and I'm afraid will not last much longer and will have to be invalided. The river is full of dead bodies.

May 13th
Marched at 6.30. Saw lots of Arabs dancing, with standards etc. They were trooping down to meet a political officer, he caught us up later and proved to be Leachman[17] (political officer to the army corps) who has lived and travelled among the Bedouin for the last 10 years or more. He took us on his launch (which came from the Thames) and we had cider and soda. An extraordinary enigmatic man whose knowledge of Arabs and the desert is legendary. He said the Russians are at Karid and not near Bagdad, nor likely to be. Gorringe and HQ are at Sheik Saad, where the 14th Division is concentrating. Nothing doing at the front. [General] Gorringe is called 'The Blood Orange' and hated by everyone. Leachman has been down to Basra for a few days, the first time for a year.

Like T.E. Lawrence, Colonel Leachman worked with the Arab tribes and initially earned their respect through his knowledge and understanding of their lifestyle and his willingness to help them. Leachman arrived in Mesopotamia in 1907 after serving in the Boer War and India. He soon made his reputation moving and living amid the tribes of the Euphrates wearing traditional Arab clothing and riding camels on long journeys across desolate uncharted areas. However, this changed as the political situation in the area drew to its inevitable conclusion after the war. His stance in supporting the ruthless British policy of quelling Arab uprisings led to a number of attempts on his life by his former Arab allies.

His rather extreme views, advocating mass slaughter as the only means of quelling rebellion, were probably instrumental in his death

16. Subadar: Indian Army commissioned rank
17. Brevet Lieutenant-Colonel Gerard Evelyn Leachman, CIE, DSO, of the Royal Sussex Regiment.

in August 1920, when he was shot dead at a police post near Fallujah. He has been described as a heroic figure, largely through his pre-war work with the Arab tribes and some of his exploits were arguably every bit as celebrated as those of Lawrence. At the time Howard met him he was very much a legendary character, but he didn't live to write his memoirs and rather faded from public prominence after his death.

May 14th

Marched at 6.30. When we got up to Sheik Saad we wasted a lot of time with a signaller trying to find out where we were to go. This is a huge place now with camps extending along the bank for miles. They told us to march up and cross by the bridge of boats, but there was a gap in the latter and eventually we crossed in a launch with a mahela tied to it. Burne and Urmson met us on the other side and we left a party to unload the mahela and marched to camp. Everyone here except Bliss and Russell[18], who are up at the Orah Canal. One Glover (34th Pioneers) with us as a railway specialist. Got a huge bag of mail – two from home. We were all inoculated against Cholera in the evening. Got 14 more men from the draft.

May 15th

Bitten all night by sandflies, we had a day off. Don't see much of the CO these days. Tents very hot and full of flies. 'Fritz' the enemy aeroplane (Fokker I believe) chased our two back to their hanger. The 36th Sikhs, next to us, fired at him. Sir Victor Horsley,[19] who is on a tour of all the fronts as a sort of Royal Commission, came to the mess in the evening. I thought he was some Colonel on the staff as I did not catch his name. He should stir up the medical arrangements here a bit.

18. Second Lieutenant Russell, No.4 Company.
19. At the outbreak of war, Sir Victor requested active duty on the Western Front, but was posted in 1915 as a Colonel and Director of Surgery of the British Army Medical Service in Egypt. In the following year he volunteered for field surgery duty in Mesopotamia, where he died unexpectedly in Amara, Iraq, on 16th July 1916. He was 59 years old.

May 19th
Called at 4am and marched at 4.30 to work on the road. Gorringe passed some way off. Met Bliss and Mackie and between us we finished the road to Sodom. Rumour in the evening that during General Gorringe's visit here the divisional commander[20] moved forward and occupied the Turkish position which was found deserted, that Gorringe in a great rage ordered them back as being without his orders. Another rumour that the Russians have appeared within 12 miles of Ali Gharbi, clamouring for topees!

May 20th
More wonderful rumours – that the Turks have abandoned Es Suin and are legging it for Bagdad. The Cavalry Brigade disappeared early this morning, also quantities of transport. We worked on the railway formation. Orders to move camp tomorrow about 2000 yards to near the bridgehead on the river bank. General Egerton, commanding our 14th Division visited us in the evening with his ADC (7th Cavalry) – a nice chap.

May 22nd
Making a railway embankment – 6 inches high! Not very exciting. Worked from 5am until 11am. The enemy seem to have left the Sannayat position and to be holding the line of the Shatt-al-Hai.

May 30th
Got a holiday! Went to the Vetinary Hospital to see my sick pony–colic and fever. Bucked [talked] with Morris (10th Mule Corps) who shares a dugout with Higgins (Vet). Morris told me that [General] Gorringe turned the sick out of the only house in Alwaz last year and lived in

20. Depending on when exactly this visit took place, and presuming it was the 7th Division who were still in the line at Es Suin and Sannaiya, the divisional commander referred to would have been either Major-General Sir G. Younghusband or Brigadier-General C. de Norie who took over temporary command on 8th May 1916.

it himself. Corps orders that troops are to work 5-9am and 6-10pm, very pleasant! Stewart came along and I went to 12 Coy Mess and bucked with him and Pemberton. Stewart was in the 60th Irish Yeomanry with my brother Stanley in South Africa.

June 3rd

Unloading railway material. Got the engine (10 tons) off the other barge successfully and made crib piers[21] for this. Worked till 12.30. Met Waller (45th Sikhs) and Micklejohn. Colonel Gunning (36th Sikhs) had all his kit stolen when he was commanding the 37th Brigade and now Colonel Stewart has had all his taken from the same tent. He woke up and found 8 Arabs in his tent but luckily for him they ran away.

June 6th

Temp. 105 degrees. Railway work 5-11am. A gunner subaltern, Cathcart[22], rode out towards Lot's Mound yesterday and was shot dead by an Arab. Much argument about who won the Naval engagement[23] on 31st but believe we did as Germans had 18 ships sunk.

June 8th

Temp 111 degrees. Road work. Bad news in the evening, Kitchener drowned off the Orkneys. Two officers per division are to get leave to Amara, fortnight at a time, 2 to go every week. The first lot of carts went up (200) to Orah at night and were met by carts from the front. The South Wales Borderers[24] (13th Division) have had most of their tents, kits, helmets, rifles etc burnt by a grass fire, lots of bombs and ammunition exploded but only one man wounded.

---

21. In this situation the crib pier would be made from wood. Pairs of logs would be parallel, then others laid over them to make a square, and this continues upwards in a style of building similar to a log cabin's construction.
22. Probably Second Lieutenant Francis John Cathcart. Royal Field Artillery. His name is commemorated on the Basra Memorial. Panel 3.
23. A reference to the Battle of Jutland May 31st 1916
24. 4th Battalion South Wales Borderers, part of 40 Brigade.

June 10th

Temp. 112 degrees. It was 115 degrees in the divisional camp. Enormous explosion in the direction of the front with a huge column of smoke. Rumour that the Sappers are going to the front. Russell came in from Sodom with fever.

June 11th

Temp. 111 degrees. No work and no breeze, I was dripping by 6.30am. Yesterday's explosion apparently due to Fritz who successfully bombed 2 of our ammunition barges. Rumour that the 3rd Division are coming down here and the 14th going up. Sappers certainly going. Heard later that the explosion was due to 5.9 shells, with Fritz spotting. Enemy got the information about the barges from the Turkish prisoners who went up on the *Mosul* the other day.

June 14th

Two fellows in the SWB [South Wales Borderers] turned up and said they were to relieve us this evening. Lots of gunfire at the front. We were relieved at 7pm and got back to camp at 8pm. Another draft of 62 has come, some for the 81st and some ours. [General] Gorringe has now ordered that the motor road to Twin Canals must go on the other side of the cart road, he is quite mad! Also no working parties of troops are to unload the barges, so shipping is hung up and I suppose the troops at the front will starve, all because [General] Gorringe had had a row with McMunn about the Cooley Corps. Berkley, formerly Chief Engineer of the Bengal Association Railway has come up and is to be in charge of all railways. The 96th and 11th Rajputs are coming up her and the 4th Rajputs have just arrived.

June 15th

Unloading railway material. Met Seabrook, Berkley's assistant. Heard some more medical scandals, 58 wounded Tommies down last night, without food, bedding or any orders where to go. 14th Division HQ moved up here about 9pm. Burne, who has had a bad go of Jaundice, has leave to go to Amara tomorrow. Got a Chitai hut built over my tent, which is an improvement.

The hardships suffered by the troops in Mesopotamia had by now begun to attract attention at home. Heavy casualties had overloaded the already wanting medical resources, and the dreadful conditions the wounded and sick troops were being subjected to had reached scandalous proportions. There was a distressing similarity here with the totally inadequate medical provision during the Gallipoli campaign. In the three months between June and August 1917, over 34,000 officers and men were invalided out of Mesopotamia.

June 19th
Went out to work but felt rotten. In the evening Godkin [medical officer] found I had a temperature of 102 so was put to bed. Gen. Maude (13th Div) and everybody is at the front except Corps HQ. He [Maude] believes the Turks are bluffing us with about 5000 men, officially they have 3 Divisions.

June 22nd
Godkin thinks I am suffering from sun. Col. Swinley, Chief Engineer Tigris Corps, came to see Berkley about the railway. Russians said to have withdrawn for the hot weather, very wise of them!

June 23rd
Moved into a new dugout. I still have a temperature and am rather a worm. We are to work 2 hours a day extra now the weather is nice and warm! 4.45am to 10am and 4.45 to 6.45pm. The men will hate the latter more than I, it is their evening rest and wash period etc which has kept them so fit up to now. Sayyid Ismail, our Salturi,[25] set off

---

25. The Bombay Veterinary College supplied fully qualified veterinary graduates and practitioners to all parts of India and neighbouring countries. It also filled the gap that existed between the few European Veterinary Surgeons and inadequately trained local personnel for veterinary work, called Salutris, who occupied a position in Veterinary profession similar to that of Sub-Assistant Surgeons in the Medical Department.

on a mule for Sodom last night and has not been heard of since.

June 24th

I am taking 30gr. Of Quinine and I think getting better. A party of 8 men sent out by No. 4 Company to look for Sayyid Ismail was badly scuppered, 4 killed, 1 wounded and 3 captured. They were stripped and let go again. They ran into 60 or 70 mounted Arabs. That side is quite open and I have thought many times that the Arabs would give trouble.

June 25th

Quite normal but buzzing with quinine and absurdly wobbly. Arabs yesterday rounded up a lot of horses and No. 1 Company had to stop work and drive them off. They are very uppish and looted horses etc all over the place last night. The Times rejoices over the capture of the Dujaila Redoubt[26] by Gen. Gorringe! The Turks abandoned it actually!

June 29th

Feeling much stronger now, the Sodom detachment came in, Bliss is down with fever, so are Mackie and Aylward. What a country. We have 86 men in hospital, not counting those in the field hospital who are struck off strength. Out of a draft of 70 128th Pioneers attached to us only 48 arrived here. 24 have gone to field hospital and 10 in our hospital. Balance 14! The 13th Division Sappers and Pioneers are to help us with the railway; the Sappers have only 20 men for work out of 150. Pioneers much the same. They are to build the blockhouses along the railway line 600 yards apart.

June 30th

Bliss and Mackie are still laid up. I told Col. Swan that I

---

26. This is a reference to the retreat of the Turkish forces from the Dujailia-Maquais line and the occupation of those trenches by Major-General H. D'Urban Keary and the 3rd (Lahore) Division.

am perfectly fit and he said, 'for God's sake be careful, I have quite enough sick, including myself'. Col. Goodbody at the hospital here calculates that at the present rate of sickness the Tigris Corps will last about 6 weeks. They asked him how many more cases he could take in his hospital, he said 10 and they sent down 1000 the next day. The 4th Rajputs who have just gone up sent down 2 lots in the first few days, one of 160 and one of 60. An NCO and man (British patrol) shot last night just opposite our lines, such stupidity to send out two men like that. Tom Haughton (in my company at Sandhurst) came to breakfast, very pleased to see him again. He says Lake and Beauchamp Duff[27] will both have to go. The War Office sent Maude a wire direct to take over the Corps and for [General] Gorringe to hand over. Maude is the junior Major-General in the Corps. A great row in India about [General] Aylmer, who will also probably have to go.

In late July 1916, Howard received the first news of the Ulster Division's attack at Thiepval. The letter from his sister Evelyn, provided detail of family friends who had been killed and an account of Charlie's brush with death:

July 26th
Got some news of the Ulster Division, a bit of a knock out. Albert Uprichard, Haughton Smyth both killed on July 1st. Clarence Craig and Charlie wounded. Wish I could see the list. The division did splendidly, too well in fact, as they went on to the German 5th line and were practically wiped out.

From August the regiment was under the orders of the III Indian Army Corps, now under the command of Major-General Maude. For the next five months they were employed almost

27. On 8th March 1914, General Sir Beauchamp Duff replaced General O'Moore Creagh as Commander-in-Chief in India.

continuously on railway work between Sheikh Saad and Es Suin and then onto Iman-al-Mansur. During this time the daily temperature rose as high as 127 degrees, making working conditions almost unbearable. Other factors such as sickness and frequent dust storms continued to conspire against the regiment's railway work. As if that was not enough, there was a shortage of materials during July and August. Despite these setbacks, their railway work was completed by early December.

In August, Sir Percy Lake was relieved by Maude. Now a Lieutenant-General, he soon announced his intention to advance on the Shatt-al-Hai Waterway and begin a new offensive. Consequently, on 13th December, the 64th Pioneers marched with the 13th Division to Iman-al-Mansur and crossed the Hai. Here they were detailed to construct bridges and crossing points.

December 13th
Busy with the men's kits and our own. They get 1 blanket and 1 waterproof sheet, we get 20lbs, which is little enough in this weather. Marched at 6.30am. In the dark until the sun rose. We followed the 13th Division up the Duyailah Depression to Iman. Got there about 10.30pm and bivouacked. Too cold to sleep.

December 14th
The infantry brigades (38th, 40th and 39th in reserve) moved off at 3am which was just about the time the Sannaiyat bombardment started, made a devil of a noise. We moved at 5.45am behind the bridging train. Arrived at Atab and started digging approaches for the pontoon bridges. Very heavy work. Worked till very late and bivouacked near the bridges. Very cold night.

December 16th
Great artillery strafes along the whole front in the after-noon. Turkish position is round the Hai-Tigris junction, where they are more or less penned in. 13th Division has about 200 casualties so far. The Welsh Pioneers camped near us in the evening.

December 17th
Moved camp to make more ramps for bridges across the Hai. Today was quite interesting as we were close to the front-line and saw the shelling etc. Saw the Gloucesters[28], who had just come in and got a pretty fair doing over yesterday. They had 100 casualties but only about 10 killed. Great crowd of troops along the Hai. Our front-line is about 400 yds. From the Turks. Some Arabs came in close on our west side but were shelled off. They had about 40 killed by shrapnel yesterday.

Towards the end of December the regiment received orders to return to Iman and begin work on the railway extension to Atab. Christmas was spent at Twin Canals.

December 25th
Worked 7-12 and 1-5. First bad accident on the railway today, the engine rolling off the line and the driver badly injured. Bannister came to dinner with Urmson's brother and Seabrook. We all a bit tight and the plum pudding turned up just in time. Got fed up and went to bed. Rather a rotten Christmas.

From the end of December the 3rd Division had been steadily pushing forward and, on 9th January, the 8th and 9th Brigades assaulted and captured the Turkish front-line trenches in front of the Khudaira Bend position. In the eleven days of fighting that followed, the Turkish troops finally withdrew across the river leaving the 3rd Division with over 1,600 casualties. For the 64th Pioneers these advances saw them working at night on the construction of defences and communications west of the Hai. Much of this work was carried out under fire. On 1st February, the 13th Division assaulted and captured the penultimate Turkish line east of the Hai. On the west bank of the Hai the assault on the Turkish trenches was not as successful. The 36th and 45th Sikh Infantry were forced to retire from the trenches they had captured in the face of strong counter-

28. 7th Battalion of the Gloucestershire Regiment

attack and it wasn't until two days later that the Turks were finally driven out by the 37th Brigade. The British casualties were inevitably heavy.

February 1st 1917

Devil of a bombardment began at about 9.30. The 36th and 45th Sikhs attacked but after hanging on for a bit were turned out again, pretty well wiped out! Saw a somewhat gruesome procession returning. Colonel Gunning, Elkington and all the other 36th who went over the top, except one, were badly hit. Colonel Rattray[29] (45th) wounded and missing, Wilson[30] and Hannay[31] killed etc. One of Conran's chaps, Johnson, was hit in the jaw. I got a new wrist watch today sent by Grindlays from Bombay.

February 2nd

We were greatly delayed going up Butt Street [a communication trench] and it took some time to set out the work, we didn't start until late. I had one man killed on the way up, shot through the head. I had nearly got the men all out and was just going to jump over a wire into the trench, which was deep and narrow, when my right thigh was smashed by a sniper's bullet. They were hooting and pipping all round me and I think it was a rifle fixed on this particular spot. The bullet went through Narayanasmi's head, who was stooping down beside me, and I went into the trench, a horrid fall, with him on top of me. Godkin soon came and cut my breeches off and stopped the bleeding and gave me a Morphia tablet. I was hit about 1.30am and had to lie in the trench until work was finished. It was bitterly cold. A recruit with me was jolly good and kept shoving his water bottle in my mouth. He asked everyone who came

29. Haldane Burney Rattray DSO, aged 46. Commemorated on Panel 56. Basra Memorial.
30. Captain John Graham Wilson, aged 31. Commemorated on Panel 56, Basra Memorial.
31. Major Ramsay Rainsford-Hannay aged 32. MiD. Commemorated on, Panel 56, Basra Memorial.

along if I was dying! Poor Subadar Musa Raza Khan was killed and many more hit. Perfect hell getting back but the men were awfully decent, a lot of them wept. Had my leg set, with some Morphia, was put in a car and taken to Iman. The Major who set my leg gave me a whiskey and soda (very gladly received) but I was sick all the way. At Iman the splint was changed, under Chloroform and I was sick again. They were all awfully decent.

February 3rd
Moved by train to Sheikh Saad, a pretty miserable journey. I felt very sorry for the young fellow alongside me, who had dysentery. I was very badly bumped when they were taking me out of the ambulance at No. 31 Field Hospital. More surgeons, I was too tired to bother about anything. A padre gave me a cigarette.

February 5th
Taken on board the *Sikkim* for the downriver journey. Crammed into an iron bunk that was too short for me so my leg was miserably squeezed up. A pretty bad night as some of the wounded were awful to listen to. The lights were put out and we were left in the darkness.

February 6th
I am next to a 4th Devon called James who is badly wounded. Got to Amara about 3.30 and the men were landed almost at once but officers, after trying various hospitals (all full up) didn't get ashore until after 8pm. Eventually admitted to No.23 British General Hospital. I was interested to see my foot was facing round the wrong way when I was taken off. A bad night.

February 8th
Awake all night. My splint, which has a big iron ring jammed against my hip and hurts a good deal. Sisters here are awfully decent, especially Miss Nash, who keeps

everyone cheerful. A corporal came to alter the padding on my splint and gave me hell. A good chap though, he had a D.C.M. There is a County Down officer in the ward who was badly hit, he has a terrific Belfast accent, haven't had a chance to talk to him yet.

February 12th
No sleep and feeling a worm. Some Colonel came round to see some of the worst cases, ignored me thankfully. Going to Basra tomorrow? Saw my X-ray, what Miss Nash called a perfect beast of a fracture, the bone all in small pieces and splinters. Am I going to lose my leg? Poor little Wilson has died of wounds.

February 15th
Got to Basra at 4pm and disembarked to No. 3 British General Hospital. An old Major told me I would be sent to England via the Cape, don't believe it though. The doctor is like an undertaker and the Matron a Gorgon. Another rotten night, wooden bed, no sleep and general misery. I shan't last much longer if I stay here!

February 18th
Embarked on the hospital ship *Takada*. In a very nice warm ward with 2 beds. My stable companion is Spencer (2nd Lt. Wilts Regiment[32]) with a bad wound in his thigh. Very nice matron, there are over 500 wounded on board. The night sister is an Australian and a good sort. Couldn't sleep.

February 20th
I've had a wash and a shave and feel much better. Spencer is very ill. They decided to change my splint after dinner, a beastly business. The old splint is covered with muck and blood. Asked if I would lose my leg, they were very evasive.

32. Probably the 5th Battalion of the Wiltshire Regiment.

February 22nd

Leg worse today, doctor investigated wound with a probe. My leg has swelled to an enormous size and there is something wrong, although the Doc, of course, says there isn't. They are going to put me ashore at Karachi tomorrow as I am in such pain and there is so much vibration on board. The skipper has been taking endless trouble altering water tanks to try and lessen the vibration. Captain Rouse is an old friend, skipper of the *Edavana* when I went from Rangoon to Calcutta. Tried to get out of Finney, the Doctor, if my leg was to be amputated, but he hedged again.

Howard's war was now over. His femur had been shattered and, as it later transpired, it was touch and go as to whether his leg should be amputated. On 23rd February, he was taken off the hospital ship and transferred to the military wing at the civilian hospital in Karachi. Here he met Major Stephen, the doctor who would give him hope of a full recovery and save his leg. It was to be a long and painful road for him; he would not be discharged from hospital for another nine months and even then his recovery would take a further year before he was back in uniform. During his stay at Karachi Hospital he continued to write his diary:

February 27th

Great news from Mespot, the river crossed at Shumran and we have Kut. Stephen told me he does not think my leg is septic. Young Cheers (S.Lancs) who is shot in the jaw, had a bad haemorrhage in the night. Cowley and Firmin of the *Julnar* have been awarded posthumous V.C.s. About time. Stephen came and measured my leg this evening and found it short. Tightened up my splint again. Slept quite well.

March 9th

Cheers had another haemorrhage which caused great consternation. The staff here consist of sisters and nurses on probation. The sisters are Otto (who looks after me most of the time), Murray, Culverhouse (theatre sister) and Blake (night). The Matron is Miss Walters. In Mespot they are within 8 miles of Bagdad. De Grey, Horner and Shand (Norfolks) are all wounded.

March 17th

Poor old Cheers sneezed in the night and started another haemorrhage from his ear and lost 3 pints of blood. Bad luck as he was beginning to get on a bit. A Mrs. Mules[33], hospital visitor, came to seem me, she has lost her only son killed in Mespot. Got my first mail from home, heard from Jim, Evelyn, Charlie and Willie. They had heard on the 6th that I had been wounded and harried the India Office for news of me. Stephen told me I would have to keep my splint on for another 8 weeks. Help!

April 7th

Charles Harvey-Kelly [an old friend] turned up in the evening, as cheery as ever, and spent about 2 hours with me. He had half of his regiment here and expects to be mobilised by the 15th. Had a long discussion with Sister Hay, who is very religious, about the Angels of Mons,[34] which she firmly believes in. Someone on the Surgical ward screaming in the night.

April 15th

Stephen nearly twisted my foot off in an effort to get it straight. Leg is hurting which I hope is a sign of returning circulation. It's still huge. Visited by Colonel Martin, he told me of Captain Buchanan[35] who went through on a hospital ship today. He has the V.C. and M.C. He was

33. The Only Mules recorded in the CWGC database is a Captain George Mules, Killed in East Africa on 2nd December 1916.
34. Supposedly a group of angels who protected British soldiers during the Battle of Mons in 1914.
35. Angus Buchanan was a Captain in the 4th Battalion South Wales Borderers. He won the VC on 5th April 1916 at Falauyah. He was awarded the MC at Gallipoli in 1915. He was shot in the head by a sniper in 1917. He died in 1944 after continuing to work as a solicitor despite his blindness.

shot through the eyes and is blind but does not know it yet. What a tragedy. Cheers paid me a visit in the evening, a rare bird, but he has been through a lot.

May 5th
Cheers can get about a bit now and has his bandages off. He has two long stories which he tells me frequently, one about how he was jilted and the other about his brother[36] who was blown to pieces in France, the pieces just filled a sandbag! Stephen told me if my leg had been septic I would not have survived it. Wicks has got his wound infected and has a temperature of 105 degrees. Dreadful screams and crying from new arrivals next door.

Another letter from home brought news of the cavalry action at Monchy-le-Preux during the Battle of Arras. Howard's sister, Evelyn, recording in her precise style the detail of Bill's wounds and news of other family members:

May 26th
Cheers left today for Kashmir. Heard from home that Bill Murland got 4 wounds at Monchy. Gerry's lot did well and Warren and the North Irish Horse annoyed at being left out of the scrap at Monchy. Discovered in the evening I could lift my leg nearly an inch!

June 6th
Had my first trial out of bed. Horrible failure, my good leg refused to support me, the blood rushed down my dicky leg which turned bright purple. The whole room went round and round. Hoo-har in the night, Dugan had a haemorrhage and lost a pint of blood, bad luck as he is very weak.

---

36. Probably Second Lieutenant Ronald Anson Vlassow Cheers, aged 26. Killed on 25th September 1915. He is buried at the Dickebush New Military Cemetery. Ref: G.19.

June 13th
Poor Duggan had another haemorrhage at 10am and Stephen and Major Good operated on him. Was told that my leg could be 1 inch shorter. Meditated on my boots, none of which will be much use now! Wonder if I shall be able to ride?

A letter from Mary Murland, writing from Badby, gave news of Bill's recovery from his wounds and Gerry's award of the Military Cross. She also passed on news of Howard's cousin, Gerald Smyth, who had been wounded yet again during the Battle of Arras. There was also an interesting hint as to the number of officers who were apparently going absent without leave after being invalided home:

June 18th
Got a mail from Cousin Mary. Gerald [Smyth] had been wounded again rather badly, Gerry has been put up for an M.C. and Bill's wounds are doing well. She says that they insist on officers going to convalescent homes as 700 officers of the New Army who went to their homes have been lost! Very sorry to hear that. News that Harvey-Kelly's brother[37] in the R.F.C is missing. Can't stand up without assistance yet.

In late June 1917 he was operated on again by Major Stephen to enable him to bend his knee and raise his foot. This surgery was successful and, despite the discomfort it caused for some weeks afterwards, it was a milestone in his recovery. On 22nd August, Howard was promoted to Major and by September was beginning to walk again. He had his final visit to the operating theatre on 22nd October, where Stephen cut some tendons to release the rigidity of his foot. A month later, weighing nine stone, he was discharged on three months leave to Bangalore. Back with friends and the close community of Wellington Lines he began to make a more rapid

---

37. Major Hubert Dunsterville Harvey-Kelly DSO. Aged 26. Shot down on 29th May 1917. Died of wounds 3 days later. Buried at Brown's Copse Cemetery, Roeux. Ref: Special Memorial 7. HK was the first RFC pilot to land in France in 1914, flying a BE2a with No. 2 Squadron. At the time of his death he was CO of 19 Squadron.

recovery. In spite of his good progress he was still concerned about his future in the Army.

> *April 25th 1918*
> I am so afraid that I shall be a crock for the rest of my life. All the doctors are so vague as to whether I shall ever be able to walk [unaided] again. I have asked to be put on duty for sedentary work.

By the end of April 1918 he was on light duties at the regimental depot having been classified as B3 by a medical board. It was to be another twelve months of treatment and exercise before he would be fit for duty again. On numerous occasions his diary betrays his impatience over what he sees as a slow recovery. Eventually in May 1919, two years and four months after a Turkish bullet shattered his leg, he is appointed DAA & QMG[38] to the Baluchistan Force in Afghanistan. He was back in the saddle.

---

38. Deputy Assistant Adjutant and Quarter Master General.

9

Aunt Helen's Boys

Gerald Brice Ferguson Smyth
and George Osbert Stirling Smyth

Gerald and Osbert grew up in close association with their Murland cousins, sharing their love of horses and hunting. Gerald was educated in England, initially at Strangways School in Wiltshire and then at Shrewsbury School from 1889 until 1901. Osbert remained in Ireland and attended the well-known Campbell College in Belfast but later became a private pupil of William Thompson Kirkpatrick. William Kirkpatrick is probably better known as the tutor that prepared C.S. Lewis for his university entrance examination and as a former Head Master of Lurgan College. Kirkpatrick was also tutor to Gerald, preparing him for the Civil Service Examination, enabling him to gain a first place entrance to the Royal Military Academy, Woolwich in September 1903.

Gerald excelled at Woolwich, becoming well-known for his intellect and force of character. He passed out fifth in his intake and was awarded the Armstrong Memorial Medal for obtaining the highest marks in Advanced Electricity along with the prize for Military Law. His commission into the Royal Engineers was gazetted in July 1905. On leaving Woolwich he completed two years at the School of Military Engineering at Chatham where, shortly before he completed the course, he was promoted to Lieutenant on 3rd February. In 1908 he was posted to the 32nd Company, then serving in Gibraltar as a fortress company, with responsibility for coastal defence work.

He remained in Gibraltar for five years, during which time he also served with the 45th Fortress Company. It was in Gibraltar that he demonstrated his early promise and quickly endeared himself to his men and brother officers. Grandfather described Gerald as a bold and fearless horseman who was often difficult to follow over the country. Fortunately for Gerald there was a pack of hounds on the Rock and he was able to indulge his zest for hunting and ride regularly with the Calpe Hunt. The Hunt owed its formation to a garrison chaplain who, in 1812, imported foxhounds to deal with the plague of foxes that were raiding the gardens and poultry sheds of the Rock families. For several seasons Gerald acted as one of the Hunt's Whips. Gibraltar agreed with him: he was able to combine soldiering with hunting and playing Polo and even found time to become fluent in Spanish.

In 1913 he left Gibraltar and returned home to take up an appointment with the 17th Field Company at the Curragh. There is no evidence that he was involved in the Curragh 'Mutiny' in July 1914 but I would be surprised if he was not. Grandfather writes in his diary that he had a long talk with Gerald about the impending Home Rule crisis and what action they would both take if civil war broke out. Regrettably, he does not record what they both said to each other. I know what grandfather's stance was and I imagine Gerald's view was not dissimilar. I can find no record of Gerald or Osbert signing the Ulster Covenant on 28th September 1912, which is not surprising since they both were still serving abroad. However, there were plenty of the family that did, including cousins Haughton and Teddy Smyth.

In 1908, Osbert followed in his brother's footsteps and passed the examination for Woolwich, beginning his army career as an 18-year old gentleman cadet in September that year. In December 1909 he was commissioned and posted to 62 Battery then serving with 3 Brigade, Royal Field Artillery in India. In India he contracted malaria in 1911, prompting his mother to go out to supervise his recovery. Malaria would continue to plague him until 1914, when he finally shook it off in time to go to France.

George Smyth died in 1895 while still a relatively young man of 54 and, not unnaturally, Helen made it her business to be involved in the lives of both her boys. While Gerald seemed to have been for the most part left to get on with his career, she attempted to exercise a considerable maternal influence over Osbert who she considered to be the baby of the family. During the period he spent with William Kirkpatrick in England preparing for his entrance to Woolwich, Helen moved with him and stayed in lodgings nearby. When he passed the examination in 31st place she wanted him to take it again in 1909 in order to achieve a higher final position. There is a note in grandfather's diary about Helen going out to Gibraltar to see Gerald and how she had looked after all the other army wives and relations on the boat. There is no doubt that she was a formidable lady, some of whose characteristics were not hard to find in her two sons.

—————

September 1914 changed the lives of the Smyth family completely. Not a great deal is known about Osbert's movements over the course of the four years of war. His service file[1] at the National Archives contains a letter from Lieutenant-Colonel Ross of the RAMC. confirming his treatment for malaria had been successful and he was now fit for active duty. Ross had been treating him since early June 1914. It would appear Osbert had come home from India at some point in 1913 or early 1914 to recover from his illness and was being treated at the Queen Alexander's Military Hospital in London. Another letter in his file refers to his posting on 2nd October 1914, to Ludgershall, where 15 Brigade RFA had joined the newly formed 3rd Cavalry Division.

The division moved to Belgium a few days later, landing at Zeebrugge and Ostend on 8th October. The 3rd Cavalry Division included the 6th Cavalry Brigade in which Bill Murland was serving with the 10th Royal Hussars. Bill and Osbert would have been serving together, possibly in the same brigade, but whether they met up is anybody's guess. They certainly knew each other, as Bill had met Osbert when he was staying at Ardnabannon in 1912 and, in the relatively small world of the BEF Officer Corps, where everyone seemed to be at least an acquaintance, I am sure their paths must have crossed.

1. National Archives Catalogue reference: WO 374/63952

Departed Warriors

Once on Belgian soil, the division was ordered to join the defence of Antwerp but arrived as the city was being evacuated. Consequently, they were ordered to defend the canal crossings at Ghent to allow the Belgian Army to retreat, and then to move westwards towards Ypres. Osbert had only just been promoted to Captain when he was badly wounded on 21st December 1915, resulting in his evacuation to England on 30th December. From the paperwork in his service file it would appear he was in a military hospital until the end of February 1916. Shrapnel in his back and left arm had resulted in nerve damage and musculo-spiral paralysis which prevented him from bending his arm beyond a right angle. This condition is apparent in a photograph I have of him, which shows him supporting his left arm with his right hand. Although he did recover some movement, he never regained full use of his arm. His paperwork also reveals he spent his sick leave at Ardnabannon with the Murland family. It was during the four months he spent recovering from his wounds at Ardnabannon in 1915, that he received news of his award of the Military Cross[2] in the King's Birthday Honours.

———

Gerald's war began in August 1914 when the 17th Field Company embarked for France as one of six Royal Engineers units in the 5th Division. Based in Ireland before the outbreak of war, this division was one of the first to see action on 23rd August at Mons. During the retreat of the BEF from Mons, Gerald was the life and soul of his company, his Irish humour apparently doing much to maintain morale and discipline. The 17th were responsible for blowing bridges to slow the German advance and were often involved in the rearguard of the retreat under continual harassing fire. A number of these bridge demolitions were carried out by Gerald with extreme gallantry.[3] For his work during the retreat he was mentioned in despatches by Viscount French on 7th September. After the retreat, the Company was in the front line during the Battle of the Aisne in September. Whether Gerald knew at the time that Barrie Combe had been killed on 30th September, at Conde, is not known, but news

2. London Gazette June 3rd 1916
3. Brigadier-General G. Walker in RE Journal Vol XXXII No 4.

194

would undoubtedly have reached him at some point. As a friend of the Combe family, he would have been deeply upset by the news of his death.

Gerald was soon to have his own brush with death. In October he lost an arm in the La Bassée sector at Givenchy, when his section was caught under heavy shellfire and took refuge under a steep bank. He would have probably escaped unhurt if he hadn't gone out to bring in a wounded NCO. His action in saving the wounded man was typical of the regard he had for his men, a characteristic which contributed to the award of the DSO in November 1914. The citation published in the London Gazette on 11th November read:

> For consistent skill, daring and hard work in reconnaissance and defensive preparations night and day through the campaign, and especially during the battle of the Aisne and in the trenches at Givenchy, although wounded on 20th October 1914 by a shell, entailing the loss of his left arm.

His arm was amputated at the elbow in a nearby field ambulance and there is a possibility that this took place at Cambrin, where Archie Goode was treated in 1916. Three months later he was back at Aldershot undertaking light duties and agitating to get back to front-line service. For many officers, losing part of an arm would have been enough to keep them on home service. Despite his mother pleading with him to remain at home, he convinced a medical board at Aldershot on 10th April 1915 that he was fit for active duty. He had been promoted to Captain at the end of October 1914 and was now posted to the 9th Division as second-in-command of the 90th Field Company. He would remain with this division until October 1918.

Despite another potentially fatal incident in June 1915 near Nieppe, when he was blown out of a window after the company bomb factory had exploded, killing five officers and a number of men, he continued as second-in-command of the 90th until the Battle of Loos. At Loos, the C.O. Major J.D. Munro was wounded and Gerald succeeded him in command, remaining with the company at Ypres during the winter of 1915-16. For his services during this period he received a brevet[4] majority, his outstanding leadership during this period being recognised by Sir Douglas Haig who mentioned him in despatches in January and June 1916. A month later, on 13th July, he was wounded again, this time in the throat during the heavy fighting around Trones Wood.

The wood was of considerable strategic importance during the July fighting in the Somme area. Trones Wood was only two miles from an important enemy nerve centre at Combles and thus heavily fortified with a network of trenches and wire entanglements concealing numerous machine guns, each with interlocking zones of fire. In short it was a death trap, particularly as the artillery of both sides could pour down a barrage of fire at a moment's notice. By the time Gerald was wounded on 13th July there were no trees intact and the ground was a tangle of shattered tree tops and barbed wire, with the dead bodies from both sides lying where they had fallen. Gerald was shot through the throat whilst encouraging his men to move forward; it is said that he was waving the stump of his left arm to beckon them to a forward position which he had reached. The bullet passed through his neck from the left side, fortunately avoiding the Thyroid Membrane. He had been extremely lucky and, despite his protests, was sent back to England for treatment four days later. On discharge from hospital he returned to Banbridge on leave and in July he was examined by a medical board in Ireland which extended his leave for a further month. His medical board in London on 26th August passed him fit for active service and, five days later, he reported to the Royal Engineers Depot at Aldershot for duty.

Grandfather's diary entry on 19th September gives an idea of some of the manoeuvring that was going on at the time to keep Gerald out of the front line. He was at Sheik Saad at the time and was obviously summarising the news from home as he also refers to Charlie's wounds and Bill's regiment. Grandfather's approval at Gerald's return to the front was not shared by Aunt Helen:

Charlie is getting on slowly. Bill is in the front line with

---

4. Brevet referred to a warrant authorising a commissioned officer to hold a higher rank temporarily, usually without pay.

the 10th Hussars. Gerald has refused to go on General Gough's staff, greatly to Aunt Helen's distress. He is determined to stick to his own crowd. He is a fine chap.

Turning down the offer of a staff appointment, he returned again to the front to resume command of 90 Field Company. His leadership skills and courage under fire had not gone unnoticed, and in November 1916 he was offered the command of the 6th Battalion of the King's Own Scottish Borderers. For a born soldier like Gerald, this was the opportunity he had been waiting for.

The battalion was part of the 27th Infantry Brigade and he joined his new command at Neuville-au-Cornet, a small village south-west of Bethune, immediately putting in place a battalion training programme. The battalion had been fighting almost continuously during the second phase of the Somme Offensive, their actions at High Wood and the notorious Delville Wood having reduced the strength of the officers and men considerably. New drafts of men and officers were arriving and it was vital to integrate them into the fighting strength of the battalion before the Spring offensive in 1917. Writing to my grandfather on 14th December 1916, Gerald reflected on the war and on the quality of the recruits the battalion was receiving:

I gather that people at home are very much depressed. We out here, who don't move much further than our own hole, are much more cheerful than last winter. Then we had Neuve Chappell [sic], the 9th of May [the Battle of Aubers] and Loos, all hideously unsatisfactory shows, to look back on.

Now we have the Somme behind us. It was not an unqualifying [sic] success, I suppose it was a failure but there was some coherent plan and although we may lament the lost opportunities and curse the staff, most of us feel that there is hope for the future if the improvement is maintained. Also now we have the men. We have the winter to train them, to get to know them. They tell us the depots are full of recruits and if they are as good as the drafts I am getting I have no complaints. Mind you, I have not a good word to say for the training at home, but if we can't lick them into shape in 3 months in the trenches and 6 weeks training at the back, the fault is ours.

I personally don't believe we will drive the Hun out of France next year – but we will make him devilish sick. If the Russky can do his bit we ought to be in sight of the finish next autumn. I admit that is a big if. We spend our Xmas in the trenches.

On the morning of 9th April, on the opening day of the Battle of Arras, the 6th KOSB reached their first objective in thirty minutes, taking the German positions around the Point du Jour. Their training under Gerald's supervision had paid dividends. On 12th April, the battalion was still holding the reserve lines of trenches near the Point du Jour and was being shelled relentlessly. Gerald, never afraid to make his opinion known, was aghast at the rising numbers of men being killed and wounded for no apparent reason. Convinced that there was no strategic value in holding the trench, he pestered Brigade Head Quarters until he was allowed to withdraw his men to a safer place until the barrage ceased[5]. This was classic Gerald Smyth, his first and last thoughts were always for his men and, if he thought they were being placed at risk unnecessarily, he would say so.

Fortunately, they were not involved in the first attack on Greenland Hill on 12th April, which left so many of the 27th Brigade dead on its slopes. Their turn came at 3.45am on 3rd May in what turned out to be a disastrous day for the battalion. Gerald was hit in the right shoulder at 5.50am and incapacitated, but refused to leave his command position until he had been relieved in person by Major Innes-Browne. Despite this serious wound, he continued to remain cool and in control of the situation.

Greenland Hill was strongly fortified and remained in German hands despite the fact the Borderers reached their objective. In any frontal attack, unless the units on both flanks also achieve their objectives, there is a great danger of becoming isolated and being attacked on three sides. This is what happened on Greenland Hill, resulting in over fifty percent casualties for the Borderers. The Hill

5. Brigadier-General G. Walker in RE Journal Vol XXXII No 4.

was finally taken by the 51st Division in August 1918. These heavy casualties together with those sustained on 9th April effectively put the remnants of the 6th KOSB out of action and, on 14th April, they were bussed back to St. Pol. Gerald's actions as commanding officer were rewarded with a bar to his DSO.

> For conspicuous gallantry and devotion to duty. Although seriously wounded, he remained at the telephone in an ill protected trench for many hours during a critical time to report the course of events to Brigade Headquarters. He realised that there was no officer of experience to replace him and his sense of duty may cost him his remaining arm, the other having been amputated as a result of a previous wound.

By the time the above London Gazette announcement appeared on 18th July, Gerald had been discharged from the King Edward VII Hospital for Officers in London and was at home in Banbridge. Apart from Shell fragments in the shoulder, which had also broken his collar bone, he was having some difficulty with mobility in his remaining right arm. It appears from notes grandfather made at the time that Aunt Helen implored Gerald not to return to the front. As usual he listened, but his heart was with his men in France and his return on 22nd October 1917, was inevitable.

He found them at Irish Farm in the Ypres Salient recovering from their part in the third Battle of Ypres. The appalling conditions and horrors of the Ypres battlefield had left their mark on the Borderers. When Gerald arrived, they had just been withdrawn from action near Poelcapelle where several had literally drowned in the mud. There is no doubt he would have found it difficult to recognise the battalion he had left six months earlier. Apart from the indomitable Innes-Browne, very few of the original officers were left and the battalion was in great need of a rest. For a man who considered the welfare of his men to be paramount, this must have been a heart-breaking reunion. But Gerald was a great motivator and the very fact he was back in command lifted the spirits of his officers and men considerably, particularly so when he told them the battalion was about to begin a two week break by the sea at Dunkirk. It was a vital tonic that was

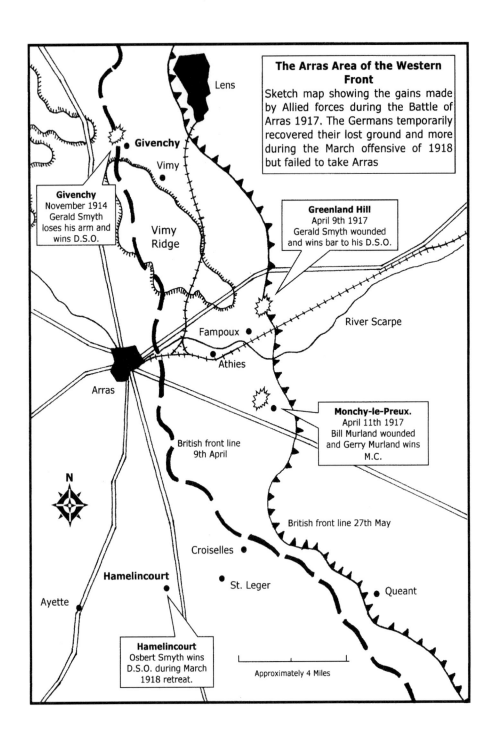

The Arras Area of the Western Front

Sketch map showing the gains made by Allied forces during the Battle of Arras 1917. The Germans temporarily recovered their lost ground and more during the March offensive of 1918 but failed to take Arras

Givenchy
November 1914
Gerald Smyth loses his arm and wins D.S.O.

Greenland Hill
April 9th 1917
Gerald Smyth wounded and wins bar to his D.S.O.

Monchy-le-Preux.
April 11th 1917
Bill Murland wounded and Gerry Murland wins M.C.

Hamelincourt
Osbert Smyth wins D.S.O. during March 1918 retreat.

Lens

Givenchy

Vimy

Vimy Ridge

Arras

Fampoux

Athies

River Scarpe

British front line 9th April

British front line 27th May

Croiselles

St. Leger

Queant

Hamelincourt

Ayette

Approximately 4 Miles

needed because, barely a month later, the German counter-attack after the Battle of Cambrai sent them scurrying back on the 6th December to Gouzeaucourt to relieve the 3rd Cavalry Division. Fortunately, the Borderers were not required to fight: the cavalry, along with the Guards, a few tanks and anyone else who could be drafted in, had checked the German advance and famously retaken Gouzeaucourt.

I'm not sure how Gerald received the news that his cousin Teddy Smyth had been killed with the 36th Division three days earlier, but news travelled fast and he wrote of his distress over Teddy's death in a letter to grandfather dated January 1918. Teddy had been previously wounded on 1st July 1916, while serving with the 11th Battalion Royal Irish Rifles. Having recovered from his wounds, he was transferred to the 13th Battalion and by 1917 had risen to the rank of Major. He temporarily commanded the battalion at Messines during the third Battle of Ypres in June 1917. On 3rd December he was killed while fighting at Marcoing on the Saint-Quentin Canal. He was 31 years old.

On 21st March, Gerald and the 6th KOSB were serving with the Fifth Army when the German offensive struck. The 9th Division, commanded by Major-General H. Tudor[6], was fortunately well up to strength and well rested. During the inevitable retreat on the Fifth Army frontage, the 9th Division was never overrun and only retreated when ordered to as a consequence of units on either flank withdrawing. Typical of this orderly withdrawal was the 6th KOSB action of 23rd March. Their sector, north of Peronne, ran from Nurlu to Moislains on the Canal du Nord. At 7am, from the advantage of their high point, they could see their South African neighbours on their right flank in Epinette Wood falling back after being attacked in force. A timely counter-attack by the South Africans plugged the gap in the line and allowed the KOSB to carry out a fighting withdrawal over the two miles down the hill to the canal. Having crossed the canal, they passed through Moislains to new positions on the heights north-west of the village. Still under great pressure from the advancing Germans, they successfully held off a German attack in the afternoon.

6. Major-General Sir Henry Hugh Tudor KCB, CMG, (1871-1965). May 1920 appointed Police Adviser to the Dublin Castle administration in Ireland.

It had been a masterly withdrawal but the final stroke was yet to be delivered. The war diary records how Gerald waited until dark and then ordered a counter-attack with two companies. He found the Germans in the Bois des Vaux and, after inflicting heavy casualties, he forced them out of the wood. Major Innes-Browne recorded the counter-attack in the war diary:

> Large masses of the enemy were encountered in the Bois des Vaux and were checked by heavy rifle and machine gun fire at point blank range. Very heavy casualties were inflicted on him. The O.C. 6th K.O.S.B. was wounded.[7]

It was an action so typical of the fighting spirit that Gerald had engendered into his battalion and one that he personally led. It was often said in the battalion that he would never ask a man to do a job that he was not ready to do himself. There was also a cost to having a commanding officer who led from the front and Gerald was wounded for the fifth time since the war began, this time in the chest. Having handed over to Major Innes-Browne, once again he left Calais for Dover and the King Edward VII Hospital, where he ran up and down the stairs to prove to a sceptical medical board he was fit for service.

Badgered into allowing him to return, the medical board finally gave in and Gerald is recorded in the war diary as arriving on 1st June 1918. On his return he found the battalion at Watou on the Winnezeele Road, just west of Poperinge, under the temporary command of Lieutenant-Colonel J. Colchester-Wemyss. Having lost over half of their strength during the course of five weeks of more or less continual fighting, they were once again badly in need of a rest and reinforcements.

Gerald would have seen notice of the death of Innes-Browne[8] in the casualty lists whilst at home and known his battalion was in the thick of the second German offensive. Captain R. Cundle, who found himself in command during the heavy fighting in April, would have given him the details, starting with 10th April when the

7. National Archives Catalogue reference: WO 95/1772
8. Lieutenant-Colonel Ambrose Robin Innes-Browne DSO, aged 35. Killed in action on 4th April 1918. Buried at La Clytte Military Cemetery, ref: IV.A.18.

9th Division relieved the 1st Australian Division entrenched on Hill 60. It was there that Innes-Browne was killed, as the battalion fought through another withdrawal when the Hill 60 positions were finally overrun. After pulling back to Viersrtaat, the battalion was again under heavy attack on the morning of the 25th when the Germans punched a hole in the line at Kemmel Village. He would also have heard how the two forward KOSB companies were cut off and fought back to back to the last man and how the C.O. Major H. Wilkie was killed when the battalion HQ was rushed.

I know there would have been a flicker of pride when he heard how the two remaining companies refused to be beaten and counter-attacked, capturing two machine guns and taking fifty-eight prisoners. This and other similar feats of stubborn and courageous resistance around the much-diminished perimeter of the Salient eventually halted the German offensive. The front-line was almost at the gates of Ypres, but the pressure point had now moved south and was now on the French Sixth Army on the Marne.

So what of Osbert during the desperate days of March 1918? I tracked him down through his Medal Index Card to C Battery, 160 (Wearside) Brigade, Royal Field Artillery, a unit he joined after recovering from wounds in 1916. Little is known about his movements in 1917, except that he was mentioned in despatches on 11th December 1917 and by the end of 1917 he was a Brevet Major. 160 Brigade were part of the divisional artillery of 34 Division, which had moved to France in January 1916. Apart from the Somme, the division also fought in the Battle of Arras. According to the brigade war diary, 160 Brigade moved from Peronne to the Hazebrouck area to take over the 59th Division's guns in October 1917. Two months later they were back at Wancourt, south-east of Arras, where they stayed until February before moving to St. Leger, a few miles to the south.

A Field Artillery Brigade, when up to full strength, would be commanded by a Lieutenant-Colonel and consist of an HQ and four gun batteries lettered A to D. Each battery, usually commanded by a Major or a Captain, could have upwards of 150 men to control and fire the guns and supply the ammunition. In reality, this number of men was rarely achieved during the war years and certainly 160 Brigade was very much below strength in March 1918. Some of the 160 Brigade batteries were two thirds below strength on the morning they were attacked.

On 21st March 1918, the six guns of C Battery, commanded by Osbert, was dug in at the small village of Croisilles, a little to the north of St. Leger in the Third Army sector. The war diary notes the enemy barrage beginning at 6am with some very accurate German counter-battery shellfire, designed to cripple the British artillery and command positions. By 8.30am two of the C Battery guns were out of action and soon after another gun was hit which also set the ammunition on fire. Despite losing three of the guns and having to put out the fire that was threatening to blow the ammunition dump, the battery continued firing on the advancing German troops. The battery war diary,[9] written by Osbert after they had withdrawn, takes up the story:

> About 2pm I saw masses of troops moving from Ecoust towards Croisilles and also up on the ridge towards Mory Copse. [I] pulled the guns out of their pits into the open, swung round and commenced firing about 2.25pm. Fired until dark without stopping their advance for more than a few minutes at a time. About 4pm I heard that three new guns had arrived at the wagon lines. Sent Lt. A.P. Humble to take them over and ordered him to get into action, which he did at 7pm. At about 5pm Lt. Humble succeeded in rescuing the two guns of the detached section under heavy rifle and machine gunfire.

They received orders to withdraw at 11pm, which they did under fire from across the St. Leger valley. In their new positions they commenced firing until the defending infantry gave way:

> At about 10pm having established an OP [observation post] an attack developed [and] the [British] troops in

9. National Archives Catalogue reference: WO 95/2447

this sector gave way. Endeavoured to stop them [the Germans] with a barrage but they broke through and ran the faster. Posted Lt. A.P. Humble mounted to watch the situation on the left and keep me informed. Collected some machine gunners to stop the stream of stragglers and line them up on the railway. At about 2pm [on the 22nd March] a series of enemy attacks on St. Leger Wood commenced. Dealt with them until relieved by 2/Lt. N.E.D. Menzies and went myself to watch the situation, afterwards taking over control of the shooting until dawn.

By 25th March, C Battery and the remnants of 160 Brigade had withdrawn to a line west of Ayette, a distance of nearly five miles from their position on 21st March. Here, the German advance was checked. A study of the casualty list for the five days the brigade was in action reveals the intensity of the fighting that took place in the face of the German advance. By 6pm on 21st March, only C Battery was still firing and there were heavy casualties in the other batteries, including two of the battery commanders. At the end of the first day's fighting, the four batteries had a total of 22 officers and men killed and wounded with another 36 missing. By the 26th the brigade had 79 officers and men killed, missing and wounded. C Battery in their defiant stand against the enemy lost over 20 officers and men.

Osbert had not only been responsible for keeping the battery firing but he had taken steps to gather up some of the retreating British troops and their machine guns to form a defensive line along the railway that ran to the east of St. Leger. Here they held up the advancing Germans for some time, inflicting heavy casualties. For his display of leadership and courage under fire his commanding officer, Lieutenant-Colonel W. Warburton, recommended him for the DSO. The award was gazetted on 16th December 1918. The citation read:

For conspicuous gallantry and devotion to duty. Under heavy shelling he went along the battery and helped to put out ammunition that had been set on fire and with three remaining guns fired on the approaching enemy with open sights, inflicting heavy casualties. Next day, by collecting men near him and machine guns, he held up the enemy for hours.

A week later he was mentioned in despatches[10] for the second time. He would later add the French Croix de Guerre to his decorations. In June 1918, Osbert was posted as Brigade Major to the 34th Divisional Artillery. For a career officer this was a good move, giving him experience of command and control at brigade level. His records indicate he remained as Brigade Major until 19th April 1919 when he embarked for Egypt in July.

The 6th KOSB war diary notes Gerald's promotion to Brigadier-General on 2nd October 1918. He was 33 years old and had risen from the rank of Lieutenant to that of Brigadier-General in four years. At the time, the battalion were engaged in the battle for Ledeghem and Hill 41 in the Ypres area, fighting a stubbornly retreating enemy. His departure to take over the command of the 93rd infantry Brigade was a sad one for the officers and men he had led for almost two years. His new command included three battalions of Yorkshire men from Leeds and Bradford and a battalion of Durham Light Infantry. Little if anything has been written about his short tenure with 31 Division, though he was mentioned in despatches on a further two occasions. He remained with them until the division was broken up in 1919. I feel sure that, if his time with the KOSB was anything to go by, then the men of his new command would have quickly warmed to this "one armed Irish warrior of dauntless courage".[11] Certainly his record had been recognised by the French and Belgian governments as he received the Croix de Guerre from both countries in 1919.

With the war over and a Staff College course behind him, Gerald, now only 34 years old, was posted in June 1920 with the

10. London Gazette 23.12.18
11. The KOSB in the Great War by Stair Gillion

rank of Brevet Lieutenant-Colonel to command the 12th Field Company, Royal Engineers, who were based at Limerick. It was while he was at Limerick that his former Divisional Commander, Major-General Tudor, who had known Gerald well during his time with the 9th Division, appointed him as Divisional Commissioner of the Royal Irish Constabulary in Munster. Aunt Helen, who had thought Gerald was now intent on peace-time soldiering, had all her old nightmares reawakened as he was plunged into the brutal turmoil of the Anglo-Irish War. She was right to be concerned: Gerald had only weeks left to live.

The Anglo-Irish War has its origins with the Proclamation of the Irish Republic during the Easter Rising of 1916 and with the formation of a unilaterally-declared independent Irish parliament, called Dáil Éireann. This parliament, known as the First Dáil, declared Irish independence by reaffirming the 1916 declaration and demanding the removal of the British military garrison. The Irish Volunteers, formed in 1913 in response to the Ulster Volunteer Force, were reconstituted as the Irish Republican Army. It is not clear that the Dáil actually intended to gain independence by military means, but an incident in January 1919 drew it unavoidably into an armed conflict that began nearly two years of appalling violence on both sides. Several IRA members acting independently in Soloheadbeg, in County Tipperary, attacked and murdered two Royal Irish Constabulary officers for refusing to surrender to the IRA. There was no going back after this incident.

In May 1920, when Tudor took up his post as Police Adviser to the Dublin Castle administration, the British regime in Ireland was on the verge of collapse. The Royal Irish Constabulary's morale and effective strength were in decline and IRA gunmen were ambushing police patrols and burning police barracks. Tudor's job was to raise police morale and to restore law and order. His approach was to employ men he had known during his army career and reinforce the RIC with units such as the Auxiliary Division. It was a heavy-handed military solution which led to excesses of violence and tit-for-tat reprisals on both sides.

The circumstances that led to Gerald's murder in July 1920 appear to have begun with a visit he made to the Listowel Police barracks on 19th June. As part of a general tour of police barracks to introduce himself and make his presence felt, he made a statement regarding the use of weapons by the RIC:

> A policeman is perfectly justified in shooting any man seen carrying arms who does not throw up his hands when ordered.
>
> A policeman is perfectly justified in shooting any man whom he has good reason to believe is carrying arms and does not immediately throw us his arms when ordered. Every proper precaution will be taken at police inquests, so that no information is given to Sinn Feiners as to the identity of individuals and the movements of police. I wish to make it perfectly clear to all ranks that I will not tolerate reprisals. They bring discredit on the police. I will deal most severely with any officer or man concerned in them.[12]

From all accounts his words were met with some resistance and one officer accused him of inciting them to murder. To some extent one can sympathise with the plight of the RIC. Over the twelve month period, ending in December 1919, the IRA killed 18 policemen in the course of their duties. Six months later, police casualties had risen to a total of 55 killed and a further 74 wounded, indicating a considerable escalation in the campaign of violence directed at the RIC. According to a report in the Daily Chronicle dated 23rd July, Gerald ordered the arrest of 14 RIC officers who refused to comply with his orders. This was extensively reported as a 'police mutiny'. In that charged political climate such an episode could not fail to draw attention to itself. Very quickly the confrontation at Listowel began to take on a new dimension. The same newspaper drew attention to the circulation of a different version of the statement Gerald had allegedly made:

> You may make mistakes and innocent people may be shot but that cannot be helped. You are bound to get the right parties sometimes. The more you shoot the better I will like you. I assure you no policemen will get into

12. Quoted by Mr. Dennis Henry, Irish Attorney-General, in the House of Commons, 22nd June 1920.

trouble for shooting any man.

It was also reported that he had told the assembled officers that the police were about to take the offensive against the IRA and martial law would soon be declared, adding:

> Lie in ambush and when civilians are seen approaching shout hands up. Should the order be not immediately obeyed shoot them down – shoot with effect.

Gerald's statement, in both its forms, was widely reported in the British and Irish press with the emphasis focussed inevitably on the more controversial version.

The Listowel statement rippled through both the Dublin administration and Whitehall, resulting in questions being asked in the House of Commons. Despite official repudiation of the accuracy of what was reported to have been said at Listowel, Gerald was now a marked man in Ireland. The IRA saw the Listowel statement as a challenge and responded a month later on the night of 17th July. Sitting in the smoke room of the exclusive County Club at Cork with RIC County Inspector F.W. Craig and two others, Gerald was shot dead by a group of IRA men who burst in and opened fire with revolvers. When the first shot was fired, Gerald apparently sprang to his feet and ran towards the door, gun in hand. He got no further than the vestibule, slumping to the floor as further shots hit him. Craig was wounded in the left leg, apparently not a target on that occasion, but Gerald was probably dead before he hit the floor. His attackers escaped as quickly as they had arrived.

There is no doubt that had he continued with his work as Commissioner of Police, despite the fact that he had already given his version of events in both Dublin and Whitehall, there would have been a more formal inquiry into the Listowel statement and its repercussions. Those in government and on the opposition benches who were against the military solution to the Irish unrest would have used Listowel to bring to public attention the manner in which irregular British forces, such as the Auxiliary Division and the Black and Tans, were being used in Ireland. The leading article in one of the London broadsheets of 19th July had this to say:

The brutal murder in the very heart of Cork of the unfortunate Divisional Commissioner Smyth is one of those insane acts which reduce the warmest friends of Ireland in this country almost to despair. Here was a case in which it seemed at last possible to bring to the bar of British public opinion in a single striking test case the whole character of the present military rule in Ireland. Colonel Smyth had denied the speech attributed to him and Sir Hamar Greenwood in the House of Commons had declared the reports of it as published 'distorted and wholly misleading'. But the matter could not have rested there; further inquiry was inevitable. The astonishment and indignation with which opinion in this country heard the original report were themselves a guarantee that the case would be sifted. This Cork atrocity will have two obvious results. By removing the chief actor, it makes the satisfactory pursuit of the inquiry practically impossible; and the manner of his removal will undoubtedly provoke a vehement revulsion of public feeling here.

Gerald's death was conveyed to my grandfather by telegram. The last time the two cousins had seen each other was on 12th April when they were both staying at the Shelbourne Hotel in Dublin. A large party from County Down had travelled south for the Punchestown Races, only to find they were to be cancelled in the light of a general strike in support of the republican hunger strikers in Mountjoy Prison. Gerald had driven over from Limerick for the races and to meet Marion Thompson who, by this time, was engaged to grandfather. He had also been staying at Ardnabannon in March when grandfather arrived home on leave from India. His diary only records they sat up late on several evenings discussing the war and old friends who were no longer with them.

The repercussions of the shooting in the Cork County Club reverberated around the north, causing an outcry of disbelief, only exacerbated by the IRA death threat made to any persons involved in the transportation of the body back to Banbridge. In the event Gerald was brought back to Banbridge by special train from Dublin. Accompanying the coffin were his uncles Norman and Stanley

Ferguson and Jim and Warren Murland. According to grandfather, both Warren and Jim were armed. Similar threats made to would-be jurors at the inquest held in Dublin on 19th July resulted in the proceedings being abandoned.

The funeral took place at Banbridge on 20th July. His coffin, placed on a gun carriage and draped with the Union Jack, took his body from his uncle's house through the town to the Banbridge Municipal Cemetery. The funeral service was probably the largest the small town of Banbridge had ever witnessed, with representatives from the Army and the RIC included in the long list of family and friends. He was buried alongside his father in a grave now recognisable by its 11 foot high celtic cross.

If ever there was a murder designed to cement the Unionist cause in their stance against a united Ireland, the shooting of Gerald Smyth provided it. The widespread violence and strength of feeling against Sinn Fein escalated, particularly in Banbridge where catholic workers in the various linen factories were made to swear not to support Sinn Fein on pain of losing their jobs. Regardless of the Banbridge Civic Guard being reinforced by troops to maintain public order, the damage claims during this period of unrest totalled £40,000.

Tributes were also received from the surviving officers and men of the 9th Division who served with Gerald during the Great War, and a separate memorial stands next to his grave as testament to the regard they felt for their former commanding officer.

Apart from my grandfather, there was one other person who was unable to attend Gerald's funeral. Osbert was still in Egypt with the 33rd Brigade RFA. Inconsolable over the manner of his brother's death, he left Alexandria on 30th July, having secured a posting to the home establishment in Ireland. There is no doubt he was hell bent on revenge and, although there is no direct evidence to support it, and plenty to suggest otherwise, he was reputedly a member of the so-called Cairo Gang.

The Cairo Gang was a group of eighteen British intelligence agents employed by the Army and trained by MI5. The majority were murdered on 21st November 1920 by the IRA. There is some dispute over the Cairo Gang's *nom de guerre* apparently resulting from a common history of service in the Middle East. Many of them did serve with British Military Intelligence in Egypt and Palestine during the Great War but it is thought the name was connected to the Cairo Café in Dublin which they used as a meeting place. The Cairo Gang's members worked undercover in Dublin, living unobtrusively while putting together a hit list of known republicans. Their names and whereabouts were eventually betrayed by an officer in the Dublin Metropolitan Police.

Osbert's service history with the RFA on the Western Front during the whole of the Great War precludes his association with the Middle East during that time and, in particular, the intelligence services. He had only arrived in England on 10th August, which would have been followed probably by a period of disembarkation leave before being appointed to the security forces operating in the Dublin area. The fact that the undercover Cairo Gang officers would have been 'in place' well before that date lends weight to Osbert not being one of them. Osbert was certainly not working undercover on 12th October, when he and Captain A.P. White of the Surrey Yeomanry, accompanied by a number of troops, went to the house of a Dr. Carolan in the Drumcondra district of Dublin.

Carolan was on the staff of St. Patrick's Teacher's Training College and a suspected IRA sympathiser. Osbert and his men were after two IRA gunmen, Daniel Breen and Sean Treacy, who were believed to be sheltering in Carolan's house. Having searched the first floor, they moved up to the second floor where they were met by a fusillade of shots that resulted in both Osbert and Captain White being killed and an NCO wounded. Professor Carolan was also seriously wounded in the neck by a stray round during the gun battle and later died in hospital. The identity of the two gunmen was confirmed as Breen and Treacy in a witness statement heard at the court of enquiry. Republican sources of the day verify that it was Breen and Treacy who were staying at the Carolan house and that Breen was injured in the gun battle. Both men escaped through a back window of the house, leaving behind most of their clothing. Treacy was shot and killed two days later, on 14th October, and Breen lived on to be elected to the Dail in 1923.

Reading through grandfather's diary, it becomes clear that

Osbert was making his presence felt in Dublin by hunting down Gerald's killers. It seems he had already dispatched one of them, although no name is given in the diary, and was on the trail of the others. His death in October was over five weeks before the Cairo Gang killings, adding to the evidence that Osbert was not associated with them. Evidence from the military court of inquiry into his death contained in his service file refers to a uniformed raiding party which again would not be consistent with undercover work. Grandfather first heard of Osbert's death through a newspaper report in London on 12th October:

> Going back by Oxford Street saw posters, "Major shot in Dublin". Got a Standard and found it was a Major Smith an ex. RIC Officer (sic) hoped it was not Osbert but at the hotel got a wire to say that it was. Rang up Onslow Court but Aunt Helen had left today, leaving no address. What a tragedy for her.

For Aunt Helen, her nightmare had been realised. Both her sons, whom she feared for during their service on the Western Front, had been killed within months of each other, not as a result of enemy action but during a civil war in her own country. It was a family tragedy that she did not recover from. As soon as she heard the news, she left London for Banbridge having been persuaded not to go to Dublin to see Osbert's body.

Osbert was buried next to his brother at Banbridge. He was 30 years old. The funeral procession from Clonaslee, his uncle's house, passed through Banbridge along a route lined by thousands of mourners. Major-General Tudor found himself in Banbridge yet again, along with numerous other senior officers representing the Police and Army in Ireland. Grandfather was unable to attend, having been summoned to an army medical board, but the Murland family was represented by Jim, Charlie, Warren and my two aunts, Florence and Evelyn.

As the notes of the Last Post drifted across Banbridge for the second time in three months it closed a chapter on two warrior soldiers who, having served their country with distinction, fell foul of Irish politics and were cut down in their prime.

10

Bomber Pilot

Charles Owen Clarke

To those who had fought in and survived the Great War, the nightmare scenario of it all happening again began to surface in the 1930s. Many had predicted a second round after the German humiliation at Versailles in 1919; a treaty that required Germany and its allies to accept full responsibility for the war, disarm and make substantial territorial concessions and reparations. Fathers, who had themselves marched off to war twenty-five years earlier, now experienced the anxiety their parents had felt, as they watched their own children get into uniform. This time there was a new service to join. The Royal Air Force that my grandfather Douglas Watts had flown with in 1918 was now an expanding force and, to many young men, it appeared to be a more glamorous option than the Army or Royal Navy. This was certainly the case with Charles Owen Clarke from Hull.

Owen was the uncle my wife never had the opportunity to meet; he was killed long before her birth in 1947. She only knew of this fair-haired young man from conversation with her father. The few photographs of him that remained were consigned to an upstairs drawer where I found them years later and asked who this RAF pilot was. My father-in-law, Albert Royle, remembered vividly the occasion when the news came through that he was officially missing in action. Apart from that, the events that led to this youngster ditching in the North Sea with his crew on the way back from a bombing raid over Hamburg, remained an unspoken family episode for years. Like so many families who had suffered the loss of a loved one on active service, they shut the painful memories away, hoping beyond hope that one day the door would open and in would walk Owen as if nothing had happened.

A chance conversation with Albert revealed that Owen's girlfriend in 1939 was a Jean Frost née Payne, and he still kept in touch with her. Jean, now over eighty and living in Exmouth, replied to my letter with clear memories of Owen and the Clarke family in the early war years. Jean and Owen had met at the Tommy Foster's Ballroom Dancing Class in Hull, which, as Jean recalls, was where:

> Most of the sixteen to eighteen year olds seemed to gravitate to on a Saturday evening. We had an hour of instruction and then just an ordinary dance from then to 11pm. Owen was a very good dancer.

After leaving the local Grammar School Owen joined the Argo Shipping Company in Hull as a junior shipping clerk; he continued living at home in the Garden Village, Hull. Number 33 Maytree Avenue was also home to his mother, Elma Clarke, and his elder sister Margaret. Owen's father, William, died in 1935 on his way to visit the Flanders battlefields. His life was in all probability shortened by the effects of gas in the trenches around Ypres. He was certainly not an easy man to live with after he returned from France, and it was this, perhaps, which encouraged the two elder boys to leave home while still quite young. Norman left to join the Nautical School in Hull when he was fifteen and Douglas emigrated to Canada in April 1934. Norman's war would see him on tanker convoys running the Atlantic gauntlet and Douglas would return to Europe with Canadian forces in the Princess Patricia's Light Infantry in 1942.

On 9th March 1939, with the threat of another European war on the horizon, nineteen year old Owen joined the RAF Volunteer Reserve. Jean recalled the occasion:

> I don't know why he joined the R.A.F., but it was the young service and he was young. His friend Geoff Crawford was keen on the Tank Corps but Owen talked

him out of the idea on the day, and they set off to sign on the dotted line.

Hull Training Command was based at Brough, some ten miles out of Hull on the main A63 Road. Today it is the home of BAE Systems and, although the runway has long gone, the Hawk, used by the RAF and Royal Navy as an advanced jet trainer, is still built there. The airfield has had a long association with flying and had been home to the Blackburn Aircraft Company since 1916. The RAF Reserve Flying School was established in 1924 and soon became one of the foremost Reserve Flying Schools where part-time pilots logged their refresher flying hours. The airfield at Brough is a bleak and windswept place on the banks of the Humber estuary, but for Owen and the other pupil pilots it provided the venue for their elementary flying training in the DH8 Tiger Moth. Jean has fond memories of this period:

> From March to September 1939 was given over to learning to fly during every spare moment. He joined the R.A.F.V.R. in March and soloed that Spring, flying Saturdays and Sundays buzzing our houses in the Garden Village at very low level. You could always read the letters on the wings. They used to joke that those who could not navigate used to follow the railway lines and station names back to Brough.

The pupil pilots used the grass airfield and usually took off towards the river bank which, being some twenty feet high, left no room for error and it was not uncommon for the pupils to make several attempts to land having misjudged their position in relation to this hazard! At the outbreak of war in 1939, the airfield was taken over by Flying Training Command and Brough became the home of No 4 Elementary Flying Training School, with the nearby airfield at Bellasize used as the relief landing ground.

As part of the search for information about Owen I wrote to the editor of the Hull Daily Mail to ask if they would run a feature on Owen and appeal for information, from anyone still alive who knew him. One of the numerous replies I received in response to the half page article was a letter from a Fred Dent who had known Owen well. Fred wrote:

> I was a boyhood pal of Nobby Clarke and I also lived in Maytree Avenue in Hull. Geoff Crawford was a friend too. One of our treats as boys was to hang around Geoff's house in Elm Avenue to see the great Yorkshire and England batsman, Herbert Sutcliffe, who was a friend of Geoff's father, George, and was always invited to stay at their home when he was playing for the county at the Anlaby Road Circle in Hull. Nobby and Geoff both joined the RAF Reserve in 1939 and started flying.

Fred also gave me the address and telephone number of Geoff Crawford's younger brother Phillip, who was still living close to the old family home in Hull. Although I had Owen's service history from RAF Records, there were still unanswered questions. Phillip had very clear memories of Owen and Geoff and was very helpful in filling in some of the gaps. It also became apparent from talking to Phillip that the lives of Owen and Geoff were so closely bound together that I had to include Geoff in any story about Owen.

The flying training scheme that Owen and Geoff were part of had been established in 1936 under the Air Ministry plan to expand the RAF. Under the new scheme, the RAF set certain standards of training that had to be completed in just two months. The elementary course required fifty hours of flying divided equally between dual instruction and solo flying. After fifty hours flying the successful pilots were sent to an RAF recruitment centre to receive basic training. For Owen and Geoff the end of their elementary flying training coincided with the outbreak of war and they were officially called up into the RAFVR a few days before war was declared. Jean still remembers that week as if it were yesterday:

> Owen and Geoffrey Crawford were called up and in uniform a week before war broke out. Owen was on holiday in Bridlington when the radio news said it would only be a week or less before war would be declared. We all rushed back to Hull when we heard that.

218

Bomber Pilot

In October, Owen received orders to proceed to No 4 Initial Training Wing at RAF Bexhill-on-Sea and Paignton. Life at Bexhill was a little different to Brough. Owen was billeted at a hotel situated on the seafront and after a month spent square-bashing he was posted to No 3 Flying Training School at South Cerney on 18th November 1939, for advanced flying training. At this early stage of the war the flying training programme was not as sophisticated as it would become by 1942, when my father learnt to fly in South Africa. Owen had only a minimum of basic tuition in a Tiger Moth at Brough and, although he was deemed a competent pilot, he was still required to go through advanced flying training.

The five months he was at South Cerney provided his instructors with the opportunity to make an assessment of his future deployment as an operational pilot. As with the huge majority of young men on Owen's course, they all wanted to be fighter pilots. Unfortunately, despite the shortage of pilots to fly the Hurricane and Spitfire, only a small number would graduate to the single-seat aircraft.

Owen's fate was sealed with his posting to No. 14 Operational Training Unit in May 1940. No. 14 OTU was based at Cottesmore, about thirty miles north east of Leicester and close to Rutland Water. As part of 6 (Training) Group it was not an operational bomber station, despite the fact that some training crews did take part in Nickel Raids over Northern France. These raids were essentially leaflet-dropping flights over France and although they provided crews with operational night flying experience they were discontinued at Cottesmore by the end of December 1940.

Now a qualified pilot with the rank of Sergeant, Owen arrived at his OTU days after the phoney war had ended with the German armoured divisions crossing into the Benelux countries and pushing the British Expeditionary Force back towards the sea. This time there would be no courageous stand by the Belgian army, and no pivotal battle on the Marne. Many feared a resumption of trench warfare, but this was never going to happen. The Wehrmacht had learnt the lessons of the Great War and had perfected all-arms cooperation with infantry, armour, artillery and air forces working together extremely effectively. This was going to be a war of movement, and it moved very rapidly.

It was too much too soon for the French and the badly equipped BEF. Dunkirk was a matter of weeks away and it seemed inevitable the invasion of the English mainland would follow. By the time the last troops had been evacuated from Dunkirk on 4th June, German forces were in control of much of north-west Europe. As Fighter Command prepared for its battle to deny the Luftwaffe control of the skies over Britain, Bomber Command took the first tentative, albeit largely unsuccessful, steps in developing its campaign to destroy the German industrial base. At the heart of this plan was the increase in trained bomber aircrews. By the end of 1940 there were eleven bomber OTUs, a number which would double over the next few years.

Cottesmore was equipped with forty-eight twin-engined Handley Page Hampdens and Herefords and twenty-four Anson twin engined navigational trainers. There was no doubt as to the demands of the flying training; the trainee crews were introduced to the complexities of handling a multi-engined aircraft together with all the associated skills of night flying, navigation and bombing. Inevitably the flying accidents began to mount up. The first accident that Owen would have been aware of involved Flying Officer Lennie and his crew on 29th May. Their Hampden crashed into trees while approaching the runway on a night exercise. Fortunately all the crew survived without injury.

This was not the first mishap at Cottesmore. Before Owen's arrival there had been four aircraft crashes, the most serious being on 6th May, when all the crew of Hampden P1274 were killed during night flying. Nor were these accidents isolated incidents. Before Owen finally passed out from Cottesmore at the end of July 1940, there were another seven crashes involving trainee crews, the majority taking place during night flying exercises. It is remarkable that more crews were not killed and injured as a result of these accidents. As it was, five aircrew were killed at Cottesmore during Owen's short stay, a number that would triple by the end of 1940. Nevertheless, Cottesmore by comparison was relatively low down the league table of air accidents. Over the same period, 12 OTU at Benson lost 29 aircraft written-off with an equal number of crew killed, while 10 OTU at Abingdon lost 11 aircraft and 14 aircrew killed. It was the OTUs flying Hampdens and Herefords that were among the units with the highest casualties, a factor which would be repeated in the operational squadrons equipped with the Hampden.

As far as we know, Owen's transition to becoming an operational bomber pilot went relatively smoothly, as there are no records of crashes involving him or any disciplinary action taken over his performance in the air. This was certainly not the case with Geoff Crawford, who was court-martialled on 24th September, for low flying a Wellington over the airfield. Geoff had been posted to 15 OTU at Harwell in South Oxfordshire, having passed out of advanced flying training at nearby Kidlington on 16th February.

At Harwell Geoff was training on the much superior Wellington 1, but his low-flying antics resulted in him being reduced to the ranks and posted back to 15 Flying Training School on 12th August to retrain. The court martial records indicate his Wellington was below 50 feet as it flew over the airfield! This was not the first time Geoff had been disciplined for low flying. While he was at Brough he was reported for dive bombing the pier at Bridlington while on a cross-country flight, causing some consternation to the people enjoying their Sunday promenade! By the end of November 1940, with his sergeant's stripes back on his sleeve, he was at 13 OTU based at Bicester, this time flying the twin-engined Blenheim IV.

At the end of July 1940, Owen left Cottesmore and was posted to RAF Finningley near Doncaster for further operational training with 106 Squadron, which had moved up from Cottesmore with their Hampdens and Ansons to train aircrews for the operational squadrons of 5 Group. His service record indicates he was only there for a month before he was posted to 144 Squadron based at Hemswell, just north of Lincoln. This was to be his last posting.

144 Squadron had been reformed in 1937 as a day bomber unit. Equipped with Hampdens, it was now one of 5 Group's front-line squadrons. Front-line it may have been but it was equipped with an aircraft that was already obsolete. 144 Squadron would soon reach notoriety by becoming the squadron with the highest number of Hampden losses in 5 Group.

The Hampden's origins can be traced back to 1932 when the Air Ministry put out to tender a specification for two medium twin-engined monoplane bombers. The specification gave birth to the Handley Page Hampden and the Vickers Wellington. In contrast to the Barnes Wallis designed Wellington, which was relatively spacious, the Hampden's fuselage was narrow with a deep profile tapering into a slim boom providing a profile similar to the Luftwaffe's Dornier. At least two were shot down in error by British fighters mistaking then for the flying pencil shape of the Dornier 17. On one of these occasions Spitfires of 602 Squadron shot down a 44 Squadron Hampden off North Berwick, unfortunately killing one crew member. It was an altogether strange looking aircraft that looked as though the rear section had not been finished off completely. Crews dubbed it the 'flying suitcase' and later the 'flying coffin'.

As far as defence in the air against fighter attack was concerned, the Hampden had serious deficiencies. The aircraft had five .303 inch Vickers K machine guns. The fixed forward firing gun was practically useless and the others, with their limited traverse, left blind spots which enemy fighters were quick to identify. The .303 was largely ineffectual against the cannon-firing Luftwaffe machines which were able to penetrate the Hampden's armour and, more importantly, the fuel tanks which were not of the self-sealing variety. Air Chief Marshal Sir Arthur Harris[1], who became Bomber Command's supremo in 1942, was not at all impressed with the Hampden and described it as a most feebly-armed aircraft and was critical of the lack of crew comfort.

Crew comfort was a major factor and, with a crew compartment that was only some three feet wide, movement proved to be very difficult. Access to the pilot's compartment was only possible after the rear upright of the seat was fully retracted, thus allowing the pilot to crawl into position. If the pilot was injured during a flight and had to be pulled out to allow the navigator to fly the aircraft, the seat back had to be laid flat again to enable the navigator to crawl over the top of the injured pilot. The navigator doubled-up as the observer/bomb aimer and occupied the front position in the nose and the wireless operator/air gunner took the upper gun position at the rear of the aircraft overlooking the tail boom. This left the fourth member of the crew to occupy the lower rear gun position, known as 'the tin', situated underneath the aircraft. Fortunately, Owen was

1. Commonly known as 'Bomber' Harris by the press. Air Officer Commander-in-Chief of RAF Bomber Command and later a Marshal of the Royal Air Force during the latter half of World War II.

only five foot eight inches tall, something that would have been to his advantage in the cramped confines of the Hampden.

The Hampden was further handicapped by its inability to deliver a bomb load of more than 4000lbs, unlike the Avro Lancaster which later in the war was able to deliver bombs as large as 22000lbs. In 1939, the only bombs the RAF had at its disposal in any quantity were the 250lb General Purpose Bomb, which was first in use during the Great War. However, despite all its shortcomings, the Hampden served its purpose in the early months of the war, holding the line with the Wellington until the next generation of bombers came on stream.

RAF Hemswell was a comparatively new airfield, having been built in the 1930s as one of the permanent RAF bases opened to accommodate the rapidly growing Bomber Command. The airfield was also home to 61 Squadron which was originally equipped with the Bristol Blenheim, but by March 1939, was re-equipped with the Hampden. Both squadrons took part in the very earliest daylight operations of the war, quickly discovering how easily the German fighters could knock them down. This was no better illustrated by the daylight operation planned for 29th September 1939, when two flights of six Hampdens from 144 Squadron left Hemswell to look for shipping targets in the Heligoland area. Heading south towards Wilhemshaven, the second of the two flights was bounced by a strong force of Me109s, and within five minutes five British aircraft had been shot down and were in the sea. Of the twenty aircrew who took off from Hemswell, only four survived to be taken prisoner. The most senior of the casualties was the Squadron Commander, Wing Commander James Cunningham.

It wasn't a good start to operations against the enemy and was a major disaster for the squadron. Incredibly, instead of prompting a reappraisal of daylight raids, Bomber Command stubbornly stuck to the maxim that the well-armed bomber formation will always get through in daylight. It was a tactic that would take several more setbacks before the daylight raids were abandoned in the winter of 1940 in favour of night attacks. By the time Owen arrived at Hemswell at the end of August to join B Flight, night operations were well underway. On the nights of the 25th and 26th August, squadron aircraft were tasked to attack and bomb targets over Berlin, a long way to go in a Hampden, particularly as Berlin was at the limit of their range. A similar raid involving 144 Squadron aircraft was carried out on the 31st August.

Desperate for good news, in a war that up until now was not going well, a grateful public accepted the accounts of targets being destroyed and an enemy that was reeling from the Bomber Command onslaught. What was slightly more disconcerting was Bomber Command itself accepting its success without real evidence. The reality was that in 1940 barely one in five aircraft actually found the primary target and, of those that did, very few managed to hit the target area.

The procedure adopted in bomber squadrons throughout the war was for new pilots to gain experience as a second pilot and fly with an experienced crew until they were judged as capable of captaining their own aircraft. In the Hampden this was difficult, as the seating arrangements did not allow easy access to the cockpit once the aircraft was in flight, which usually resulted in the new pilot acting as navigator/second pilot. This was the scenario in the Hampden P1172 on the night of 5th September when Owen joined the crew of Pilot Officer John Newton-Clare. Newton-Clare had arrived some weeks before and had already captained the aircraft on numerous operational flights. On this occasion the squadron was to be part of a widespread effort to bomb targets in Italy and Germany. A force of 82 aircraft, which included Wellingtons, Whitleys and Hampdens, were to attack targets from Turin to Stettin, with 144 Squadron aircraft tasked to bomb installations at Hamburg.

What actually happened on that flight we shall probably never know. Hemswell records show the aircraft was on the return journey from Hamburg in the early morning of 6th September, when it was lost. There were no German night fighter claims for that night, ruling out the option the aircraft was shot down by an enemy fighter. The only other possibilities were damage from flak over the target area resulting in engine failure on the way home, damaged fuel tanks or even a navigational error that ate into their fuel to such an extent they ran out over the sea. On 8th September, Group Captain E. Rice, the Commanding Officer of RAF Hemswell, wrote to Owen's mother in Hull:

May I express the very sincere sympathy of myself and of

all the Officers and Airmen on this station with you in the grievous anxiety you must be suffering through your son being missing.

He was on a bombing raid over Germany during the night of 5/6th of September and radio communication had been established on the return journey at 4.51am. An SOS signal was received. It is supposed they came down in the sea at that time and immediately a search was inaugurated in the area from which the message was believed to have come, in the region of 50 degrees north.

I regret to say that so far the search has been without result. It is of course possible that your son and the others of the crew were able to take to their rubber dinghy and were picked up by some vessel without a radio or by an enemy ship, it is therefore too soon to give up hope and you may be sure that any information that comes in will immediately be passed onto you.

I can only say how much I hope such news will be good and how sorry I am that this should have happened on your son's second operational flight, for he had already shown the qualities of gallantry and courage that make for success and of which you must be proud.

Similar letters were written to the families of the other three crew members. What the CO had not mentioned in his letter was Owen had only been a member of the squadron for eight days. He had hardly had time to unpack and settle in before his kit was being packed up again and sent to the Central Repository, where it would wait until it was claimed by the family. The reference to Owen having already flown one operation was incorrect. Although the family were always under the impression that Owen was shot down on his second operational flight, this was not supported by the evidence in the squadron operational record book. At the National Archives the ORB confirmed that it was Owen's first flight over mainland Europe and he was flying as navigator. There was no previous entry indicating Owen had flown with the squadron prior to 5th/6th September. The ORB logged the end of Owen's short career with the squadron:

Flying Battle Casualty – Hampden P1172. P/O Newton-Clare, Sgt Clarke, Sgt Thompson, Sgt. Powell. Aircraft took off on schedule to take part in operations against Germany and the correct W/T procedure was carried out prior to crossing the coast. Later the aircraft appeared to be in difficulties and at 0456 hours a request for a bearing was received, the aircraft was asked for a call sign but signal gradually faded out and nothing further was heard.

The other NCO crew members were both youngsters: William Thompson, the aircraft's wireless operator/air gunner, aged 18 years old and Leslie Powell, the second air gunner, who was only a year older. What did catch my eye while reading the ORB was the note in the margin regarding the crew of P1172 being apparently rescued and reinstated on the strength of the squadron. Below this a further note in a different hand had been added to the effect that this information was false and a line had been drawn through the names of the crew. There had obviously been some news of the crew that had turned out to be unsubstantiated.

The rescue arrangements for the early period of the war were just not up to the task of searching and rescuing the increasing numbers of aircrew who found themselves ditching in the sea. The Sea Rescue Organisation had only come into existence in August 1940 and already was finding itself unable to cope with demand. It wouldn't be until nearly a year later that the Air Sea Rescue Directorate was established with the support of designated ASR Squadrons such as 278 Squadron, which my father would fly with in 1944.

For Owen and the crew of P1172 all this came too late. The chances of the crew being found in a small dinghy in the North Sea were slight, that is if they were uninjured and able to escape after the aircraft had ditched. The vision of four men in a dinghy slowly succumbing to the elements over a period of days is not something to dwell upon, but it was the fate of many crews who did not make it home.

There were some remarkable rescues made after crews had been afloat, in some instances, for days. The ditching of a 77 Squadron

Whitley V on 24th September 1940, some 80 miles off the East Coast, resulted in the survivors being adrift in their dinghy for four days. The aircraft had been hit by flak over Berlin and the fuel tanks holed. A three-and-a-half day search ensued with the two survivors being eventually picked up in a very poor condition by the destroyer *HMS Ashanti*. Tragically the pilot, Pilot Officer A. Dunn, died within hours of being found, leaving the rear gunner, Sergeant Riley, as the sole survivor of the crew of five.

On the night that Owen and the crew of P1172 ended up in the sea, two other Hampdens had a similar fate. According to *Bomber Command Losses 1939-1940*, an aircraft from 49 Squadron ditched off Calais and the crew were taken prisoner, while a 44 Squadron Hampden ditched off Lowestoft, the crew being rescued by a passing ship. This is most likely where the false report of the rescue of Owen and his crew originated: there could have easily been confusion between 44 Squadron and 144 Squadron, with Hemswell thinking it was their crew that had been rescued. Owen's name and those of the crew are commemorated on the Runnymede Memorial to the missing.

In Hull the news reached Maytree Avenue by telegram. Owen had not told his mother he was on operations and the news that he was missing completely devastated her. My father-in-law remembered being woken by a phone call from Elma late at night and he and Margaret, Owen's sister, going round to Maytree Avenue to console her. Jean Payne's mother kept the news from her until she had returned from work the next day. Jean knew instinctively what had happened as soon as she walked in and saw her mother's face.

Geoff Crawford was still at 13 OTU when the news of Owen's death reached him by letter from home. Back at Elm Avenue on the morning of Saturday 7th September, the Crawford family were one of the first to hear the distressing news. Owen's mother had walked round to the Crawford household with the telegram in her hand, clearly distraught over the news it contained. In her distress Elma Clarke told them that Geoff would be next. Geoff's brother Phillip still remembers her knocking on the door that morning and how horrified his mother was at Elma's pronouncement. Phillip was the younger of the two Crawford boys and about to go into the RAF himself as a wireless operator/air gunner. At around this time Geoff returned to Hull on leave and one of the first things he did was to visit Jean, promising to see her again on his next leave. Sadly, she never saw him again as, five months later, Geoff was reported missing himself.

—*—

I would have been content to have concluded Owen's story there, but a conversation with Phillip Crawford had intrigued me. Apparently, the family never really discovered what had happened to Geoff and the crew of his Wellington bomber in March 1941 when it was shot down. All enquiries by Geoff's father to the Air Ministry were replied to but any detail was veiled under the cloak of classified information. Eventually they gave up and, although they were finally told he had been shot down over the Mediterranean, nothing further was forthcoming. It was Geoff's service record that provided the key to the missing information.

Having behaved himself and kept on the right side of the Chief Flying Instructor, Geoff finally completed his OTU training without further mishap and was posted to 99 Squadron in January 1941. It must have been a relief to have finally reached an operational squadron, not that life at Bicester had been without hazard. During the period that Geoff was there, ten aircraft had crashed with the loss of fourteen aircrew killed and five injured.

His new squadron was based at Newmarket Heath in Suffolk. The airfield was literally on the Newmarket Racecourse with the famous Rowley Mile being used as a runway. Today, at the entrance to the Rowley Mile enclosure, is a propeller blade from Wellington T2888 R-Robert, mounted as a memorial to the aircrew of 99 Squadron who did not return.

When Geoff reported to 99 Squadron on 11th January, the majority of the ground-crew were sleeping in the open grandstand, which wouldn't have been so bad if the winter of 1940/41 had been a little milder. Fortunately the aircrew were billeted in the nearby Jockey Club premises but, despite the slightly improved accommodation, aircrew serving with 99 Squadron that winter remember the aircraft covered in snow and the bitterly cold wind howling over the heath with ground-crews working in deplorable conditions to keep the aircraft serviceable. At the National Archives an examination of the 99 Squadron ORB detailed how poor weather conditions had handicapped the squadron's operational ability to such an extent that they were only able to get airborne on five occasions in January 1941.

Geoff's first operational flight was on 16th/17th January, as second pilot of Wellington P9281. The target was Wilhelmshaven, and the Wellingtons from Newmarket joined the 81-strong bomber force that took part in the raid. Although the squadron lost no aircraft to enemy action, only six returned to Newmarket, two landing at Debden, another at Kenley and one crash-landing after returning early.

On 29th/30th January, he was in the air again as second pilot of T2554. This time the aircraft were after the German battleship *Tirpitz* which was berthed at Wilhelmshaven. In what was a fairly typical outcome of bombing operations at the time, of the thirty-four aircraft that were in the attack only nineteen found the target area and the *Tirpitz* was not located by anyone. One of the aircraft that failed to find the primary target was Geoff's T2554 which bombed Emden instead, reporting large explosions and 'pinky-red sheets of flame' erupting from the centre of the town. Another flown by Pilot Officer Coote failed to find any target at all in the very bad weather conditions over Germany and returned home with a full bomb load, which must have given them a few anxious moments as they touched down. The squadron lost no aircraft but only seven of the nine returned to Newmarket. The others found alternative landing grounds in Suffolk.

On 4th February, they had better flying conditions and the squadron attacked shipping at Brest, but apart from making a lot of noise and setting fire to dock installations, no shipping was reported hit. They all returned home safely. Geoff's final operation with 99 Squadron was on 2nd March. On this occasion the target was the dock areas on both banks of the Rhine of the cathedral city of Cologne, which was more successful. Aside from losing two aircraft over the target, the real problems began when the returning aircraft found their airfields obscured by dense fog. Fortunately, Geoff's Wellington managed to land safely at Newmarket but fourteen others from participating squadrons crashed landed at their various airfields, with twelve aircrew losing their lives. It had been a costly night.

In 1941, volunteers were being recruited for Middle East Command to fly reinforcement Wellingtons to Malta and North Africa. I imagine the warmer climate sounded quite attractive to Geoff, who was still accommodated in the Jockey Club at Newmarket Racecourse! Whatever his reason for volunteering to go to the Middle East, it was shared by all his crew except the first pilot, Sergeant Malcolm, who elected to stay with 99 Squadron, a decision he would not have cause to regret.

Geoff's service record shows him posted to 3 Group Support Flight based at Stradishall in Suffolk on 9th March 1941, along with the crew he had flown with since January. Malcolm's place was taken by a 26 year-old New Zealand pilot, Sergeant Richard Alington, who had also volunteered for Middle East service. Alington was an experienced 99 Squadron pilot with 29 operations to his credit and was the aircraft's captain for the long flight to the Middle East. The sixth crew member was Group Captain Dudley Humphreys who was, I assume, going out to the Middle East to take up a command post. Humphreys, a career officer who joined the RAF in 1918, had just completed a tour as the CO of 217 Squadron at Tangmere.

They took off from Stradishall in Wellington W5644 on 13th March for the first leg of the flight that would take them to Gibraltar and then to the island of Malta before finally flying the last stage to Egypt. Ferry flights were the only way of getting new aircraft to Middle East Command and once clear of Gibraltar they had to run the gauntlet of marauding German fighters based in Sicily. The flight was a bit of a lottery: over the course of 1941, delivery flight casualties totalled 45 aircraft lost, 108 aircrew killed and 168 aircrew either interned by neutral countries or captured. Records indicate W5644 arrived at Gibraltar on 14th March, and after refuelling and resting, they took off for Malta between 2027 hours and 2039 hours in the company of two other Wellingtons and an escorting Martin Maryland, a twin-engined American-designed aircraft. At some point before their arrival at Malta they were picked up by a German radar installation in Sicily. A message received at 0545 hours stated W5644 was under attack some 70 miles out from Luqua Airfield.

Nothing more was heard.

They had fallen prey to one of the most prolific Luftwaffe fighter aces of the war. If the crew had seen their attacker they would have glimpsed the yellow nose of the Me109e of Oberleutnant Joachim Muncheberg. Muncheberg was based at the Gela airfield in Sicily, the home of Jagdgeschwader 26, one of the most successful Luftwaffe fighter wings to fly in the western theatre of operations. Muncheberg in his report of the encounter stated he shot down the Wellington in flames, 10km north-west of Gozo Island, and that he had seen the aircraft ditch, observing some of the crew getting into their dinghy. They were never found. The JG 26 war diary records a formation of Wellingtons being detected near Sicily on 15th March and one was attacked from below by Muncheberg pulling up from Gela in a near vertical climb. Müncheberg was later killed on 23rd March 1943, over Tunisia in combat with USAF Spitfires from the 52nd Fighter Group. He had 135 aerial victories to his credit.

The names of the crew of W5644 are also commemorated on the Runnymede Memorial. Apart from Geoff Crawford, Richard Alington and Group Captain Humphreys, the other aircrew reported missing were: Sergeant Kenneth Herbert Vaughan, Sergeant Harold Edward Meason, Pilot Officer Robert Henry Blandy, and Sergeant Charles Gillespie.

So why did the family have difficulty in gathering information about this flight? Humphries was most likely going out to take up a strategic command position in the Middle East and I can only guess that his loss was not something that the Air Ministry would want to advertise to the enemy, hence the secrecy. As for W5644, despite going down relatively close to Malta, the surviving crew would have little chance of rescue unless found by passing shipping. Air sea rescue in the Mediterranean was practically non-existent in early 1941 and there were precious few available aircraft on Malta to go out and look for them. As with Owen and the crew of his Hampden six months earlier, those that survived the attack and escaped from the aircraft would have drifted in their dinghy until they too succumbed to the elements.

Armed with Geoff's service record and other material from the National Archives and the RAF Museum, I drove up to Hull to visit

Phillip and explain the circumstances of his brother's death. Most of our previous communication had been by letter and telephone and although the events over the Mediterranean took place well over sixty-five years ago, I felt this was something that should be done on a personal level. Phillip was visibly moved as I described the events that led up to Geoff's aircraft being shot down and the probable fate of his brother and the crew.

Driving home again that evening I reflected on what had been a rather sad meeting. During the course of my research I had come to know these two boys well. I had met and spoken to individuals who had known and loved them, I had been to the family homes where they had been born and visited the school where they had been educated. For me, the story of these two RAF pilots, both of whom had ended their young lives in the sea, needed a more formal closure. That closure came a few weeks later with a visit to the Air Forces Memorial at Runnymede, where we left flowers and said goodbye.

11

Fighter Pilot

Howard (Hugh) Ferguson Murland

My father was one of those individuals who kept absolutely everything relating to his RAF career and, like his father before him, he also kept a diary and took photographs. More importantly he was still alive at the time of writing and could fill in some of the missing pieces himself, although inevitably, after his death in 2006, a number of questions arose which only he could shed light on. However, his collection of photographs presented me with a chronological pictorial record from his early days at the Edinburgh University course to eventual demobilisation in 1947. In addition, they were a fascinating archive of the evolution of an operational fighter pilot, from fledgling pupil to confident master of his trade.

One of the first tasks I set myself was to transcribe his diaries into a more readable format and then to check those individuals mentioned by name against the Commonwealth War Graves Commission database. This proved to be a rather sad task, as again and again, the Roll of Honour confirmed the individual in question had not survived the war. Very often news of friends killed in flying accidents or killed in action would filter through some time after the event. These would be recorded in his diary by a single short sentence, a sentence that betrayed nothing of the inevitable sorrow that was felt. By the end of flying training, it was obvious that Hugh had developed the wartime pilot's apparent casual attitude to death, an attitude that helped him, and others like him, deal with the unavoidable collision with death they all faced. After Hugh died, I contacted the surviving members of the Edinburgh University course to let them know our sad news. It was through this and subsequent correspondence with Peter Thorne[1] and George Harris that further details emerged to supplement the diary and provide some additional background to the Commonwealth Air Training Plan that turned these boys into operational aircrew.

—⁂—

Howard Ferguson Murland was born at Bangalore, India on 12th April, 1923. At the time of his birth his father, Howard Ferguson Murland (senior), was still serving in the Indian Army as a Major in the 64th Madras Pioneers. In 1925, the family moved to Mandalay when he became commanding officer of the 2nd Battalion Madras Pioneers. In 1933, Hugh was sent to be educated at Swanbourne House School near Buckingham and in 1936, aged thirteen, he moved to Wellington College in Berkshire. With his parents still in India, he and his sisters spent the school holidays with the Shackleford family at Kingswalden. He was still at Wellington when war broke out in 1939, but he would have to wait nearly two years before he was old enough to join the RAF Volunteer Reserve. During those early days of the war the students were certainly not immune from the everyday hazards of wartime Britain. Air attacks were commonplace and during one of these air raids in October 1940, the Headmaster of the college, R.P. Longden, was killed. Many years later, Hugh recorded the event for the *Old Wellingtonian* Magazine:

> Enemy aircraft were frequent visitors by both day and night. On the tragic night the Master [headmaster] was killed we were in shelters when the bomb exploded. In our shelter a squealer [a new boy] had just climbed up the short emergency ladder to the hatchway and was peering out into the darkness above. The explosion blew him down the ladder, I suspect more from fright than blast effect.

Another incident at Kingswalden had all the hallmarks of a Boy's

1. Air Commodore Peter Thorne OBE, AFC.

Own adventure. With London only forty miles away, the sight of enemy aircraft returning from attacking the capital was quite commonplace and, as members of the Home Guard, Hugh and the Shackleford boys were always on the lookout for shot-down enemy airmen. On one particular night in April 1941, Hugh had a close encounter with a German airman after a Dornier crashed in the nearby deer park:

> One night during the holidays the noise of an aircraft grew louder and ended in an explosion. We dashed out in different directions to find the crash and as I was passing a field a figure advanced on me calling 'Hans! Hans!' A white blur in the trees behind was his parachute. I held out my hand for his 'arms', he put out his hand and I withdrew my hand quickly, this was the enemy and no handshake was intended! But he had no weapons or the wish to resist. The family's bag that night was two captured.

Hugh's choice of service with the RAF had met with considerable resistance from his father, now a retired Lieutenant-Colonel. His father had already persuaded an old army friend, now commanding a battalion of the Leicestershire Regiment, to sponsor Hugh's commission as a Second Lieutenant into the regiment. There had been no discussion with Hugh about this event and part of the problem, I suspect, was the RAF Commonwealth Air Training Plan and its decision to recruit all prospective aircrew into the ranks until they had completed their training. Even then, there was only a percentage chance of being commissioned immediately. His father clearly had difficulties coming to terms with the prospect of a son not being commissioned, on top of which he was also of the opinion that the RAF was not a serious career option. Although a large number of students from Wellington did volunteer for the RAF, the emphasis at the college was always on the Army as the preferred service, and the school's close connection with the Royal Military College at Sandhurst, was well-established.

Nevertheless, despite this vehement opposition and with the welcome support of his House Master, Hugh arrived at Edinburgh on 16th April, 1941, four days after his eighteenth birthday, and took up residence at Cowan House in George Square, to begin the University Short Course as 1385606 Aircraftsman Second Class Murland.

In September 1941, with the course successfully completed, he received his Proficiency Certificate from the University Air Squadron and was posted to No. 1 Aircrew Reception Centre in London, based at Lord's Cricket Ground. Here they messed at London Zoo and waited to hear news of when they would begin their flying training. From London, the cadets were moved south to Brighton to what was, rather grandly, called an Aircrew Disposal Wing – in reality one of the older Brighton hotels requisitioned by the Air Ministry.

At Brighton, they were initiated into the long-established service tradition of waiting around doing very little. It was at the Aircrew Disposal Wing that they were given a choice of where they would complete their flying training. Hugh noted at the time that the cadets did not really believe they were going to be able to choose their destination and thought the whole process was a wind-up. He rather flippantly opted for South Africa as it sounded nice and warm. It was with some surprise that these choices became reality.

The consequences of the choices they made in Brighton would have a direct bearing on which theatre of war they would eventually find themselves in. Of the Edinburgh course cadets, George Harris gained his wings in the USA and returned to the UK to fly Lancasters, winning a DFC with 101 Squadron. David Calder went with him, but tragically in October 1942, he was killed in Alabama flying a Harvard during advanced training. Peter Boyle chose to remain at home for his flying training and would also fly Lancasters with 50 Squadron. Peter Thorne would eventually end up in Canada after beginning his training in Carlisle, to return home to fly Typhoons with 193 Squadron. Those that chose southern African destinations would be posted either to the Mediterranean and North African theatre, Hugh to 81 Squadron, Dave Edye to 142 Squadron or, in the case of Joe Simpson, to 194 Squadron in India .

What the future, in terms of life or death, might hold in store for them was not a consideration in Brighton; the cadets only felt excitement at the prospect of becoming pilots and were impatient at the seemingly slow progress they were making towards that goal. Diary entries gave an indication of everyone's frustration about the lack of information regarding their postings overseas:

> *Dec. 11th*
> Not wanted today. In bed until 8.30 so to NAFFI for buns for breakfast. No news of postings, are we actually going?

> *Dec. 15th*
> Others inoculated morning. Self 2.30 (arm). No further news of postings. Not much sleep – v sore and stiff.

> *Dec. 16th*
> No breakfast. V. Stiff and headache. Cleaned room for Wing/Cmdrs inspection. Sgt. Richard (Postings) gone – no-one knows anything about it!!

Finally, even the top brass seemed to have become impatient with the lack of movement. It was no coincidence that the Air Commodore's[2] son, Peter Boyle, was also in the group that graduated from Edinburgh and was kicking his heels along with the rest of them in Brighton.

After a short embarkation leave and an issue of tropical kit, the South African bound cadets were on board the *SS Otranto* by 8th January 1942. The *Otranto* was an Orient Line Passenger liner of some 20,000 tons. Brought into service as a troopship in 1940, it survived the war, being scrapped in 1957 at Faslane. The ship spent its final years ferrying the so called 'Ten Quid Tourists' to Australia under the Australian postwar immigration scheme. The accommodation offered to the post-war passengers would have been a little more lavish than the overcrowded below-decks mess areas, that the cadets shared for the next five weeks. Sleeping several decks down in hammocks that swayed above their mess tables, they quickly grew accustomed to shipboard routine. The weather did

---

2. Air Commodore the honourable Jack Boyle DSO CBE (1884-1974). His brother, Alan, built the first monoplane in Britain and set a number of distance records on it. Jack gained Royal Aero Club Certificate No 558 in November 1912. Prior to this he had held Aeronauts' Certificate No 34 and had also qualified as an Airship Pilot (Certificate No 19). His eldest son was killed during the crossing of the Rhine in 1945.

not help for the first few days, as the numerous troopships ploughed their way through heavy seas to join the convoy off the Irish coast. Hugh was one of the few in his mess not to become sea sick. He noted on the 12th:

> Move from off Belfast 1am. Wake up to see coast of Scotland again. Slight swell, weakest of us seasick. Hugging Scottish Coast. After lunch swell increases, nearly all seasick (self just not) Most people in bed. Self on guard, but by 6pm all disorganised, as all guards sick.

The *Otranto* was sailing in a large convoy of several troopships escorted by light cruisers and, a week later, by the battleship *HMS Resolution*. The *Resolution* had already seen considerable action. In 1940, whilst supporting troops in Norway, she was bombed near Narvic and four months later, on 25th September, she was torpedoed during an unsuccessful attempt to land a Free French force at Dakar, on the coast of the Vichy French colony of Senegal. After safely delivering the convoy to South Africa she would remain in the Indian Ocean until 1944.

In common with Douglas Watt's experience on the *Olympic* in 1915, the big fear was enemy submarines and the sighting of an enemy aircraft on 16th January caused some concerns, fuelling the very efficient rumour machinery that had already established itself on board:

> On guard 8-10. Parade 10-11, so no exercise. Condor sighted 11.30 to port. Light cruiser firing, no hits. My telescope used. Had to go below until all clear. No lunch. Missed the fresh air on deck. There are rumours of 2 torpedoed troopships.

The Focke Wulf Condor was a maritime reconnaissance bomber used to find and attack convoys. It would also signal a convoy's position to surface ships and U-boats. It was after this incident that everyone had to carry their lifejackets with them at all times. What was probably not appreciated at the time was the cadets' ability to read and understand Morse. So while those in charge were vainly trying to keep the cadets in the dark about submarine sightings, the boys were reading the signals between ships in the convoy and often were better informed than their officers. On the 17th Hugh noted:

> Battleship HMS Resolution joined us – feel safer! Sailing alongside us: studied them through telescope. Watching her most of the day and reading her signals! It seems there are subs in the area and the destroyer screen is working hard. I hope we do not all end up in the drink. My telescope in great demand. Clock back another hour. Lost 5/- playing Pontoon.

By 20th January, most of Hugh's mess were sleeping on deck. The weather was getting progressively warmer as they steamed further south. The warmer tropical weather allowed the heavy blue serge of uniforms to be replaced with the more comfortable tropical kit which, to the delight of the cadets, meant there would be no more buttons to clean. Five days later, on the 25th, they dropped anchor in the large sheltered harbour of Freetown, Sierra Leone:

> Various types of fish seen. Sweepstake on when we drop anchor at Freetown. I bought 2 tickets but won nothing. Arrived 1.40. Large estuary but insignificant town. Very hot. Dozens of ships here. Bumboats and natives selling fruit (strictly forbidden!!!) and diving for coins. Everyone hanging over rails most of the afternoon. 1 Walrus & 2 Sunderlands at anchor. No blackout! and no carrying lifejackets.

Despite the ban on buying fruit from the locals, most of the cadets ignored the order, and twenty-four hours later, Hugh discovered why. A violent gastric attack together with a temperature put him in the ship's hospital for a week. Despite his discomfort, the clean sheets and beds were a welcome relief from the mess deck. The spell in hospital denied him the opportunity to take part in the Crossing the Equator Ceremony, but by 4th February, he had been discharged and was back sleeping on deck and complaining about being a mess orderly again. Four days out of Durban, the Capetown bound troopships left the convoy and on board the *Otranto* preparations for disembarking were in progress:

> Damp and muggy, floor of mess deck slippery and foul smell from hold. Mess orderly again! Trousers filthy, what if we are going ashore in them? Parade in blues and afterwards packing up kit. Everyone washing clothes – self included. Very warm in mess deck all of us in singlet and shorts. Got blues ironed for 6d – couldn't get iron myself. I really need a bath and to get off this blasted ship.

The *Otranto* docked early in the morning of 13th February, and by 9am the RAF contingent was on parade with full packs before being dismissed to shore leave. Hugh makes no mention in his diary about Perla Gibson, the 'Lady in White', or whether she greeted the *Otranto* with her usual welcome. I'm sure that if he had seen and heard her he would have recorded the event. By 1942, The Lady in White had become part of the troopship experience for those arriving and departing from Durban.

The Perla Gibson story began in April 1940, when troops on board a troopship persuaded Perla Siedle Gibson, a soprano, to sing to them. Perla was happy to oblige and broke into song. There was silence and then the troops joined in, their voices being heard above the hustle and bustle of wartime Durban. It was the start of a ritual which she would continue doing as long as there were troopships to sing to. Dressed in white and wearing a white hat, she sang patriotic songs for more than one thousand troopships and over three hundred and fifty hospital ships.

Durban was quite a shock to the cadets. Having travelled over eight thousand miles from a blacked-out Britain, it was almost as if they had disembarked onto another planet. Hugh and others made a beeline for the Royal Hotel to order their first decent meal in weeks: unrationed food was a welcome relief from shipboard messing. The following morning they paraded again and entrained for the long rail journey to Lyttleton Camp. Hugh and Dave Edye managed to find a compartment together:

> Paraded at 11am on the wharf. Got on the first train, missed all others except Dave, but a good lot in our carriage. Journey very interesting, first mountains, then Velt (rather interesting). Very hot all day then suddenly an electric storm and downpour. The train stopped (electric) because of lightning (continual in distance all evening) took plenty of photos. Later we let the bunks down in the carriage and had a very comfortable night.

It was with some disappointment that the Edinburgh cadets found themselves at Lyttleton Camp to repeat their initial training, as they had expected to go straight to a flying training wing and begin flying. The South African Air Force clearly had other ideas and lumped everyone in with their own trainee programme. There was little point in complaining – they just wanted to get on with it and get airborne. By the beginning of April, the initial and advanced basic training was out of the way and Hugh, along with Dave Edye and Joe Simpson, were posted to 6 Air School at Potchefstroon to begin elementary flying training, arriving on 11th April. The next day was Hugh's nineteenth birthday:

> My birthday today. Up at 8am. Suddenly remembered when I woke up that I was at EFTS! Took it very easy all day, very tired: didn't move from mess and hut, latrines filthy. Mess not bad, four baths, and sometimes there is hot water. In bed 8.20pm, SHEETS! Very comfortable, didn't like to get up Monday morning.

Potchefstroom was one of six elementary flying training schools in South Africa. Hugh's instructor was a Lieutenant Nesser, an individual he immediately recognised as someone he was going to get on with, and the aircraft he would fly would be the familiar Tiger Moth that he had first flown at Edinburgh. The Tiger Moth is probably the most well-known and best-loved of the training aircraft used by the RAF and was still in service with Flying Training Command as late as 1947. Fully aerobatic, this rugged little biplane was the standard initial trainer during World War 2 and most RAF pilots would record their first solo flight in a 'Tiger'.

Hugh, after some initial difficulties with landings, went solo on 25th April, after some ten hours dual instruction. With the pressure to go solo now gone, and like thousands before and after him, he discovered that mastering the skills of flying was about to begin. Taking off from the airfield, flying straight and level round the circuit and landing in one piece was relatively straightforward. Instrument and formation flying, spins, stalls, aerobatics and cross-country exercises were yet to come, demanding an ability to develop what was called an 'air sense'. Those that did not progress quickly enough or demonstrate the right aptitude were 'washed out' and re-mustered as navigators, wireless operators, air gunners or air bombers. On the 14th May, Dave Edye, despite having gone solo, fell foul of the demanding pace after repeated difficulties with the finer points of aircraft control. Hugh discovered his friend's demise after returning from a cross-country flight:

> Solo X-Country to Baragwanath – got on fine. Wind giving 10 degrees drift. Saw no other pupil pilots there. Very high wind and a tricky landing. Back at 12.55. Later, Night flying 45 mins, good fun but different. Dave Edye washed out this morning – lack of air sense. Damn bad luck, be sorry to see him go. Only self and Joe left from the Edinburgh course now.

In the capable hands of Lieutenant Nesser, Hugh's progress continued without mishap with frequent cross-country solo flying and the occasional dual instruction, formation and instrument flying. When not airborne the cadets made good use of Link Trainers to gain additional simulated instrument experience. The Link Trainer was the brainchild of the American pilot Edward Link who constructed the first machine in the 1930s. More or less resembling an aircraft, it could imitate its movements around its three axes. Now firmly established as an integral part of flying training, the Link Trainer provided valuable additional flying time for pupil pilots without taking up valuable aircraft time. Over the eleven weeks of the course at Potchefstroom, Hugh logged some fifteen hours in a Link Trainer, which would be increased to a total of forty-three hours by the time he had gained his wings.

By late June, with over seventy hours flying time in his logbook, his diary recorded his last cross-country flight and the final mess party to celebrate the end of the course:

> *Tuesday 23rd*
> Final X-country completed and summarising my log book, getting it checked in the flight office. No more flying for me – now finished initial training, will be sorry to see the last of the Tigers but looking forward to flying Masters. Total hours 70.50. Party in mess in the evening, everyone tight, two fire extinguishers used up.

> *Wednesday 24th*
> Trouble over extinguishers. All leave cancelled by CO but luckily withdrawn later after deputation from pupil pilots. Mess in a hell of a state. CO in a very, very bad mood.

High spirits such as these from the cadets were not uncommon. The majority of them took every opportunity to tap into the local social life and frequent visits to Johannesburg, Potchefstroom and later Bloemfontein were recorded in Hugh's diary. The cadets certainly enjoyed a varied and active social life while in South Africa, invitations to stay with local families were frequent and there was no shortage of young women keen to meet these fledgling aviators.

Over the period of time that Hugh was in flying training, wherever he and his friends found themselves, they would use the local Toc H Services Club as a focal point for meeting people and spending the occasional night away from camp. An international charitable society, Toc H was founded on christian principles during the Great War in the Belgian town of Poperinge. The first Toc H was called Talbot House[3] where a young Army chaplain, the Reverent Tubby Clayton, established a centre for soldiers that was open to all ranks and provided basic comforts for the young men going to and

3. The first Toc H was named Talbot House after Lieutenant Gilbert Talbot who was killed in Action on 30th July 1915.

RAJ4259—1941-2—10,000.

FIDENTIAL.

R.A.F. Form 1499

REPORT ON THE FLYING AND GROUND TRAINING OF PILOTS

Name: MURLAND

Christian Names: HOWARD FERGUSON

ber: 1385606

Rank: P/P L.A.C.   R.A.F.

AT

No. 27 SERVICE FLYING TRAINING SCHOOL (SOUTH AFRICA).

ed: 6.7.42   Left: 29.1.43

NG TIMES: Course No. FOUR

	Type of Aircraft.	Day.		Night.		Formation.	Instrument.	Passenger.	Link Traine
		Dual.	Solo.	Dual.	Solo.				
evious lying	D.H.82A	39.15	28.35	3.00	-	5.40	5.35	-	15.00
S.F.T.S.	HARTER II	60.40	88.00	6.35	5.25	25.10	16.35	-	28.00
	Total............	99.55	116.35	9.35	5.35	30.50	22.10	-	43.00

GROUND EXAMINATION MARKS

Airmanship A.E. & M. .. 52 %

Maintenance Armament (Written) 74 %

Armament (Practical) 71 %

Signals (Pract) Buzzer 10wpm Lamp 8 wpm %

Navigation (Part 1)(Theory) .. 79 %

,, (Part 2)(Plotting). 82 %

Signals (Written) .. .. 71 %

NIL. 51 %

G APTITUDE (on conclusion of Course)—							Exceptional.	Above Average.	Average.	Below Average.	Poor.
Natural Aptitude	..	..	..	..	..	..			Yes		
Skill in Landing	..	..	..	..	..				Yes		
Airmanship	..	..	..	..	..				Yes		
Cockpit Drill	..	..	..	..	..				Yes		
Instrument Flying	..	..	..	..	..			Yes			
Night Flying	..	..	..	..	..			Yes			
Aerobatics	..	..	..	..	..				Yes		
Formation Flying	..	..	..	..	..			Yes			
Map Reading	..	..	..	..	..				Yes		

2, 3, 4, 5 and 6 should be specially considered when recommending pilots for larger type aircraft.
5, 7 and 8 should be specially considered when recommending pilots for fighter aircraft.

·This report need not be shown to the pupil unless it accompanies a recommendation to cease instruction.
For full instructions regarding compilation and distribution of this form see Training Headquarters Instructions (which are adapted
A.M.O. A. 321/41).

Hugh Murland's final report from 27 Air School in which he is recommended for a commission. Despite this good final summary of his flying training he had to wait until 1944 to receive his commission.

from the battle lines of the Ypres Salient. By the outbreak of the Second World War, the movement had become international and Talbot Houses were established wherever there were troops.

Fighter Pilot

MOTIVE QUALITIES—	Exceptional.	Above Average.	Average.	Below Average.	Poor.
rsistence (Does he keep on trying or is he easily disheartened ?)			YES		
nse of Responsibility (Has he common sense or is he over-confident ?)			YES		
ndurance (Does he put up a consistently satisfactory performance under conditions of strain ?)			YES		
adership (Has he taken the lead in any activities ? Would he make a good captain of aircraft ?)		YES			
thod (Does he work systematically to a plan ?)			YES		
liberation (Does he act decisively for reasons or on impulse ?)			YES		
terprise (Does he want to try things on his own ?)			YES		
sh (Is he quick and decisive in action ?)			YES		
stribution of Attention (Does he find it difficult to do more than one thing at a time ?)			YES		
lf -Control (Does he get flustered ?)			YES		

—Items 1, 2, 3, 4, 5 and 6 should be specially considered when recommending pilots for larger type aircraft.
Items 7, 8 and 9 should be specially considered when recommending pilots for fighter aircraft.

SSMENT OF SUITABILITY FOR FURTHER TRAINING FOR (State pe of Squadron) :—	Exceptional.	Above Average.	Average.	Below Average.	Poor.
F. B. G. S.			YES		
A. G. B. S.			YES		
B. B. S.			YES		
As Potential Instructor					

ral Remarks (if any required)

. . This pupil should be watched as he is inclined to be over confident.

ority to wear Flying Badge was granted w.e.f. _____ 29.1.43

P.O., whether recommended for regrading_____ N/A

her (1) Strongly recommended for Commission.
(2) Recommended for commission. ....Yes
(3) Not at present recommended for Commission.
(4) Not recommended for Commission.

(Sgd.) A.F. Maurice. GROUP CAPTN

Signature

_____9.1.43_____

Officer Commanding.
No. 27 Air School, Bloemspruit.

With initial flying training completed, only four of the ten pupil pilots in B Flight at Potchefstroom, moved on to 27 Service Flying Training School at Bloomspruit, near Bloemfontein. Initial flying training had identified those who were likely to make the grade as fighter pilots, whilst the remainder would be trained at 22 Air

School on twin-engined aircraft to prepare them for their future with larger multi-engined aircraft. It was at this point that Hugh and Joe Simpson parted company and, although they corresponded regularly, they would only meet once more before the end of the war. Joe would eventually find himself flying the robust twin-engine DC3 Dakota in the Far East with RAF Transport Command and would survive the war intact.

At Bloomspruit the cadets began their advanced flying training with the Miles Master II. The difference between the Master and the Tiger Moth[4] was evident from their first familiarisation flight; with a maximum speed of 242 mph and a rate of climb of 1500 feet per minute, this two-seater monoplane took a little getting used to. With a totally new cockpit layout, an unfamiliar range of instruments, a retractable undercarriage and a different view through the windscreen, Hugh not unnaturally wondered if he would be able to fly the machine. He recorded his first flight on 9th July:

> First flip in a Master. Flying for 45 mins. Power excellent and climbs well. Fumes bloody awful but in general a grand aircraft. Did one spin – not like a Tiger's!

The Master was indeed different to the Tiger Moth and frequently less reliable in terms of engine failures. Training flights were regularly cancelled as aircraft became unserviceable, with corrosion, oily plugs and cylinder wear being commonplace. On 4th August, there was only one serviceable aircraft available in Hugh's flight and that quickly joined the others!

> This afternoon 4 aircraft out of 5 u/s. Mine was the only serviceable one – took it up and almost at once it started popping and cutting. Quickly brought it down again.

The Master also suffered from the warm South African climate which warped the wooded structure, again rendering the aircraft unserviceable. The technical problems the Masters were experiencing and the resulting delay in pupil pilots' progress had begun to

---

4. The maximum speed of the Tiger Moth was 160 mph.

impact on the flow of trained pilots from the Service Flying Schools based in South Africa and, although the difficulties were eventually remedied, the Master was replaced with the more reliable Harvard towards the end of 1943. Despite these setbacks, Hugh went solo after two hours forty minutes dual instruction and, by the end of flying training at 27 Air School, had completed over 200 hours in Masters.

Regardless of its apparent unreliability, the Master was still a demanding aircraft to fly and it was not long before minor accidents began to feature in the daily flying programme. Bill Coulter[5] was the first pupil pilot to be shaken up in an accident when one undercarriage leg gave way on landing. Hugh had a near miss a week later when a faulty carburettor caused the engine to cut out at 1500 feet while he was instrument flying under a cockpit hood. Not realising immediately what had gone wrong, he only just made it down safely with a successful forced landing. In August, Jimmy James collided with an Albacore when his brake pressure failed during taxing and damaged the wing tips of both his, and the other aircraft.

These minor scrapes were overshadowed by the first fatal accident in September, when one of the South African cadets, F.J. Scheepers, died after crash landing on the aerodrome. As if this was not enough to bring home the serious and dangerous nature of flying, a second fatal accident occurred only two weeks later when Alan Dicky Dick[6] was killed. Hugh records the event with a single unemotional line in his diary, but a photograph taken the next day of Dicky's funeral with Hugh and others acting as pall bearers betrayed the shock that they obviously felt over their friend's death.

With the beginning of night flying in November, a new set of challenges presented themselves, and the first to fall victim was 21 year-old Eric Scarfe, whose engine caught fire at 50 feet, resulting in a stall and a fatal crash. A month later Dan Pienaar, another South African pupil, and a local boy whose parents lived at Kroonstadt, was killed during a night flight across open country.

On 1st January, 1943, Hugh had one more near miss when he landed partly on a fence during a night approach to the aerodrome

---

5. Flying Officer Bill Coulter was killed in action with 81 Squadron in Burma on 17th March 1944.
6. Alan John Steven Dick, age 19, Eric Osmond Scarfe, age 21 and Clifford Mandefield, age 21 are buried in the Bloemfontein Cemetery, South Africa.

after a solo cross country flight, damaging the prop and right wing. As with all accidents, the pilot was required to immediately write a statement detailing how the incident occurred. Consequently Hugh had very little sleep that night and after completing his account he finally got to bed in the small hours.

The following morning he discovered that on the same cross country exercise another pupil and his instructor, Lieutenant Bains, had crashed and been killed. Tragedy struck again later in the month; ten days before the course passed out, 21 year-old Clifford Mandefield from Halifax in West Yorkshire was killed after his aircraft stalled at 50 feet during a forced landing. Flying accidents were an unfortunate facet of flying training and certainly not confined to 27 Air School. In November, Joe Simpson wrote from 22 Air School at Vereeniging that Gordon Cornish,[7] who had been at 6 Air School, Potchefstroom with Hugh, had been killed flying the twin-engined Air Speed Oxford.

Despite these accidents, which in many ways prepared the cadets for the future when operational losses would inevitably impact on their lives, the remaining cadets on the course kept their noses to the grindstone and continued with the demanding pace of the ground and flying syllabus that would end with the final exams. Life was extremely competitive and the fear of being 'washed out' motivated every cadet to work hard, each one fired by the overriding ambition to qualify as a pilot.

As the wings parade and graduation to an operational training unit drew nearer, the question of which cadets would be commissioned began to surface. Hugh had been strongly recommended for a commission after completing initial flying training and his final report from 27 Air School endorsed this recommendation. Much to his frustration, despite passing out fifth in the course, he was overlooked. No reason was given despite the earlier positive indications. In the end only three of the cadets were commissioned and the remainder were promoted to Sergeant Pilots. Hugh would have to wait until 1944 before the CO of 278 Squadron made the necessary recommendations and supported his application.

———

7. Gordon William Cornish, age 20, is buried in the Vereeniging Old Town Cemetery, South Africa.

Overcoming his initial disappointment, he joined the seven others destined for Clairwood Camp at Durban, safe in the knowledge that he would soon be flying fighters and hoping that they would be Spitfires. Clairwood was an Imperial Forces Transshipment Camp based at the Durban Racecourse.

Durban was full of service personnel, most of whom were either just arriving from the UK or awaiting a posting to another unit elsewhere. The waiting around was not unpleasant; Hugh and the others spent their time on the beach and at local dances in the company of a number of young women from the WRNS, taking full advantage of the bright lights of Durban. Hugh writes typically in his diary on 14th February:

> Into town at 11.30am. Lunch at the Hotel Louis with Kay and Margery. On the beach all afternoon, a very fine day. A friend of Margery's joined us as well. Bathing and surfing etc. Dinner in the hotel and others to a concert while self and Kay strolled on the beach until 2100hrs.

The pleasant holiday atmosphere of Durban came to an abrupt end with a posting to 21 Personnel Transit Centre at Kasfareet in the Suez Canal Zone. This move provided Hugh with his second troopship experience, this time in the *H.M.T. City of Paris*, an old refrigeration ship, late of the Ellerman Line. The ship was in a poor state having arrived from the UK barely a week previously and, apart from being in a filthy condition, was also having engine trouble. The 240 sergeant pilots en-route to operational training units were crammed into the mess decks below, while the officers enjoyed a little more comfort in cabin accommodation, albeit cramped.

At some point during the fifth day the ship fell behind the convoy, and for the next twenty-four hours steamed on, isolated from any convoy protection. It wasn't until the early hours that the ship finally rejoined and took up its station with the other troop-ships, much to the relief of all on board! By the time the convoy arrived at Aden to refuel, most of the aircrew were sleeping on deck. As it became more apparent the ship was having trouble maintaining its convoy speed, spending time below decks had not become a popular option. A lone ship was easy prey for U-boats and to be caught below decks during a torpedo attack did not increase chances of survival should the ship sink.

Eventually, on the last leg of the journey, they moved through the Straights of Bab-el-Mandeb and into the Red Sea where the ship lost the convoy completely; a beer issue helped to take their minds off submarines a little, although on 18th March, Hugh noted with some alarm that the ship had been overtaken by a rather tired looking owl and estimated the ship's speed at 1 knot! Nevertheless, two days later the ship docked at Suez and a very relieved group of aircrew disembarked for Kasfareet. The *City of Paris* was finally scrapped in 1956 and many of those who travelled on her while she was a troopship would have been more than pleased to see her scrapped much earlier.

The accommodation at Kasfareet was largely tents although the pilots noted with some relief they were in a building, which was just as well, as wind, dust and rain greeted their arrival. It was at Kasfareet that the extent of the log jam of qualified pilots became apparent. By 1943 the Joint Air Training Plan in South Africa was turning out large numbers of aircrew from its numerous training schools. Having overcome the aircraft maintenance problems, the number of pilots graduating from Service Flying Training Schools such as 27 Air School was impressive. By the end of 1943, over two thousand pilots had qualified in addition to the four thousand navigators and air bombers. Personnel Transit Centres such as Kasfareet were becoming full of aircrew awaiting postings to operational training units. Nevertheless, being close to Cairo and the Pyramids they took full advantage of the tourist opportunities arranged for them, which helped pass the time, but it was obvious they were impatient to begin flying again.

It was not until May 1943 that Hugh and the others were at long last face-to-face with the aircraft they all wanted to fly: the Supermarine Spitfire. There had been some doubt about this, as the Kittyhawk Wing operating in the Western Desert was short of pilots and some of those who had hoped to fly Spitfires were selected to

8. The Curtiss P-40 was an American single-engine, single-seat fighter and ground attack aircraft which first flew in 1938, and was used by the RAF mainly in North Africa.

train on the Curtiss Kittyhawk[8] and in due course ended up with 112 Squadron who sported the prominent shark's teeth insignia on their aircraft. For Hugh, there was only one fighter he wanted to fly and, after his posting to 73 Operational Training Unit, he achieved his dream and went solo in a Spitfire on Empire Day 1943.

At Abu Sueir, all flying took place between 5.30am and 1pm. There was no flying on Sundays and after flying was finished the remainder of the day was free. Here he was taught the squadron tactics of battle formation flying, dog-fighting and ground attacks using the cab rank system[9]; something he would later put to good effect in 1945, flying with 74 Squadron in Belgium and Germany. The Chief Flying Instructor was Squadron Leader Neville Duke[10], later to become the chief test pilot with the Hawker Aircraft Company. Duke, a veteran fighter pilot who was credited with numerous 'kills', set high standards and instigated a flying programme designed to give the novice pilots the greatest chance of survival in air combat. Duke's record was impressive. His first DFC was gazetted in March, 1942 and his second in February 1943, with his DSO being awarded two months later, in April 1943. He also received a third DFC in June, 1944 and the AFC in June, 1948.

Hugh's log book records some fifty hours intensive flying in Spitfires, some of which were not without incident. On one occasion, having been airborne for over an hour working on the Fluid 4 fighter tactic, he made a good landing but a tyre burst on the undercarriage causing the aircraft to end up on its nose. Following the customary completion of reports, he was fortunately cleared of all blame. Others were not so lucky:

Friday 14th
Cross country with 2/Lt. Hough, ex 27 Air School, good fun and some really low flying. Bongo Scales pranged in a Kittyhawk and washed out! Hell of a bind from the

9. The cab rank system gave two-way communications between air and ground forces that would identify strategic targets. Ground forces would call up aircraft rather like hailing a cab.
10. Squadron Leader Neville Frederick Duke DSO, OBE, DFC & Two Bars, AFC (1922 –2007) He was the top Allied flying ace in the Mediterranean Theatre, having shot down at least 27 enemy aircraft, and was acknowledged as one of the world's foremost test pilots after the war. In 1953, he became holder of the world air speed record when he flew a Hawker Hunter F Mk3 at 727.63 mph.

C.O. Apparently one crash and your wings are gone! Then in the afternoon another prang, Sgt. Cotton!!

Saturday 15th
Band pranged in a Spitfire but OK. Washed out.

For pilots to be washed out at this stage of training was very bad luck indeed. It usually resulted in remustering and being trans-ferred to a bomber operational training unit or to Transport Command, a bitter pill to swallow after flying fighters! Even with this threat hanging over them, accidents continued to take place. In early June, a South African pilot, Lieutenant Orchard, was court martialled after a taxying accident and Hugh burst another tyre after landing, this time without damage to the aircraft. Life at 73 OTU was hard work, but the pilots were allowed their freedom providing they didn't break the rules. The usual youthful exuberance was tolerated, but any occurrence of poor flying discipline was quickly dealt with:

Friday 18th
Final cross country exercise which was very very good and enjoyed by everyone. On return to the aerodrome we pulled off a low level shoot-up, there was hell to pay. Punished by having to walk round the perimeter of the aerodrome carrying our parachutes, all twelve of us! Very hot and very tiring.

They were lucky not to have been court martialled as Geoff Crawford had been in 1940, but with a posting only days away, this undisciplined display of flying was dealt with leniently and, as Hugh said, they could hardly sack all twelve of us!

The new course had already arrived at Abu Sueir and in the space of the next two weeks those who had successfully completed their OTU training found themselves first at 22 Personnel Centre at Almaza and then at 40 PTC at Azizia. They hardly had time to unpack before they were posted again to 53 RSU at Sorman in North Africa, where they found another one hundred and fifty Spitfire pilots also waiting for squadron postings! RSU Sorman supplied replacement pilots to 322 and 324 Fighter Wings and provided additional flying time on Spitfire Mark Vs and IXs.

Hugh records plenty of dogfighting and formation flying in his logbook and on numerous occasions he was flying over the sea, which was a new experience with its own set of dangers. On 5th August, he records using the K Type Dinghy on his parachute harness for the first time and noted how uncomfortable it could be on long flights to be sitting on both parachute and dinghy.

The dinghy pack was vital if pilots had to bale out over the sea. It was attached to the pilot's Mae West so it could not float away after the parachute harness had been released. By late 1943, air sea rescue services in the Mediterranean theatre of war had developed significantly from the meagre resources that had been available three years previously. With the invasion of Sicily underway and the increase in Allied air operations over the sea, No. 254 ASRU[11] with its 68-foot high speed launches arrived from the UK and added significant support to the ASR operation already in place. This improvement in the rescue capability was reassuring for aircrew; had Hugh ditched or baled out over the sea and survived, his chances of being found and picked up were greatly increased. Spitfire pilots were advised to bale out if possible, rather than ditch the aircraft as, being nose heavy, the Spitfire tended to dive beneath the surface very quickly and a number of fatal accidents had resulted from this submarine-like characteristic.

At Sorman, Hugh received news of Dave Edye,[12] who had been posted to 142 Squadron as a Sergeant air bomber. The squadron was involved in the bombing campaign over Sicily and the Italian mainland, flying the Wellington medium bomber. The letter from Dave's mother had been halfway round the African continent before finally catching up with him. It was sad news. Dave had been killed on operations over Italy on 30th April 1943. He was 19 years old and was the first of the Edinburgh cadets to be killed in action. Hugh continued to write to Dorothy Edye until well after the war.

Once the Sicily landings had been established, the ground forces of Operation Husky overran the large Italian airfield complex at Lentini. Almost immediately 322 and 324 Wing began operations

11. Air Sea Rescue Unit
12. Sergeant David Vincent Edye is commemorated in the El Alia Cemetery, Algeria and on the East Grinstead War Memorial in Surrey.

from the airfield. Replacement pilots from Sorman brought the squadrons back up to strength in preparation for the Italian campaign that would begin in early September. In late August, Jimmy James and Neil Gray, both ex-27 Air School, were posted to 93 Squadron. Hugh and Dennis Howling[13] were on the same transport, both destined for 81 Squadron.

Flying via Castell Benito, they landed at Lentini West, home to nearly ten Spitfire squadrons. 81 Squadron, flying a mixture of Spitfire Vbs and IXs, had already seen considerable action since their arrival on the island. A week before Hugh arrived, 322 Wing, led by its Wing Leader Colin Gray, had been involved in a sweep of the Milazzo area on the island's north-east coast where they intercepted and shot down twenty-one Junkers 52 transport aircraft attempting to supply German forces. They also shot down five of the escorting fighters including the Me109 of Heinz-Edgar Berres[14], a pilot of the renowned Jagdgeschwader 27 with fifty-two kills to his credit. The new boys had certainly got themselves into some action.

Hugh's first squadron flight was with Dennis Howling under the umbrella of their flight commander. It was essentially a local pinpointing exercise to familiarise the new pilots with the area and probably for the flight commander to get a good look at his new charges in the air. The 81 Squadron pilots had a reputation for aggressive flying, the squadron's Spitfires were distinctive with red spinners and the Ace of Spades painted on the cowling. The next day he flew patrols over the north of the Island but, to his disappointment, both he and Hector were stood down for the squadron show on 28th August and placed on readiness. The operation was successful and the diary notes the squadron's total of four confirmed kills and no losses.

On 29th August, all operations were abandoned as heavy rain swamped the airfield generating a sea of mud. This persisted into the next day and, despite all available personnel on mud-clearing duties, further rain prevented any flying. However, by 31st August, although the airfield was still very muddy the squadron was tasked for an operational sortie to attack and destroy enemy shipping. Hugh describes it in his diary:

13. Sergeant Pilot Dennis Howling survived the war.
14. Heinz-Edgar Berres (1929-1943) was credited with 52 victories in 354 missions.

Taking off the wheels get bogged in the mud and the aircraft goes over on its back and I feel a sharp pain in my back. Damn, Damn, Damn!

Having already had success in finding the record of Douglas' crash and being aware that a number of aircraft accident reports for 1939-1945 were held at the RAF Museum in Hendon, I emailed the museum with details of the accident, in the hope that Hugh's might still be available. A few weeks later a copy of Hugh's accident report arrived in the post. The report recorded the poor state of the runway and noted that Hugh was flying a Spitfire Vb[15] which was a complete write-off. The sharp pain in his back came from two broken vertebrae, which was confirmed by X-Ray at 30 Mobile Field Hospital, located close to the airfield. Evacuated the next day, he found himself being flown to Tunis via Malta in a DC3. To his surprise the familiar face of Andrew Frazer was in the driving seat. Andrew was an old school friend from Wellington and had been on the *Otranto* with Hugh in 1942. Andrew left him in Tunis, promising to visit him in hospital.

Number 1 RAF Hospital occupied the Maison Lavigerie missionary hospital buildings on Byrsa Hill, overlooking the ancient site of Carthage. The more serious cases were treated in the main building while other less serious cases were accommodated in tents and Nissan-type huts below. Maison Lavigerie, as it was then, was part of the Cathedral of St. Louis complex of buildings built by the French in 1890 and had long been established as a hospital run by the Missionary Sisters of Our Lady of Africa (White Sisters). When Hugh arrived, he was admitted to a ward in the main building. His hopes of getting back to the squadron quickly were dashed with the news that he would be in plaster from chin to hip for at least three months and would be moved to the orthopaedic ward. The orthopaedic ward was an ex-German tent with no flysheet and open to wind and rain:

Tuesday 7th
I move down to the tents, I'm now being treated as

15. Spitfire LZ 847 was a Category E write-off but the engine was only Category B and repairable.

convalescent. The tents are lousy accommodation, washing and latrines are not good and we queue for meals, washing our own plates in cold greasy water. Am I really going to be here for three months?

The answer to his question was no, but it would be two months before he was on his way back to the UK. A week later, one of the 81 Squadron pilots arrived with malaria. Sergeant Sandy McDonald had news of the squadron's latest engagements and gave a graphic account of the four FW190s[16] that had recently been shot down by squadron pilots. Hugh was still hoping to return to the squadron once the plaster had been removed and the steady stream of pilots from 322 Wing arriving at the hospital with malaria or injury not only kept him in touch with what was going on across the water in Sicily, but also served to fuel his frustration. He must have known that his chances of returning to 81 Squadron were slim, a view which was shared by the medical staff:

> Told by the Squadron Leader Medic that I would be three more months in plaster which will make a total of four months! I told him that I would be a lunatic by then if I was left in this place. He also told me that when the hospital moves to Italy I will probably be sent home to England. Now I know I'm going to be out of it, I hope to get home.

And so it was. Resigned to the fact his flying was temporarily over and excited by the fact he was now going home, he left the leaking tent at Carthage in October 1943 and was flown to No. 2 RAF Hospital in Algiers at Maison Carree, where he was delighted to find several old friends from 73 OTU and Sorman, who were also awaiting transportation back to England. Amid rumours they were destined for air evacuation, they were moved down the coast to a convalescent unit in the small seaside village of Guyotville. Run by the British Red Cross Society, this pleasantly situated centre provided good quality accommodation and medical support for aircrew and Royal Navy submarine crews recovering from illness

---

16. The Focke-Wulf Fw 190 was widely regarded as Germany's best fighter.

and injury. For the next fortnight they sat in the sun on the terrace of their villa and whiled away their time in Algiers and in the local estaminet until it was time to board the *SS Samaria* on the final leg of the journey home.

———

The *Samaria* was an ex-Cunard Line steamer of nearly 20,000 tons and a huge improvement on the cramped squalor of the *SS City of Paris*. That evening they passed through the straights of Gibraltar and a week later Hugh was back in Liverpool, a shadow of his former self! He had now completed an entire circumnavigation of the African continent since setting out for South Africa in 1942. Still in plaster he was transferred to the Hoylake Rehabilitation Centre near Liverpool, next to the Hoylake Golf Course. His plaster was finally cut off on 20th November, which he celebrated with a film in a West Kirby cinema and chips and beer afterwards.

A letter from Dennis Howling in January 1944 provided the latest information about 81 Squadron and the news that the squadron was moving to Burma as part of the new Third Tactical Air Force to support the offensive against the Japanese in the Burma campaign. Had Hugh remained with the squadron and survived the fierce air battles over Italy he would in all probability have gone with them to join 165 Wing at Ramu. For Neil Gray,[17] who remained in the Mediterranean theatre and was one of Hugh's close friends at 27 Air School, luck ran out on April 1944, when he was shot down and killed flying with 93 Squadron over the Anzio bridgehead in Italy. The fortunes of war and the hand of fate had decided otherwise for Hugh, and he was now destined to remain in Europe until the end of hostilities.

No. 2 Tactical Exercise Unit at Baldoro Bridge in Scotland was very different from the heat and dust of the Middle East. Hugh had no experience of British weather conditions or flying in the blackout and had not been in a cockpit for nearly six months. As an advanced flying unit, Baldoro Bridge was designed to acclimatise pilots

17. Flying Officer Neil Gray was killed in action on 12th April 1944, aged 20. He is commemorated at the Beach Head War Cemetery, Anzio.

returning from overseas or from periods of non-operational duty before being posted to operational squadrons.

The airfield was coated in snow when Hugh arrived and after the preliminary chat with the Chief Flying Instructor he found himself being checked out in the familiar Miles Master II. Back on the ground he was declared competent and, after a short introduction and cockpit check, immediately went onto flying a Hurricane I. This was another new experience for him. Noting in his diary that the aircraft was very aerobatic but had no guts in her, in his view there was no comparison to the Spitfire. His logbook records five hours on Hurricanes and another three flying a Spitfire 1b. When the weather allowed they flew tactical formations, chased each other in low level dogfights, flew attacking and evasive drills using a camera gun and practised air firing. On the ground they improved their shooting eye with clay pigeon shooting and claimed to have found the best scones in Kinross. The inevitable posting brought all these fun and games to an end and this time it was to 278 Squadron based at Coltishall in Norfolk:

> *Friday 17th*
> Get up just in time for a rather ropey breakfast and spend all morning chasing around getting clearances. Hand in flying boots. Catch the 18.20 train with Chuck Freeman, Sid Ainsley and Harry Harrison, twelve bits of kit between us, and change at Falkirk and Polmont to get to Edinburgh. Unload and load kit between us each time. We have a meal in Edinburgh and catch the 22.20 train, huge crush and only just get seats. Rough journey, we change at Ely, Norwich and Wroxham, eventually arriving at Coltishall at 3pm on the 18th. Walk to camp and find billets, have a meal and a bath and to bed.

Hugh noted with some dismay that the squadron was an air sea rescue unit but then, with some relief, learned that in addition to the Walrus and Anson aircraft already on strength, the squadron was to be re-equipped with Spitfires. 278 Squadron was first formed in October 1941 from an ASR[18] flight at Matlask for ASR duties off the

18. Air Sea Rescue

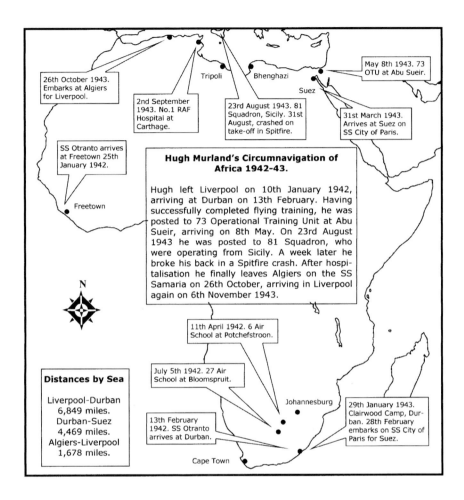

26th October 1943. Embarks at Algiers for Liverpool.

Tripoli

Bhenghazi

Suez

May 8th 1943. 73 OTU at Abu Sueir.

2nd September 1943. No.1 RAF Hospital at Carthage.

23rd August 1943. 81 Squadron, Sicily. 31st August, crashed on take-off in Spitfire.

31st March 1943. Arrives at Suez on SS City of Paris.

SS Otranto arrives at Freetown 25th January 1942.

Freetown

Hugh Murland's Circumnavigation of Africa 1942-43.

Hugh left Liverpool on 10th January 1942, arriving at Durban on 13th February. Having successfully completed flying training, he was posted to 73 Operational Training Unit at Abu Sueir, arriving on 8th May. On 23rd August 1943 he was posted to 81 Squadron, who were operating from Sicily. A week later he broke his back in a Spitfire crash. After hospitalisation he finally leaves Algiers on the SS Samaria on 26th October, arriving in Liverpool again on 6th November 1943.

N

11th April 1942. 6 Air School at Potchefstroon.

Distances by Sea

Liverpool-Durban
6,849 miles.
Durban-Suez
4,469 miles.
Algiers-Liverpool
1,678 miles.

July 5th 1942. 27 Air School at Bloomspruit.

Johannesburg

29th January 1943. Clairwood Camp, Durban. 28th February embarks on SS City of Paris for Suez.

13th February 1942. SS Otranto arrives at Durban.

Cape Town

East Anglian coast, as part of the huge increase in ASR resources required to rescue aircrew who came down in the sea. Any flying operations leaving the UK mainland would involve two flights over the sea. Aircraft in trouble would inevitably endeavour to reach home and in some cases, if they were close to the English coast, preferred to risk ditching to baling out over enemy territory and spending the remainder of the conflict in captivity.

Captivity was something that had already become reality for Peter Boyle,[19] another of the Edinburgh cadets. Flying as Captain of

19. Flying Officer P.N. Boyle was shot down on 21st December 1943. He remained in the RAF after the war and was killed in a flying accident in 1959.

his Lancaster[20] with 50 Squadron on a bombing run to Frankfurt in December 1943, his aircraft was shot down and crashed near Bodenrode in Germany. Peter was one of only four who survived and spent the remainder of the war in Stalag Luft 3 at Sagan.

Coming down in the sea was a hazardous business and despite the increased effectiveness of ASR missions and the growing success rate of crews retrieved from the sea, there were still too many who disappeared without trace. The role of the 278 Squadron Spitfires would be to provide fighter protection for the Walrus[21] amphibians and search and location operations to pinpoint aircrew that were afloat in dinghies. Many of these operational flights were undertaken at very low level and often within sight of the enemy coast, and consequently there was always the risk of being bounced by enemy fighters. The Spitfire IICs that the squadron were to fly (later, ASR Mk II) had been adapted for air sea rescue duties, with 1,240 hp Merlin XX in place of Merlin XII and with rescue packs in the flare chutes and marker bombs under the port wing. 12th April 1944, was Hugh's twenty-first birthday:

> My 21st but not much to tell it by, one letter from home and a telegram from Dad. At 14.30 five Spitfire pilots were summoned to dispersal and the squadron is moving to Martlesham Heath in Suffolk at last, and with Spits. Whit Whittacker has to stay behind with Chuck Freeman and bring the Anson down later with our kit. Arrive Martlesham late afternoon, have tea and find billets. Drinking in the mess later.

Martlesham Heath was also home to the American 356th Fighter Group who flew fighter escorts to the daily American daylight bombing raids over the German mainland in their P-47 Thunderbolts. On arrival at the 'Heath' the 278 Squadron pilots were sent almost immediately on flying sector patrols, being tasked for search and rescue operations. Many of Hugh's logbook entries show

20. Lancaster III serial DV234, code VN-M, took off from RAF Skellingthorpe and was shot down on 20th December 1943.
21. Supermarine Walrus - Single-engined reconnaissance seaplane used extensively in ASR Units.

long flights trying to locate small dinghies. Where they were successful, one of the squadron's Walruses would attempt a pick-up. There were numerous occasions when the sheer number of aircrew being picked up prevented the Walrus from taking off again.

On 22nd April, Sergeant Wally Hammond, flying a Walrus, landed on the sea to pick up the crew of an American B17 that had been located earlier in the day. Unable to take off again with ten American aircrew packed into the fuselage, he had no alternative but to taxi back from the Dutch coast on the surface until he was taken in tow a few miles off Felixstowe some ten hours later. He was later awarded the DFM[22] for this very courageous act.

In May the squadron received their new Spitfire IXs and were heavily involved in the D-Day operations providing ASR cover. Later that month, one flight of the squadron was moved down to Warmwell to support 277 Squadron. Hugh went with them:

> *Thursday 22nd*
> Wizard day. After the first flip I landed with only seven gallons left in the tanks! On from 1pm with Spike and flying most of the time. We picked up an American Thunderbolt pilot who I had seen bale out earlier. Nosing around Alderney and Cherbourg. Arrived back at base after last flip at 11.15 and had to land on the flare path. Later I saw the pilot we had picked up and was thanked by him.

The next day they were airborne again:

> Up at 04.30 and on readiness. Standing by and then tasked for search around Cherbourg sector. Found a dead body in the water, marked it but had to return through fuel shortage.

In September 1944, the Squadron was again involved in providing ASR cover for invading allied forces. This time it was Operation Market Garden, the airborne assault on Arnhem involving both parachute and glider-borne troops. From Martlesham, those on

22. Distinguished Flying Medal.

the ground watched the hundreds of gliders being towed across to Holland, while the squadron's Spitfire pilots provided relays of cover to locate gliders that had come down in the sea. Such was the effectiveness of the planning for this operation that the troops in many of the gliders that had to ditch were located and picked up very quickly. The squadron recorded one of its busiest periods during this time. A day later, the weather closed in for the remainder of the week which would have made successful search and rescue far more difficult to accomplish. Flying low over the sea in poor visibility, while constantly scanning the surface for downed aircrew, was both hazardous and very tiring:

> *Friday 7th*
> Scrambled at 08.55 and found the cloud base very low, some 500 feet or less. Searched 70 miles out but no joy in such poor viz. We patrol sector and pancake at 10.35. There was no horizon visible the whole time and I found it rather a strain flying and searching low over the sea. Very tired on return. Released 2100hrs.

On 5th October 1944, Hugh and Vic Vickery were scrambled to search for an American Mustang pilot from the 339th Fighter Group who had baled out and was reported to be unable to get into his dinghy. The pilot was Second Lieutenant Steve Ananian, who still vividly remembers the experience:

> I was flat on my back, struggling to dump the chute, and swallowing the North Sea like a pint of Half and Half at the Checkers [the local Pub back at Fowlmere] I was in real trouble and on the verge of drowning…I could not climb into the raft because the chute went down and started to pull me under. I just hung on to the raft for my life.[23]

The American had been unable to release his parachute harness and the canopy was doing its best to pull him below the surface. For

23. Personal correspondence with the author and www.littlefriends.co.uk

the next hour he fought to keep himself above water by clinging onto his dinghy. Hugh and Vic were having trouble locating him, as the American Search and Rescue aircraft had dropped several dinghies in the hope that the downed pilot could get into one of them. This in fact delayed the rescue operation while the two Spitfires located and destroyed each of the empty dinghies until they finally spotted Ananian.

Once the American pilot had been found, Warrant Officer Bedford and Leading Airman Westbrook were able to land their Walrus HD 933 in very heavy seas and secure the ailing pilot, before transferring him to the trawler *HMS George Adgell*. On attempting to take off the Walrus lost its port float and, despite being taken in tow, turned turtle and sank before reaching the coast. Steve Ananian had been in the water for over an hour and was lucky to be alive. It was also his first mission! Despite this rather wet introduction to operational flying, he was back in the air with the 339th two days later.

Martlesham Heath pilots had traditionally migrated to the popular Bull Hotel in nearby Woodbridge, and 278 Squadron were happy to carry on with this custom. Woodbridge provided a number of pubs within a short distance of each other and the Bull, managed by my grandparent's Douglas and Margery Watts, was also the venue for regular dances. Douglas and Margery's daughter was a staff nurse in the general hospital at Ipswich, and through her contacts, there was a steady stream of nurses from the hospital who were happy to meet the fighter pilots from the 'Heath' and other nearby RAF stations. It seemed inevitable that Hugh would meet Adrienne Watts. They met at a dance in April 1944 and from that moment they were almost inseparable.

The Bull soon became a second home to the 278 Squadron pilots; they would stay overnight, eat egg and chip dinners in the hotel kitchen, help out in the hotel garden and were often seen serving behind the bar. Regular visitors to the Bull were Johnnie Beattie,[24] a New Zealand pilot who became a close friend of Adrienne and Hugh, Sid Ainsley, Wally Hammond, who later married Dusty, a nurse colleague of Adrienne's, Harry Harrison, an

---

24. Flying Officer John Nesbitt Beattie was killed on 9th February 1945. He was 22 years old and came from Auckland, New Zealand. He is buried at Brookwood Military Cemetery near Woking.

Australian pilot, Vic Vickery and Whit Whittacker. During this period there were numerous occasions that Adrienne remembered of Hugh flying low over the Bull, after returning from an operational flight, to announce his imminent arrival in the hotel bar some forty five minutes later.

In July 1944, Hugh was commissioned, along with Johnnie Beattie and Harry Harrison. With Allied forces now established in Europe, any aircraft in difficulties after operations over Germany now had the opportunity of landing at airfields in the Allied sector or baling out in the knowledge they would not have to try and evade capture. There was now no need to fly home over the sea with the aircraft in a critical condition. With these changing circumstances, the 278 Squadron Spitfires were going elsewhere, the pilots being required to replace losses in the front-line fighter squadrons that were supporting advancing ground forces.

In early 1945 Harry Harrison was posted to 127 Squadron and found himself on the Norwegian 132 Wing flying Spitfires. Hugh went to 74 'Tiger' Squadron, which was part of the predominately French 145 Wing, and Sid Ainsley to 181 Squadron flying the temperamental Hawker Typhoon. Johnnie Beattie had also been destined for the same squadron, but tragically, he was killed on his first Typhoon solo flight while still at 83 Group Support Unit.

No. 74 Squadron had landed on French soil in August, 1944, flying their first sorties from Sommerveieux, just outside Bayeux, the home of the famous tapestry. It was during this period that Sparks Parker,[25] another ex-27 Air School pilot who completed flying training with Hugh, had been killed on a squadron sortie near Rouen, his aircraft crash landing after being hit by ground fire. Hugh would not learn about his death until he joined the squadron.

The final fifteen months of the war leading up to the cessation of hostilities in Europe were very costly for Fighter Command,[26]

25. Flying Officer Alan Mackinlay Parker was killed in action on 25th August 1944. He is buried in Massey Churchyard, 23 miles north east of Rouen.
26. In 1943, RAF Fighter Command was retitled 'Air Defence Great Britain' until October 1944 when the name RAF Fighter Command was used again.

with some two and a half thousand aircraft lost to enemy action. By 1945, German anti aircraft gunners were proving to be very effective in their defensive barrages and the vast majority of flying casualties experienced by the front-line fighter squadrons were as a result of this often deadly flak.

181 Squadron was particularly hard hit. Between December 1944 and May 1945 they lost fourteen Typhoons and twelve of the squadron's pilots were killed or taken prisoner. One of the more fortunate was Sid Ainsley, who survived a forced landing near Enschede on 31st March, after being hit by flak. Pilots successfully baling out or surviving a crash landing also ran the risk of summary execution by German ground forces, or even by the German civilian population, once the Allied forces had taken the war across the Rhine. Tragically this had already happened to Dennis Burman,[27] one of the New Zealand pilots flying with 74 Squadron. He fell foul of enemy ground forces on 16th August 1944, and was shot out of hand by the Waffen-SS[28] after baling out near Douai.

Since Sommervieux, the squadron had progressively moved forward with the advancing Allied forces as part of the 2nd Tactical Air Force, and by the time Hugh arrived on 21st January the squadron had been based at Deurne near Antwerp for nearly two months. The weather was dreadful; snow and freezing temperatures had effectively grounded their Spitfire IXs, giving them a short period of respite from the hard routine of eat, sleep and fly they had been in since November.

Initially Hugh was billeted locally, and then a week later some of the squadron pilots moved into Antwerp to take up residence in the Hotel Century. Antwerp and its adjacent port was at this time being treated to a sustained V1 and V2 attack, and there was a constant risk of one of these projectiles landing close to where you were. On one occasion Hugh and some colleagues had the unsettling experience of watching V1s flying below them from their top floor Hotel Century windows!

The thaw started on 1st February and operational flying

---

27. Warrant Officer Dennis Cecil Burman was 22 when he was executed by German ground forces on 16th August 1944. He came from Invercargill, New Zealand. He is buried at Biache-St-Vaast Communal Cemetry, near Arras.
28. The Waffen-SS ('Armed SS') was the combat arm of the Schutzstaffel.

resumed the next day with the loss of Frank Hardman,[29] who crashed in flames behind enemy lines near Zaltbommel during a raid on an Army HQ. Flying Officer John Bennett remembered Hardman being hit by flak:

> Frank Hardman was flying on my port side as we weaved our way in line abreast through the flak. When he started to fall like a leaf we were all yelling at him to bale out, but we lost sight of him.[30]

A week later the squadron moved again, this time to Schijndel in support of Operation Veritable. Air Chief Marshal Tedder[31] visited the squadron on 7th February as part of a high level briefing to underline the importance of the coming offensive, which was focussed on driving the enemy back over the Rhine. Launched the next day, it was hard going and progress was not easy; mud and flooded ground hampered the advance and at times troops floundered through water several feet deep. Furthermore, the American drive from the south was held up and the enemy was able to reinforce his positions. Nevertheless, the outer defences of the Siegfried Line fell, and Allied troops were able to achieve significant gains. Subsequently, in a foot-by-foot advance through the Reichswald Forest and the water-logged countryside, the British and Canadian soldiers fought their way forward until, on 21st February, they had cracked the much-vaunted Siegfried Line.

Hugh's logbook provides precise detail of his part in this battle. On 8th February, as part of the squadron's opening show, he flew two armed reconnaissances led by Flight Lieutenant Pat Preet, the A Flight commander. Tasked to shoot up anything that moved and destroy enemy communications, the squadron's aircraft were armed with one 500lb and two 250lb bombs in addition to the standard 20mm Hispano cannon and 0.5 calibre machine guns. On occasions,

29. Flight Lieutenant Frank Hardman aged 26 from Auckland, New Zealand. Shot down on 2nd February 1945. He is buried in the Wadenoijen Protestant Churchyard.
30. Personal correspondence with the author.
31. Later, Marshal of the Royal Air Force Arthur William Tedder, 1st Baron Tedder of Glenguin, GCB (1890–1967)

in place of the two 250lb bombs, the Spitfires were fitted with rockets which were not popular with the pilots, as not only were they largely inaccurate, but they also seemed to have a mind of their own! Hugh wrote of occasions when:

> Suddenly, from the back of a formation, a rocket would launch itself spontaneously (or so the offending pilot would have us believe!) and you would undergo the unnerving experience of seeing a missile whistling past your ear! Any spontaneous launchings were caused by electrical faults.

The squadron was airborne whenever weather permitted and individual pilots often flew twice each day. Front-line patrols in fighting pairs were very successful in keeping Me 109s away from harassing the troops on the ground, but there was always the danger of getting bounced by marauding enemy aircraft. On 13th April, Joe Eyre became separated from his wingman in cloud and, while heading back to base on his own, was attacked by four Me109s. Fortunately he found cloud again before they could inflict any serious damage and escaped unhurt. Hugh was flying at the time with the Squadron CO, Squadron Leader Tony Reeves, on an armed reconnaissance. Reeves heard the call for assistance from Eyre but by the time they arrived the 109s had disappeared, leaving a very lucky Eyre to be escorted home.

The role of the Spitfire as a fighter bomber in the closing stages of the war was no better illustrated than by the squadron's two attacks on the village of Hassum near the Reichswald Forest. The allied advance was being held up by a German infantry battalion dug in and around the village. Flying at low level, the squadron delivered a crushing blow to the German ground forces, reducing most of the buildings to rubble and strafing fleeing troops as they sought cover. Hugh notes in his logbook that his 500lb bomb hit the target and there was no flak. A later repeat of this sortie contributed much to the eventual surrender of German forces in Hassum and to the Canadian forward advance. In April the pilots were invited by the Army to visit the village to see the damage they had inflicted. Hugh was in the party:

We go to Hassum to see for ourselves the damage from our bombing. Little wonder they threw the towel in after our visits. Army very pleased with us.

With Operation Veritable having achieved all of its strategic aims, the squadron continued to fly against German communications and troop movements, but even with virtual air supremacy these missions were not without considerable danger from ground fire:

Wednesday 21st
Weather duff in the morning and on readiness for afternoon recce. Tasked to Geldern to Venlo railway line. 1X500lb and 2X250lb bombs. Later a second run to the Zwolle to Meppel line. Also fired two rockets. Wizard day. 2.05hrs flying.

Sunday 25th
Armed recce to Arnhem-Wesel-Zutphen railway line and later similar again. Bill Cortis and Ivan Butler missing. Bill later a POW but Butler killed after crash landing.

Bill Cortis had been badly injured after crash landing and was eventually liberated by advancing troops in early April when they overran a German military hospital. He briefly returned to the squadron before being packed off home to England. Unfortunately, Ivan Butler[32] was not quite so lucky; he died from head injuries the next day.

In March the squadron was re-equipped with Spitfire XVIs and the blister hood appeared for the first time, giving the pilots enormously increased all-round visibility. Needless to say, this modification was very popular with all the squadron pilots. Hugh continued to fly on a daily basis, attacking mechanised enemy transports on the road, trains and armoured vehicles, as well as flying escort to the numerous bombing raids on enemy strongholds. By

---

32. Warrant Officer Ivan William Butler died from wounds on 26th February 1945, he was 22 years old and came from Auckland, New Zealand. He is buried in the Nederweert War Cemetery.

early April they had to fly with 90 gallon drop fuel tanks slung under the aircrafts' bellies to enable them to reach enemy positions, making for a long round trip:

Monday 9th
Armed recce west of Oldenburgh, 90 gallon tanks on. Hit two trains on the line, bags of flak.

Tuesday 10th
Two very long trips both with 90 gallon tanks on. It's a long way to go these days. Flying for 2.05hrs.

The additional fuel allowed a greater range for the aircraft, but the tanks became a liability if they were unable to be released. On at least one occasion Hugh's tanks remained stubbornly stuck on his Spitfire, putting him at some disadvantage if they happened to meet enemy fighters. There were other problems associated with carrying the additional fuel load, particularly on take-off. The Spitfire was noted for its tremendous torque to starboard on take-off, which has to be corrected with full left rudder and full left rudder trim. With the fuel in the drop tank slopping left and right and the subsequent effect on stability, it was easy to overcorrect and crash on take-off. The pilot's dread was a crash with the plywood drop tanks full of fuel or to be hit by ground fire before the tank had been jettisoned.

Despite the war in Europe drawing rapidly to a close there was still some spirited opposition from the Luftwaffe, and it was not uncommon to be faced by the twin-engined Me 262[33] jet fighter. Squadron pilots were jumped by 262s on more than one occasion but gave good account of themselves and, although no-one was credited with a kill, there were no losses. On 11th April the squadron was successful in destroying five Me109s on the ground and damaging four others, with Hugh recording in his logbook one 'flamer' and two damaged.

---

33. The world's first operational jet-powered fighter. It was mass-produced in World War II and saw action from late summer of 1944 in bomber/reconnaissance and fighter/interceptor roles, almost sharing the title of the first operational jet with the British Gloster Meteor that became operational some weeks later. German pilots nicknamed it the 'Turbo', while the Allies called it the 'Stormbird'. The Me 262 had a negligible impact on the course of the war, shooting down an estimated 150 Allied aircraft for the loss of 100 Me 262s.

Five days later the squadron was moved to Drope, on German soil, enabling them to reach the front-line within fifteen minutes flying time. The squadron was in tents but the grass airstrip was described as 'wizard'. Hugh notes with relief that they were no longer using drop tanks. Within twelve hours of landing they were in action against German railway communications, Hugh's section successfully destroying three locomotives and damaging another. Close support sorties followed, working directly with ground forces, destroying gun positions and hitting fuel dumps and troop concentrations. Such intense low level activity was not without cost: Luke Barnes[34] was posted as 'missing believed killed' on 19th April, making him the squadron's last pilot to be killed in action.

Thursday 19th
Wizard day, very warm, we spend the early part of the morning picking shrapnel off the runway. Armed recce, we get four MET damaged and the section gets three flamers. F/O Barnes missing believed killed.

Tuesday 24th
Two trips, both close support sorties. I get direct hits and see a big explosion, was it petrol? On the second trip I get another direct hit followed by a terrific explosion. On our return we strafe everything moving.

Barnes was hit by ground fire near Oldendorf, his aircraft crash landing into a wood and bursting into flames. This was particularly unlucky as, by the beginning of May, the rumours of a German surrender were finally realised:

Friday 4th
No Flying again, weather duff. We hear the war is over in our sector, big parties all over camp.

Saturday 5th
Weather clearing but no ops to do anyway! I can hardly

34. Flying Officer Luke Barnes was killed in action on 19th April 1945, he was 22 years old. He came from Christchurch, New Zealand. He is buried in Becklingen War Cemetery near Soltau.

believe it, its all over bar the shouting, it seems I'm going to survive it all.

It had indeed finished and he had survived. Armistice was declared on 8th May and, after listening to Churchill's speech on the radio, the squadron received their orders to return to England. They were to lose their Spitfires and begin training on the Gloster Meteor, the RAF's first all-jet fighter. But first they had to get home. Hugh's memories of the day when 74 Squadron left Germany to return to England remained vivid. Years later he told me it was as if he was flying home to begin another life in another world:

> We had flown our last operational sortie a few days earlier. An air of anti-climax still prevailed; we hadn't yet got into the swing of victory celebrations, but we had certainly started to relax. Thanks to the close links with Rheims, established by the other French squadrons in our Wing, Champagne was only a few shillings a bottle. There was still a war to be won in the Far East, but our immediate future lay elsewhere. With pleasure and perhaps unjustified pride we had learned that we were to fly Meteor jet fighters.
>
> Life was full of question marks. How could we attempt to guess what the future might hold, when so many of us had been swept straight from school into action? After four years that involved 30 moves and flying in eleven different countries, could I accept a more static existence? Why had we survived, when so many others had not? There had been just one day when I woke with a strong premonition of death. During that day's operations I had waited for it, but was unscathed. Thereafter I had maintained a stoical fatalism.
>
> We exchanged our Spitfires with those of another squadron [485 Squadron]. Their old warhorses would get us back to England and would probably be put out to grass in some quiet Maintenance Unit. Our Australian and New Zealand fellow pilots were remaining behind, to be repatriated separately. The main ground party had

departed from the airfield leaving a nucleus for the final clear up. For a reason perhaps best known to some equipment officer, it was deemed necessary on the last morning to take down even those tents that were still occupied by the Aussies and Kiwis. So they slept on at the corner of the airfield, their camp beds surrounded by their possessions, folding chairs, canvass washbasins, and all open to the skies.

For the last time we climbed into our warplanes. We would certainly miss the incomparable Spitfire, legendary and lethal yet so graceful and unforgettable. Max our Dutch liaison officer and interpreter, moved from one to the next, saying goodbye. We took off and my engine immediately started misbehaving. Soon I left the formation and landed at Ghent. For two hours the mechanics tinkered with the engine while I sat in the warm sun thinking of the bottles of champagne cooking under the metal covers of the ammunition bays in each wing, the only available storage space in a single seat fighter.

I took off again, and again the engine was misfiring. I headed for Calais and the narrowest bit of sea. No doctor ever studied a heart beat with such close attention as a pilot gives to his single faltering engine. They are as closely connected as Siamese Twins, for the silence of one could easily result in the eternal silence of the other. I was alone, yet not lonely, I felt truly in my element. And thus I crossed my Rubicon. Behind lay the strife and sorrow, boredom and excitement of war. Spreading out below me was the welcoming English countryside. Ahead, the unfamiliar form that beckoned was peace.

Landing in England for a final engine tinkering at Lasham on the Sussex coast, he eventually made it to Colerne on 12th May, where the squadron was to be based with the new jet fighters.

I often wonder if his accident in Sicily was instrumental in his ultimate survival. The air combat over Sicily and Italy during the allied advance was fierce and sustained, with the beleaguered

Lufwaffe fighting hard to support the German ground campaign and ward off the increasing strength of the Allied air forces. 81 Squadron was in daily contact with enemy forces and once they had moved to Burma they again found themselves in the thick of the aerial fighting, this time with the Japanese Army Air Force. It was in Burma that ex 27 Air School pilot Bill Coulter was killed, when Japanese aircraft strafed the airfield and left him dead in the cockpit of his Spitfire.

Had Hugh remained with 81 Squadron he would almost certainly have moved to Burma, as did Dennis Howling and Joe Simpson. Hugh's ten months with 278 Squadron took him away from offensive fighter activity over the European mainland during 1944, but there was always the risk of running into enemy fighters during ASR sorties and ending up in the sea himself. Between January 1943 and June 1944, twenty-eight fighter aircraft were shot down while on ASR sorties with a loss of eighteen pilots. Fortunately, there were no 278 Squadron Spitfire losses recorded during this period.

His war concluded with some intense fighting as the allied forces moved through the Low Countries into Germany. 74 Squadron incurred several losses during this time, mostly due to heavy and accurate ground fire. For Hugh and the other squadron pilots there was the daily possibility of becoming a casualty. Whatever it was that intervened in that fine line between life and death, many of his friends and fellow pilots lost their lives and, of the original Edinburgh University cadets that completed the course in 1941, only six survived to see the armistice.

12

Epilogue

In writing *Departed Warriors* I felt compelled to visit as many of the battlefronts and memorials that are connected to the family as I could. Unfortunately, some are just not possible to visit. It was with some regret that I was unable to travel to Iraq but, at the time of writing, it is a war zone once again and likely to remain a deeply troubled region for some time to come. Nevertheless, I should one day like to visit the Basra Memorial[1] to pay my respects to the many friends of my grandfather that were lost in that gruelling campaign.

I was also advised that visiting Gaza, where Douglas Watts found himself in 1917, was not recommended by the Foreign Office. Sadly, visits to parts of North Africa are not prudent for casual tourists and I have been unable to trace my father's footsteps during his time in Algeria in 1943. The political situation there prevented me from visiting the El Alia Cemetery to leave flowers for Dave Edye. I should like one day to make that journey. Nevertheless, I did manage to visit Tunisia and, in particular, Carthage, where Hugh spent time in hospital recovering from his Spitfire crash. From his photographs I was able to pinpoint almost exactly where the RAF Hospital had been sited.

In contrast, Gallipoli, although a little off the beaten track, is very accessible. My wife, Joan, and I drove down to the peninsula from Istanbul to find Lynton's name at Lone Pine Cemetery and visit

---

1. Until 1997 the Basra Memorial was located on the main quay of the naval dockyard at Maqil, on the west bank of the Shatt-al-Arab, about 8 kilometres north of Basra. Because of the sensitivity of the site, the Memorial was moved by presidential decree. The move, carried out by the authorities in Iraq, involved a considerable amount of manpower, transport costs and sheer engineering on their part, and the Memorial has been re-erected in its entirety. The Basra Memorial is now located 32 kilometres along the road to Nasiriyah.

the ground on which he had fought and died. Lone Pine was a deeply moving experience. It had been almost two years since I had found the photograph of Margery Goode and her two brothers and now, with Lynton's name in front of me, part of the journey was over. I stood there in the bright September sunlight for several minutes, amidst the ghosts of the 15th Battalion, with tears streaming uncontrollably down my face.

Also at Lone Pine is the gravestone of grandfather Murland's friend, Everard Digges La Touché, who died on 6th August with D Company of the 2nd Battalion AIF. He had only been at Anzac for twelve hours, having arrived the night before from Egypt. His name, along with his brother's name, is also on the Newcastle War Memorial in County Down and on a plaque erected in St. Patrick's Cathedral in Dublin by their mother.

Later that day, on the summit of Chunuk Bair, I saw at first hand the terrain the 4th Australian Brigade was faced with on the morning of 7th August and I am not at all surprised at the outcome. Walking in the footsteps of the 15th Battalion it becomes quickly apparent that anything more than a stumbling pace is impossible, as successive deres and thorny tortuous hills are encountered. There is surely an object lesson to be learnt here on the prerequisite for detailed first hand reconnaissance and accurate intelligence before committing troops to the offensive. Lieutenant-Colonel Cannan and the 15th Battalion had no realistic chance of reaching their objective against the huge physical odds facing them. The battleground today is almost as it was ninety years ago and it is still possible to find spent rounds and other relics of the conflict. Sadly, it is also not uncommon to come across human skeletal debris still amongst the scrub.

Further south at Cape Helles, Gully Ravine is still pretty much as it was in 1915 and the front-line positions that my maternal grandfather, Douglas Watts, defended are still recognisable. We visited Lancashire Landing where he came ashore and followed the path the Sussex Yeomanry took to Gully Ravine. The ravine is for most of the year, a dry watercourse running up to the front-line and it was still possible to complete the three mile walk up to Border Barricade. All along the ravine are old trenches and the remnants of dugouts, still visible over 90 years after the last British troops were evacuated. Some of the dugouts would have been constructed by Douglas and the men of his company and used by them up until their evacuation in December 1915. It was in Gully Ravine that they anticipated spending the winter of 1915/16. It must have been with great relief they received the orders to leave.

I have managed to find and visit many of the war graves in Europe that have family and regimental links. Visiting the vast 'silent cities'[2] of the war dead is a poignant reminder of the sacrifice that so many young men made. What has impressed me is the work the Commonwealth War Graves Commission does in maintaining the hundreds of British and Commonwealth war graves around the world. No matter how small or how inaccessible, each cemetery is kept in pristine condition. Typical of these is the British Cemetery at Vailly-sur-Aisne on the north bank of the River Aisne. Buried here is one of grandfather Murland's greatest friends, Captain Robert Frank Hawes, known as Eustace to his friends and family. The news that Eustace had been killed on 24th September 1914, while serving with the 6th Division, reached him in India ten days later:

> Alas I got very bad news at the club in the evening, poor old Hawes of the 1st Leicesters has been killed, one of my best friends. We spent such a long time together at Sandhurst and Belgaum. I just missed seeing him in Dublin this year. He had been married[3] for just a year, poor old Eustace. Long casualty lists at the club containing so many of my friends I have not been noting them down.

The Great War battlefields in France and Belgium are surprisingly intact, with the Somme and Ypres areas, in particular, clearly benefiting from battlefield tourism. In October 2007, I visited the Somme with a group of friends to walk the 1st July British front-line, which took us from the northernmost attack at Gommecourt down through Thiepval to Maricourt in the south. The route on the second

2. Silent Cities is the title of a guidebook to war cemeteries and memorials to the missing in France and Flanders written by Sidney Hurst. The phrase 'silent cities' was first used by Rudyard Kipling when describing the work of the CWGC.
3. He married Norah Rimmer in December 1913.

day of the walk took me past James Davidson's grave at Serre Number 2 Cemetery and to the trenches at Hamel that Archie and the 13th Royal Sussex men occupied in September 1916. Here, we were close to Mailly Maillet Wood where they spent the night before the disastrous 39th Division attack on 3rd September. It was at Hamel that Joan's great-uncle, Charles Weatherill, lost his life on 13th November 1916, serving with the Royal Fusiliers and where her grandfather had served with the Royal Garrison Artillery.

As we descended into the Ancre Valley and crossed the river, we were soon on the Royal Irish Rifles front-line at Thiepval Wood, the point from which Charlie and the 13th Battalion began their attack on that historic morning. Standing at the edge of the wood and looking up the slope ahead, it was difficult to imagine the horror of destruction that unleashed itself on so many young lives that fateful morning. An image difficult to relate to the undisturbed pastoral scene that greeted us.

Climbing up Mill Road, we visited the Ulster Tower memorial which overlooks the battlefield it commemorates. From there, the chalk shadows of the old trench lines were visible in the autumn plough of the surrounding fields. After a short break and a cup of tea with Teddy Colligan, the ever-interesting Belfast born custodian of the Tower, we walked up to visit Albert Uprichard and George Rogers in the Mill Road Cemetery, situated close to the site of the infamous Schwaben Redoubt.

Standing by the gate of Mill Road Cemetery, the imposing Thiepval Memorial dominates the skyline ahead. This is where we found Haughton Smyth, Rex Neill and Cecil Ewart, who have their names listed with the missing on Pier 15. From this vantage point we were not far from Martinsart where Charlie was taken after being found alive in No Man's Land on the night of 1st July. In the Martinsart British Cemetery, buried in the first row of graves, are the fourteen men of Charlie's battalion that were killed in Thiepval Wood on 28th June by a stray enemy shell.

That evening back in Arras we visited the Faubourg d'Amiens Cemetery near the Citadel, where the names of the 10th Hussars and Northamptonshire Yeoman, killed during the battle of Monchy-le-Preux, are commemorated. In Bay 1 I found Second Lieutenant James Goodman, together with the eight men who died on 11th

Epilogue

April and the twenty-eight men of the 10th Hussars who died in their charge from Orange Hill and during the defence of the village perimeter.

The previous year, I had visited the trench lines in the La Bassée area where Archie Goode was wounded at Cuinchy and where Gerald Smyth lost his arm and won his first DSO at Givenchy in 1914. The infamous brickstacks are now on private land so I was unable to see first hand that notorious part of the British front-line. However, just to the west is the small town of Cambrin which, in 1915, was only about 800 yards from the front-line. It was here that Archie was treated for his head wound on 29th May 1916. In the Cambrin Churchyard Extension is the headstone of Edward Punch, the soldier who was wounded with Archie and died later that day.

A couple of miles to the north is the Le Touret Memorial, located in the grounds of Le Touret Military Cemetery, at Festubert. This is probably one of the most striking and moving memorials to the missing I have seen, and is where Barrie Combe has his name commemorated on Panel 1. After leaving Le Touret we moved to Richebourg L'Avoue to try and find the position from where Archie and the 13th Royal Sussex had gone over the top into a hail of machine gun fire. Around Richebourg, the military cemeteries are testament to the enormous casualties the Royal Sussex Regiment sustained during their attack on the Boar's Head Salient. In the nearby Richebourg St Vaast Post Military Cemetery alone, there are eighty-two headstones of Sussex men who were killed on 30th June. After the Armistice in 1918, another seventy-three who had been killed in the Boar's Head attack were brought in from various small isolated burial grounds and re-buried at the Cabaret-Rouge Cemetery at Souchez, some twenty miles to the south. It was a sobering journey to find the site of a battle that few have heard of, but one that left the flower of Sussex youth in permanent memorial.

On the way back to Arras we stopped at the Loos Memorial at Loos-en-Gohelle, a village a few miles north-west of Lens. The memorial is contained within the Dud Corner Cemetery and there, on panels 69 to 73, were the names of the Royal Sussex men whose bodies were never recovered after the Boar's Head attack. The name of Archie's company commander, Cyril Humble-Crofts, together with Norman Ayling and Robert Agate from West Chiltington are commemorated there.

The next day we drove over to Monchy-le-Preux. I wanted to see where Gerry Murland and his brother Bill had fought and, in particular, I wanted to walk the route of their cavalry charge. Orange Hill and Monchy-le-Preux are clearly visible from the Arras to Cambrai Road, and it is not difficult to appreciate why the village was of such a strategic importance in 1917. Today, Monchy sits astride its hilltop with views out and across the adjacent country-side. The only remaining signs of the furious battles of 1917 and 1918 are the still rows of white headstones that populate the five Commonwealth War Graves Commission Cemeteries surrounding the village. If you walk from Orange Hill, through its quiet streets towards the square, you will come across the memorials to the 37th and 29th Division infantry who fought there. It is a strangely evoca-tive place, full of the ghosts of men and horses. I found the place where Fantail was killed and located the probable position where Bill was wounded. It was impossible to identify exactly where Gerry gathered up the wounded of his regiment and led them to safety, but it must have been somewhere on the western outskirts of the village.

Further north, across the Scarpe River Valley, the slopes of Greenland Hill are visible from Orange Hill. This was the scene of the pre-dawn attack on 3rd May by the 6th Battalion KOSB where Gerald Smyth was wounded yet again and won the bar to his DSO. There also is the 9th (Scottish) Division Memorial at the Point du Jour, constructed with stone brought from Scotland.

From Monchy it was only a short drive to Fifteen Ravine British Cemetery at Villers-Plouich to find Teddy Smyth's headstone. He was never able to wear his Military Cross which was gazetted on 1st January 1918, a month after he was killed at Marcoing. His family and friends in County Down were deeply affected by his death. After hearing the news, grandfather recalled in his diary the occasions when he and Teddy, in the company of Haughton Smyth, had spent time shooting duck and riding in the local hunt together, concluding with:

> Another fine man and brave soul has given his life. I shall always have fond memories of dear Teddy.

Epilogue

Any visit to the Great War battlefields has to include Ypres and the Salient. Today, the perimeter of the old front-line is studded with cemeteries filled with the men who fell in the almost continual and bitter fighting that took place in the four years of war.

Joan's grandfather, Harry, found himself in the Salient on several occasions with the 146 Heavy Battery guns, as did both Gerry and Bill Murland during the first and second Battles of Ypres. The 'Shiny 10th' cavalrymen covered themselves in glory at Zandvoorde and Kleine Zillebeke and I wanted to see for myself the battlegrounds of October and November 1914.

Zandvoorde itself sits on a slight rise and the church is located in the centre of the village. Searching for the fallen of the 10th Hussars, I found four of them buried together in a corner of the Churchyard. There were Frank Rose, Christopher Turnor, Lance Corporal Waugh and Private MacKenzie who had fought alongside Bill on Monday 26th October 1914, in that bloody and costly battle. Turnor was the grandson of the 13th Earl of Westmorland and inside the church of St. Bartolomomeus is a splendid stained glass window that was erected in his memory by the family.

It is not clear exactly where Gerry served with his squadron of the Northamptonshire Yeomanry during the second Battle of Ypres in 1915. All we know is that he was billeted to the west of Ypres and was in action around Pilkem and Hill 60. Second Ypres saw the 10th Hussars in the trenches near one of the most notorious spots in the Salient, Hellfire Corner, on the Menin Road. I found the Frezenberg Ridge where the famous counter-attack of 13th May took place and, later that afternoon, located the valiant Colonel Shearman, his adjutant, Captain Gerald Stewart and Lance Corporal Meads in the Vlamertinghe Military Cemetery to the west of Ypres. Buried here as well is another 10th Hussars officer, Major Clement Freeman-Mitford DSO, who was also killed during that May counter-attack. His father, Lord Redesdale, donated the two sets of iron gates to the cemetery in his honour.

The vast majority of the remaining men of the 10th Hussars were never retrieved from the battlefield and are now among the 54,896 names of the missing that are commemorated on the Menin Gate memorial. Included among the names of the Royal Irish Rifles on Panel 40 of the Gate, I discovered Lieutenant Averill Digges La

Touche, the brother of Everard, who was killed in September 1915 serving with the 2nd Battalion. Back in Ireland, their mother Clementine never really recovered from the shock of both of her boys being killed within weeks of each other.

The Menin Gate is an unforgettable experience, particularly if you are present at the daily Last Post Ceremony. From 11th November 1929, the Last Post has been sounded at the Menin Gate memorial every night and in all weathers. The only exception to this was during the four years of the German occupation of Ypres from 20th May 1940 to 6th September 1944. The daily ceremony was continued in England at the Brookwood Military Cemetery, Surrey. Walking past the names of the missing, I was reminded very much of Will Longstaff's *Menin Gate at Midnight* which he painted in 1927 after attending the unveiling ceremony. His vision of steel-helmeted spirits rising from the moonlit cornfields along the Menin Road, inspired the evocative painting that now hangs in the Australian War Memorial's art collection at Canberra.

South of Ypres, along the road to Armentieres, is the turning to Kemmel. Just past the village, on the Hooghofstraat, is the Wulverghem-Lindenhoek Road Military Cemetery where we found the gallant Holt Waring[4], who was killed on 15th April 1918. An old friend of grandfather's and former commanding officer of the 13th Royal Irish Rifles, he fell during a heavy artillery bombardment while defending the Kemmel front-line near Messines. Four years earlier Holt's younger brother, Ruric Waring, was lost at sea when *HMS Hawke* was sunk off Peterhead by the German submarine U-9 in October 1914. Only 73 out of a crew of 544 were rescued. When the news of Holt's death reached grandfather in India, his diary betrayed a weariness with the war that had not been previously evident:

> Poor Holt Waring has been killed, having survived for so long. All the old families are being wiped out in this bloody war, all my friends.

Soon after her husband's death, Margaret Waring received a

---

4. Major (temp Lieutenant-Colonel) Holt Waring, aged 41. Buried in the Wulverghem-Lindenhoek Road Military Cemetery ref: II.E.7.

letter from Andrew Gibson, a Lurgan man who was serving with the battalion as chaplain. He concluded his letter with:

> Throughout the regiment today wherever one goes, whether amongst officers or men, there is the same voice heard of admiration for his splendid heroism, and deep sorrow that we have lost him. I feel that I do not put into words the courage of the man or do justice to his great personality and the charm of his fine character, as soldier and leader of men. Your husband is one of our most shining examples.

In 1919, when he returned to County Down on leave, grandfather visited Margaret Waring and Mary Combe, both of whom were still grieving for their husbands. Holt and Margaret had been married for four years and had no children. Barrie left two sons.

My visit to the little-known and almost forgotten Italian Front of 1917-18 retraced the route the Northamptonshire Yeomanry took over the Piave River in their 1918 advance to the Tagliamento River crossing. Driving across the Venetian Plain through sleepy Italian villages, I crossed a very dry Piave and headed for the Monticano River. The bridge where Lieutenant Gillespie won his MC has been replaced with a modern road bridge, but the foundations of the original 1918 construction are still visible in the river bed. I had lunch sitting by the river surrounded by vines, wondering how such a peaceful spot could have possibly been host to the violence of October 1918.

Arriving in Sacile later that afternoon, it was difficult to compare the modern bustling town with the Sacile that was the scene of the confrontation with Austrian prisoners. Much of the old town is still more or less intact, despite attempts to modernise it, and I can personally vouch for the quality of the ice creams. Before we left the stifling heat of the plain and headed up into the mountains, we visited the Tezze British Cemetery near Bassano, to find the headstones of four yeomanry troopers who lost their lives on 30th October at Sacile. The youngest of these was 21-year old Thomas Smith, who served with Gerry in A Squadron.

It is only by visiting the war cemeteries and memorials that an impression of the sheer scale of the dead of the two world wars can begin to be appreciated. Although the RAF casualties of 1939-1945 tend to be scattered far and wide, it is at the Air Forces Memorial on the banks of the Thames at Runnymede where the 20,000 names of the aircrew lost from bases in the UK and north west Europe are commemorated. Over 750 aircrew that flew in the Hampden Bomber have their names recorded on the memorial. This is the Menin Gate of the Commonwealth Air Forces and the impact of so many names of young men, who died, despite their fathers' and uncles' sacrifice in the Great War, is a profound one. Although our visit was specifically to find the names of Owen Clarke and Geoffrey Crawford and their crews, as Joan and I wandered through the cloistered walkways, past the sea of names engraved in the stonework, I began to realise perhaps why my father had not shared his wartime experiences with the family. In the midst of the names that surrounded us were many of those he had known at school and flown with in the Middle East and Europe. After visiting Runnymede there was one last visit to make. On a damp February day in 2008 I found myself at the Brookwood Military Cemetery, near Woking, to find Johnnie Beattie, the New Zealand pilot who had flown with Hugh in 278 Squadron and was killed in a flying accident.

—⚔—

With so much of my past linked to County Down, I went back in 2006 to see what was left of the Murland mills and to visit Ardnabannon, Greenvale and the other family homes. This was also an opportunity to meet two individuals who had been extremely helpful in providing me with additional family information. Paul McCandless, the author of *Smyths of the Bann*, had very kindly sent me a copy of his book and spent time with us tracking down the final resting places of the Murlands. Through him we were introduced to Albert Paulson, the owner of the now derelict Murland mills. At his invitation, we were treated to a fascinating guided tour of the mills. It was hard to imagine that in 1887 the now deserted and crumbling buildings played host to 1000 workers in the manufacture of linen.

I had been in contact with local historian, Jason Diamond, for some time via e-mail and soon realised he was something of an authority on the Uprichard and Ferguson families. He was able to fill in some of the gaps I had in my family history and was particularly helpful in identifying individuals and locations in some of grandfather's photographs. Being a Banbridge man, he was able to point us in the direction of the Municipal Cemetery where Gerald and Osbert Smyth are buried.

After the Great War, those that had survived came home again to take up their lives where they had left off. For Warren Murland it meant returning home to the family business, which had been left in the hands of elder brother Jim during the war years. Charlie's work as a procurement agent for the Royal Flying Corps had kept him on the home front, based in Belfast. After being demobbed he had little difficulty in taking up where he had left off in 1915. The Armistice was celebrated widely across the county, and in 1919, at Annsborough, the local press reported a large Union Jack being flown from the tall chimney at the Murland mills:

> ....and a very worthy place for it, too, for few firms have a better war record than Murland's Ltd. Individually each member of the family did his bit, and a bit over. Besides, every returned soldier got his old job back, or a lighter one was found if he was not fit for the old one.

Prosperity continued until the collapse of the Irish linen industry in the 1930s when the family firm was taken over by the Ulster Weaving Company in 1937. Jim, Beatrice and their son Mick[5] continued to live at Ardnabannon until Jim's death in 1942, after which it was sold.

The end of the family business unfortunately produced a rift in the family that was never healed. Both Charlie and my grandfather believed that Jim and Warren had sold out needlessly to the Ulster Weaving Company. I don't think this was necessarily the case, as the business from all accounts, was very much in decline. In fact the

5. James Robert William Murland (1909-1985). Captain, 5th Royal Inniskilling Dragoon Guards, later Lieutenant-Colonel, Royal Engineers, 1944-46. Author of *The Royal Armoured Corps* (Methuen 1942).

original mill had closed down in 1927 and the second mill stopped production three years later. There were also early warning signs that all was not well in 1923, when small firms associated with the industry began to go out of business. A note in grandfather's 1923 diary recorded the demise of several firms, and one in particular, which had connections with the family since 1850.

As far as I am aware, the two sides in the family row never spoke to each other again, which was a great shame since Warren had been best man at both grandfather's wedding in 1920 to Marion Thompson and Charlie's in 1922, to Eleanor Wilson. The rift also denied me the opportunity of meeting all my family and thus delayed the discovery of the full extent of my Irish heritage until much later in life. Warren was married to Susan Mary Ewing in 1925 and moved to Newcastle, County Down, where he died in February 1962. He is buried in the Ewing family plot at St Colman's Church of Ireland, Newcastle. Charlie lived in Belfast for the remainder of his life, where he and Eleanor had two children. After the war he was very much involved in the Royal Irish Rifles Regimental Association and in supporting old soldiers of the 13th Battalion. He died in October 1969, aged 88 and at his request, his ashes were interred in the family vault at Clough.

My grandfather, Howard, remained in the Indian Army, during which time he wrote a comprehensive regimental history of the Madras Pioneers which was first published in 1922 under the title *Ballie Ki Paltan*. He retired in 1928, with the rank of Lieutenant-Colonel, to become a partner in the Wooligooly Coffee plantation near Coorg in southern India, where he was a founder and chairman of the Coffee Grower's Association and a founder member of the Indian Coffee Board. He was awarded an OBE in the King's Birthday Honours in 1942. He and Marion had two girls in addition to my father, and his photo albums are full of pictures of the three children growing up in India and, later, in England. Grandfather died in 1958 in London and my grandmother, Marion, died eight years later aged 73. My last memory of her was of a rather distant old lady who treated us to a cream tea in Richmond Park.

—··—

Epilogue

On 15th November 1918, the Northamptonshire Yeomanry made their last move to Contrabisara, a medieval town north-west of Vincezsa. After a review of the British troops by the King of Italy, they began the process of demobilisation. Gerry was amongst the last group to return home in March 1919, being finally demobbed on 13th March. While he resumed the running of the Badby Estate, Bill was still recovering from wounds received at Honnechy six months earlier. In November 1918, he had been mentioned in despatches for a second time and the long overdue award of the Military Cross came in June 1919. He returned to the regiment in late 1920 sporting a black eye patch, looking more like a buccaneer than a cavalry officer.

The 10th Hussars was by this time based at Curragh in the West of Ireland, where the regiment faced a rather different hostility, this time from the local population and Sinn Fein. For Irishmen like Bill, this was an unpleasant and difficult time, only tempered by the occasional opportunity to indulge in his great passion in life, horse racing. In spite of the debilitating effects of his wounds, which were still giving him some mobility difficulties, in May 1921 he won the Irish Grand Military Steeplehase at Punchestown in an impressive display of cross-country riding. But, as with so many of his contemporaries, the lasting effects of wounds received in battle impacted directly on his quality of life and, in Bill's case, his ability to continue as a regular cavalry officer.

In 1922 he retired from the Army with a gratuity of £1000 to become assistant to the well-known racehorse trainer, George Lambton. Lambton was the fifth son of the Earl of Durham and after Eton and Cambridge, he had some success as an amateur jockey before being appointed trainer to the Earl of Derby in 1893. The two men had much in common and Bill worked with Lambton for a number of years, having a hand in the training of Hyperion, the 1933 Derby and St. Leger winner.

In 1924, Mary Murland died after a long illness and Willie followed in 1926. They are both buried in the Holy Cross Churchyard at Daventry. Gerry married Marjorie Waldron in 1926. Marjorie was the widow of Major Francis 'Ferdy' Waldron[6], who

---

6. Major Francis Fitzgerald Waldron, aged 29. Transferred to the RFC from 19th (Queen Alexandra's Own Royal) Hussars. Only son of Brigadier-General F. Waldron. Buried at the HAC Cemetery, Ecoust-St-Main. VIII.A.26..

was shot down in July 1916. Ferdy Waldron was the first commanding officer of 60 Squadron RFC and a friend of Hubert Harvey-Kelly, the first RFC pilot to land in France in 1914. Two months before Ferdy's death Marjorie gave birth to their daughter, Patricia. He is buried close to the poet Arthur West in the HAC Cemetery at Ecoust-St-Mein, near Arras.

After Gerry and Bill's father died, the estate was sold and Gerry moved a short distance away to Redhill House at Byfield. Bill, it seems lived with them for a while until he moved to London to take up permanent residence at the Cavalry Club. At some point in the late 1940s, Bill emigrated to South Africa where he remained a bachelor and bred horses. He died in Durban on 5th January 1967, aged 76. Records in the Natal Archives give his place of death as the Balmoral Hotel, Durban, and record his entire estate being bequeathed to Mariana Audrey Jamnik. To date I have been unable to successfully contact any member of the Jamnik family.

At the outbreak of the Second World War, Gerry volunteered for service again. He had previously resigned his commission in 1926, having seen the yeomanry convert from a mounted regiment to an armoured car company. In August 1939, he was commissioned with the rank of Major into the 4th Battalion Northamptonshire Regiment and, according to his service records, was posted to the School of Military Admin at Hythe. Much to his annoyance he was considered too old for active service, despite his overall fitness and good health. He was appointed Local Defence Commander at Firbeck Aerodrome, near Rotherham in February 1941. In September 1946 he was awarded the Territorial Efficiency Decoration in recognition of his long service history as a territorial officer.

As a child I remember visiting Gerry and Marjorie when they lived in Suffolk, where we were often invited for tea. My memories are of a grand old gentleman who was rather formal and always surrounded by dogs, and of Marjorie, who was very kind and seemed to be forever smiling. In later life they moved to sheltered accommodation and their affairs were looked after by my father. Gerry died, aged 92, in September 1980 and Marjorie a year later in January 1981, aged 93.

Epilogue

My maternal grandmother, Margery, married Douglas Allen Watts in February 1922, at Worthing in Sussex. Douglas returned home in 1919 to the family Drapery business in Arundel and for a time he and Margery lived in Arundel. Sometime in the early 1930s they both moved to Woodbridge in Suffolk to run the Bull Hotel in partnership with Joe Davies, Joe leaving his share of the hotel to them when he died. I have very fond memories of Douglas and Margery; they were both wonderful grandparents and significant people in my childhood. Douglas died in April 1956 and Margery continued to run the Bull Hotel until she retired in 1967. She died in September 1981. Their only child, Adrienne Mary, was born in May 1923, and became my mother in May 1946. Her marriage to Hugh took place in Woodbridge on 23rd July 1945.

Their marriage went ahead despite Hugh's mother and father being very much against it and refusing to attend. His father was of the opinion that Adrienne, being the daughter of an hotelier, was 'not of our class' and consequently refused to have any further contact with his son again. It was not until he was dying in 1958, that he asked to see Hugh. I have no idea what they said to each other but I hope they made their peace. Although my birth was recorded in grandfather's diary for 1946, we never met each other. I have only come to know him through his diaries and letters and, despite his stubbornness and ingrained attitudes, I should have liked to have had the chance to have met him.

Hugh remained in the RAF flying the Meteor jet fighter until 1947, after which he was demobbed. He returned to the RAF in 1952 to eventually retire in 1981. My mother died at home in 1991 at Sherringham, Norfolk, and Hugh followed her fifteen years later, in 2006. Adrienne is buried at the cliff top churchyard at Beeston Regis and Hugh is commemorated on her headstone.

Ada Goode, my maternal great grandmother, died in December 1952, and I can still remember staying with her at Worthing when I was about five years old. By then Lynton and Archie were a distant memory, very rarely spoken of and almost erased from the family consciousness. It was as if there was a wall of silence shielding the family grief, a grief that had haunted them since their deaths. It didn't surprise me to discover that I was the first member of the family to visit the Gallipoli battlefields to find Lynton's name on the

15th Battalion Memorial. Apart from my two aunts, Violet and Ethel, I only ever met one of my grandmother's six brothers. The occasion in 1954, when I was eight years old, caused great consternation and my grandmother told me her brother was coming to stay. All I recall of the event was a tall man in a dark overcoat. Passenger records for the *SS Queen Elizabeth* sailing from Southampton on 29th April 1954, confirm a Charles Goode and his wife Gladys were onboard, returning to New York. Charles' nationality was given as British and his wife was recorded as being a Canadian national. No ages or dates of birth were recorded and they gave a home address in Vancouver. Was this Charles Herbert and his second wife returning home after visiting England? In all probability it was; he would have been 66 years old but no-one really spoke of the episode to us children, and another piece of family history went unrecorded. As for Walter, I have had no success in discovering his whereabouts between being released from prison and his marriage to Josephine's mother in 1948. One day the missing pieces of the puzzle will slot into place.

For completeness, I should add that I was last of the Twentieth Century family warriors. After leaving school I served with the Parachute Regiment in the 1960s. This short adventure was a memorable experience that took me to parts of the world that are generally avoided by tourists and endowed me with a self-belief that enabled me to achieve in later life.

I hope this book will play a small part in keeping alive the memory of a nearly a century of family service.

Further Reading

A small selection of websites that I have found particularly useful for online research.

Ancestory.com (subscription) www.ancestry.com
Anglo Boer War Website www.angloboerwar.com
Australian War Memorial www.awm.gov.au
Bombercrew.com www.bombercrew.com
British-Genealogy.com www.british-genealogy.com
British Medal Forum www.britishmedalforum.com
Commonwealth War Graves Commission www.cwgc.org
Family Search www.familysearch.org
Findmypast.com (subscription) www.findmypast.com
First World War .com www.firstworldwar.com
FreeBMD www.freebmd.rootsweb.com
Gazette Online www.gazettes-online.co.uk
Landforces of Britain, the Empire and Commonwealth www.regiments.org
Liddel Hart Centre for Military Archives www.kcl.ac.uk/iss/archives
National Archives of Ireland (Eire) www.nationalarchives.ie
Public Records Office Northern Ireland www.proni.gov.uk
RAF Commands www.rafcommands.com
RMA Sandhurst Archives www.sandhurst.mod.uk/tour/archives
Roll of Honour www.roll-of-honour.com
RootsChat.com www.rootschat.com
The British Library www.bl.uk
The Imperial War Museum www.iwm.org.uk
The Long Long Trail www.1914-1918.net
The National Archives www.nationalarchives.gov.uk
The RAF Museum www.rafmuseum.org.uk

The Regimental Warpath 1914-1918 www.warpath.orbat.com
The War Poetry Website www.warpoetry.co.uk
Ulster Historical Foundation (subscription) www.ancestryireland.com
World War Two Talk www.ww2talk.com

A SELECTED BIBLIOGRAPHY

Research guides.
Spencer.W. *Air Force Records for Family Historians.* (PRO 2000)
Spencer.W. *Army Service Records of the First World War.* (PRO 1999)

The Boer War and Great War
Banks. A. *A Military Atlas of the First World War.* (Leo Cooper 1997)
Barker.R. *The Royal Flying Corps in WW1.* (Robinson 2002)
Bean. C. *Gallipoli Mission.* (AWM 1948)
Bell. D. *The Reminiscences of Capt. D.J. Bell* (Mourne Observer 1962)
Bennett. W. *Absent Minded Beggars.* (Leo Cooper 1999)
Bewsher. F. *The History of the Fifty First (Highland) Division 1914-18.* (Naval & Military Press reprint)
Brown. M. *The IWM Book of 1918.* (Pan 1999)
Blunden. E. *Undertones of War.* (Folio 1989)
Carlyon. L. *Gallipoli.* (Doubleday 2002)
Coombs. R. *Before Endeavours Fade.* (After the Battle 2006)
Chataway. T. *History of the 15th Battalion, Australian Imperial Force.* (William Brookes 1948)
Evans. M. *The Boer War, South Africa 1899-1902.* (Osprey 1999)
Gliddon. G. *The Aristocracy and the Great War.* (Gliddon Books 2002)
Graves. R. *Goodbye to All That.* (Penguin 1960)
Gillion. S. *The KOSB in the Great War.* (Nelson 1930)
Holt. T&V. *Battlefields of the Great War.* (Pavillion 1995)
Liddle. P. *The Airman's War 1914-18.* (Blandford Press 1987)
MacDonald. L. *Roses of No Man's Land.* (Macmillan 1980)
Middlebrook. M. *The First Day on the Somme.* (Cassell 2003)
Moorehead. A. *Gallipoli.* (Wordsworth 1997)
Murland. H.F. *Baillie-Ki-Paltan.* (Higginbottoms 1932)
Orr. P. *The Road to the Somme.* (Blackstaff 1987)
Powell-Edwards. H. *The Sussex Yeomanry and the 16th Battalion Royal Sussex*

Further Reading

Regiment 1914-18. (Melrose 1921)

Sheffield. G. *The Somme*. (Cassell 2003)

Simpson. A. *The Evolution of Victory*. (Donovan 1995)

Whitmore. F. *The 10th PWO Royal Hussars and Essex Yeomanry During the European War 1914-18*. (Benham 1929)

Wilcox. R. *Battles on the Tigris*. (Pen & Sword 2006)

Wilks. J&E. *The British Army in Italy 1917-18*. (Leo Cooper 1998)

World War II

Bowyer. C. *The Wellington Bomber*. (Kimber 1986)

Caldwell. D. *The JG26 War Diary Volume 1 1939-42*. (Grub Street 1996)

Chorley. J. *RAF Bomber Command Losses*. Volumes 1-7. (Midland 1992-2002)

Franks. N. *Another Kind of Courage*. (Patrick Stephen 1994)

Franks. N. *RAF Fighter Command Losses*. Volumes 1-3 (Midland 1997-2000)

Franks. N. *Spitfires Over The Arakan*. (William Kimber 1988)

Golley. J. *Aircrew Unlimited*. (Patrick Stephens 1993)

Gunby. G & Pelham.T. *RAF Bomber Command Losses in the Middle East and Mediterranean Volume 1 1939-1942*. (Midland 2006)

Middlebrook. M & Everitt. C. *The Bomber Command War Diaries*. (Penguin 1990)

Moyle. H. *The Hampden File*. (Air Britain 1999)

Pitchfork. G. *Shot Down and in the Drink*. (National Archives 2003)

Price. A. *Late Mark Spitfire Aces 1942-45*. (Osprey 1995)

Scutts. J. *Bf 109 Aces of North Africa and the Mediterranean*. (Osprey 1994)

Ward. C. *Squadron Profiles Number 49 – 144 Squadron*. (Chris Ward 1999)

Wilmot. C. *The Struggle for Europe*. (Wordsworth 1997)

Covering both World Wars

Cossey. B. *Tigers. The Story of 74 Squadron RAF*. (Arms and Armour 1992)

Doherty. R. *The North Irish Horse*. (Spellmount 2002)

King. M. Ed. *County Down at War*. (Down County Museum 2004)

Lake. A. *Flying Units of the RAF*. (Airlife 1999)

Index

Roman numerals in italics refer to pictures, numbers in brackets to maps and illustrations.

Index

Index

Index

Index

Wilhelmshaven, 229.

Wilkie, Major, 203.

Wilson, Eleanor, 286.

Woodbridge, 263, 289.

Woolwich, RMA, 191, 192.

Y

Y Ravine (Gallipoli), 65, 71.

Ypres, 9, 131, 132, 146, 194, 195, 199, 203, 216, 277, 281, 282, (134).

Ypres, first battle of, 131, (134).

Ypres, second battle of, 132, 137, 281, (134).

Ypres, third battle of, 90, 201, (134)

Ypres Salient, 131, 203, 243.

Z

Zandvoorde, 131, 281, (134).

Zillebeke, (134)